OCCURRENCE OF CACTUS SP... VEGETATION TYPES ...

P = primary occurrence; S = secondary occurrence; ... ...ence

Species and Varieties	Page	Rocky Mt. Montane Forest	Sierra Montane Forest	Calif. Oak Woodland	Calif. Chaparral (disturbed areas)	Pacific Grassland	Juniper-Pinyon Woodland	Sagebrush Desert	Mojavean Desert	Colo. Desert
O. oricola	153				P					
O. chlorotica	155				s		s		P	s
Hybrid populations of naturalized O. Ficus-Indica	158									
"occidentalis"	164				P					
"demissa"	171				P					
O. tomentosa	172				P					
Cereus giganteus	173									s
C. Emoryi	175				P					
Echinocereus triglochidiatus	178									
a. var. melanacanthus	179						P			
b. var. mojavensis	181	s			S		P		S	
E. Engelmannii	182									
a. var. Engelmannii	183								s	P
b. var. acicularis	186								s	s
c. var. armatus	186								P	
d. var. Munzii	187				P					
e. var. chrysocentrus	188								P	
Mammillaria dioica	190				P					P
M. microcarpa	191									s
M. tetrancistra	193								s	P
Ferocactus acanthodes	197									
a. var. acanthodes	198									P
b. var. LeContei	198								P	s
F. viridescens	199				P					
Echinocactus polycephalus	201								P	
Sclerocactus polyancistrus	206								P	
Neolloydia Johnsonii	208								P	
Coryphantha vivipara	211									
a. var. desertii	212								P	
b. var. Alversonii	213								S	P
c. var. rosea	213					P				

The Native Cacti of California

The Native Cacti

of California

Lyman Benson

751

ford, California, 1969

Stanford University Press
Stanford, California
© 1969 by the Board of Trustees of the
Leland Stanford Junior University
Printed in the United States of America
L.C. 69–13176
SBN 8047–0696–4

Preface

This book is intended for both semipopular and semitechnical use. Fundamentally it is an abridged technical treatment of the cacti growing as native plants in the Californian flora or introduced into it by man, but occurring without his intentional aid. Technical terms are reduced to a minimum, but the arrangement of the book is formal. Keys are provided for determining the scientific or popular name of any cactus occurring in the state, and each species and variety is described in moderate detail. Most of the species are illustrated by photographs, line drawings, or both; the more common cacti may be recognized without the use of the key, though much greater precision is obtained if the keys are employed in identification. Distributional maps indicate the areas in which the species and varieties are known definitely to occur, that is, those areas in which distribution is documented by herbarium specimens. Though species actually may occur in other areas, the ranges indicated on the maps include only areas verified by clear-cut proof—usually documentary evidence in the form of herbarium specimens.

The cacti of California have been one of my principal interests since 1931, and though their classification is complex, it is my hope that this book may make some contribution toward understanding the problems involved in organization of the species.

The book may be used alone or in conjunction with the similarly organized *Cacti of Arizona* (1st ed., 1940; 2d ed., 1950; 3d ed., 1969) or the *Cacti of the United States and Canada*, a larger and technically more comprehensive work soon going to press.

Research grants-in-aid of several types have contributed to the preparation of this book. These have included a number from the Claremont Graduate School; one from the Society of Sigma Xi, for 1950; and three from the National Science Foundation, covering the periods of 1956–59, 1959–64, and 1965–67. This aid in all phases of the work is acknowledged with gratitude.

Beginning in 1956, curating of the collection of cactus specimens and photographs of the late David Griffiths of the staff of the United States Department of Agriculture during the first two decades of this century was undertaken at the request of Dr. A. C. Smith for the United States National Herbarium, Smithsonian Institution, United States National Museum. The use here of the photographs and of the paintings by Mr. L. C. C. Krieger, which appear in the color plates, is through the courtesy of Dr. Jason R. Swallen, emeritus Curator, Division of Plants, and is much appreciated. If not otherwise indicated, the other photographs are by the author. For these others, acknowledgment is given in the legends; the privilege of using them is much appreciated.

The line drawings are by Mrs. Lucretia Breazeale Hamilton of Tucson, Arizona. The author is grateful to her for excellent work in preparation of these illustrations.

L.B.

December 28, 1968

Contents

Detailed Description of Color Plates

Plates 1–8 follow p. 100

1. CHOLLAS: 1 & 2. Cane cholla, *Opuntia Parryi* var. *Parryi*, in flower and in fruit. 3. Snake cholla, *O. Parryi* var. *serpentina*. 4. Coastal cholla, *O. prolifera*, with a detached bud. 5 & 6. Diamond cholla, *O. ramosissima*, the joint tip (6) with a young spineless fruit; most but not all fruits are densely spiny. Paintings by L. C. C. Krieger for use by the late David Griffiths, courtesy of the U.S. National Herbarium, Smithsonian Institution (see comment under Plate 5).

2. CHOLLAS: 1 & 2. Silver cholla, *Opuntia echinocarpa* var. *echinocarpa*, in flower. 3. A south-facing hillside with a dense population of teddy bear cholla, *O. Bigelovii* var. *Bigelovii*; northeast of Aguila, Maricopa County, Arizona. 4. Teddy bear cholla with the fallen joints rooting and forming new plants. 5. A buckhorn cholla, *O. acanthocarpa* var. *major*, in flower. Photographs: 1, Reid V. Moran; 2 & 3, Robert A. Darrow; 4, from Lyman Benson, *Plant Taxonomy, Methods and Principles*. Copyright © 1962. The Ronald Press Company, New York. Used by permission.

3. DRY-FRUITED PRICKLY PEARS: 1. Beavertail cactus, *Opuntia basilaris* var. *basilaris*, in flower; Mojavean Desert near Death Valley. 2. Plains prickly pear, *O. polyacantha* var. *rufispina*, in flower; west of Grand Junction, Colorado.

4. DRY-FRUITED PRICKLY PEARS: Mojave prickly pear, *Opuntia erinacea* var. *utahensis*, in flower; near Zion National Park, Utah. 1. Natural habitat. 2. Sectioned flower, showing the same parts and a longitudinal section of the ovary and ovules. 3. Joints, spines, flower buds, and a flower, showing the petaloid perianth parts, stamens, and stigmas. Photograph: 2, Carolyn R. Trapp.

5. DRY-FRUITED PRICKLY PEARS: 1–3. Beavertail cactus, *Opuntia basilaris* var. *basilaris*: joint, flower bud, and flower. 4–6. Kern cactus,

O. basilaris var. *Treleasei*, the spiny variety: two mature joints, an immature joint with leaves, and a flower bud. 7 & 8. Little prickly pear, *O. fragilis*: joints. Paintings by L. C. C. Krieger for David Griffiths, courtesy of the United States National Herbarium, Smithsonian Institution. Because the flowers close up rapidly indoors, Mr. Krieger painted only this one complete flower, using a heavy iron ring to hold the flower open. For other prickly pears he painted only one petal. The other paintings by Mr. Krieger are tinted photographs, i.e., paintings made directly upon very pale prints.

6. JUICY-FRUITED PRICKLY PEARS: *Opuntia littoralis*. 1. Var. *austro-californica*, the flower red, flame, or tending toward magenta; the joints spineless and glaucous (with particles of a bluish wax on the surface). 2. Var. *Vaseyi*, the flower yellow with a red center; the joints spiny and green.

7. JUICY-FRUITED PRICKLY PEARS: 1–4. *Opuntia phaeacantha* var. *major*, the most widespread and common prickly pear in the Southwestern Deserts of the United States: joints, with the characteristic spreading, long, reddish-brown spines restricted to the upper portion of the joint; a flower bud; a single petal (see comment under 5 concerning problem of painting the complete flower); a mature fruit. 5–7. The Indian fig or mission cactus, *O. Ficus-Indica*, spineless form: joint and two fruits (for other colors see Plate 8). Paintings: joint of the mission cactus, Lydia M. Green; others, L. C. C. Krieger for David Griffiths, courtesy of the United States National Herbarium, Smithsonian Institution (see comment under Plate 5).

8. JUICY-FRUITED PRICKLY PEARS: Indian fig or mission cactus, *Opuntia Ficus-Indica*. 1. Spiny form: the large plant at the left, about ten feet tall, introduced in the mouth of a small canyon near Puddingstone reservoir, Pomona, Los Angeles County. The small blue-green plants in the right foreground are hybrids with *O. littoralis* var. *Vaseyi*; the yellow-green plants behind them are of var. *littoralis*; those visible above the grass on the hillside beyond are hybrids; plant of var. *Vaseyi* is hidden and almost enveloped in the grass. 2 & 3. Spineless form: joints with two colors of fruits; these plants result from selection by man from among the many strains of fruit tree cacti long cultivated in Mexico. Photograph: 3, David L. Walkington.

Plates 9–16 follow p. 164

9. JUICY-FRUITED PRICKLY PEARS: The prevailing hybrid type in the extensive hybrid swarms on the coastal side of the mountains in southern California; derived about three-quarters from the small *Opuntia littoralis* var. *Vaseyi* and one-quarter from the large, treelike, introduced

Indian fig or mission cactus, *O. Ficus-Indica*. Plants with various similar gene combinations cover large areas, crowding out the grasses, which carry fire, which in turn would destroy the cacti; these plants have thus gained the ascendancy from the small native species, which tends to be killed outright by grass fires. Plants in bloom near Claremont, Los Angeles County.

10. JUICY-FRUITED PRICKLY PEARS: The prevailing hybrid type described for 9, *Opuntia littoralis* var. *Vaseyi* × *Opuntia Ficus-Indica*: joints, a flower bud, and the characteristic reddish-purple fruits. The white spots on the upper fruit are the white woolly female cochineal insect, which yields cochineal dye of commerce. The juice of the insect is bright red; depending on the treatment used in killing the insect, various colors may be produced—crimson, scarlet, orange, etc. Formerly, prickly pears were cultivated (as for example on the islands of the Caribbean) for the cochineal insects, but this source of color has been replaced largely by aniline dyes. Paintings by L. C. C. Krieger for David Griffiths, courtesy of the United States National Herbarium, Smithsonian Institution (see comment under Plate 5).

11. CEREUS AND JUICY-FRUITED PRICKLY PEARS: 1 & 2. Saguaro or giant cactus, *Cereus giganteus*: 1, near Tucson, Arizona; 2, fruits, showing the red inner surfaces of the opened fruits (not flowers, as identified in the picture postcards offered for sale). 3. A cultivated prickly pear, *Opuntia tomentosa*, sparingly escaped near Claremont, Los Angeles County. 4. A coastal species, *O. oricola*, with mature fruits.

12. CEREUS EMORYI: 1. Thicket on the coast southwest of San Diego, in fruit. 2. The branches and exceedingly spiny fruits. 3. Flower showing the spiny ovary, the sepaloid and petaloid perianth parts, the stamens, and the stigmas. 4. Fruits, and scars where two have been removed, showing the position within the spine-bearing areole where the flowers and fruits of *Cereus* are produced. Photograph: 3, Reid V. Moran.

13. ECHINOCEREUS TRIGLOCHIDIATUS: Plants of the red-flowered group, having plastid pigments in the flowers, these not water-soluble. 1. Var. *melanacanthus*, in flower; Chisos Mountains, Brewster County, Texas. 2. Var. *mojavensis*, in flower and showing the twisted, nearly white spines; Joshua Tree National Monument, Riverside County. 3. Flower and the subtending areole (of an Arizona variety); the flower bud bursts through the epidermis of the stem rib just above the areole, leaving a jagged scar; this is characteristic of the genus.

14. ECHINOCEREUS ENGELMANNII: Plants of the purple-to-magenta-flowered group, having soluble, probably betacyanin, pigments. 1. Var. *armatus*, in flower; near Victorville, San Bernardino County. 2. Var.

chrysocentrus, in flower. Note the large, white, swordlike, lower central spine in each areole. The name *chrysocentrus* is a misnomer; the spines are not necessarily yellow, and they are not yellow in the type specimen.

15. SEVERAL GENERA: 1. *Mammillaria microcarpa*, in flower; near Superior, Pinal County, Arizona. 2. *M. tetrancistra*, in fruit; Whitewater, Riverside County. 3 & 4. Barrel cactus, *Ferocactus acanthodes* var. *Le-Contei*: 3, showing the red central spines and the less conspicuous, flexuous radial spines; 4, a tall and characteristically slender plant, among young chollas growing from fallen branches of the teddy bear cholla, *Opuntia Bigelovii*, northeast of Aguila, Maricopa County, Arizona. 5. Barrel cactus, *Echinocactus polycephalus*, showing the curving central spines; near Victorville, San Bernardino County. 6. *Mammillaria dioica*; plant in the Rancho Santa Ana Botanic Garden.

16. SEVERAL GENERA: 1 & 2. *Neolloydia Johnsonii*; southeast of Death Valley, Inyo County. 3. Pincushion cactus, *Coryphantha vivipara* var. *rosea*, in flower. 4. Pincushion cactus, *C. vivipara* var. *Alversonii*, in flower. 5. Pincushion cactus, *C. vivipara* var. *desertii*; Beaverdam Mountains, Utah. 6. *Sclerocactus polyancistrus*, in fruit; near Victorville, San Bernardino County. Photographs: 1–4, Stanley J. Farwig.

Introduction

Introduction

The Structure of Cacti

Cactus stems are SUCCULENT,* and this succulence sets the cactus family apart from most other plants. However, some plants of other families have succulent stems or leaves, and some even have the appearance of cacti. For example, the African succulent spurges (*Euphorbia*) seem almost identical with some cacti. Commonly, the spurges are distinguished by their milky juice, but a few cacti have juice that appears to be similar.

Succulence of stems or leaves occurs in several plant families, including the lily family (Liliaceae or its segregates), e.g., the yuccas and century plants; the carpetweed family (Aizoaceae, subfamily Ficoideae), e.g., leaf succulents such as the ice plants, *Mesembryanthemum*; a few members of the milkweed family (Asclepiadaceae); and some plants of the sunflower family (Compositae). Succulence especially of the leaves occurs throughout the stonecrop family (Crassulaceae). Succulent tissue usually is correlated with need for storage of water, but not necessarily so. As pointed out below, in the cacti succulence occurs in combination with a wide-spreading shallow root system capable of rapid absorption of water after even a light rain. According to Axelrod, the climate of the Pacific Coast has become gradually drier during the 100 million years since Cretaceous time, and through this period there has been gradual adaptation of some plants to desert

* All botanical terms used in this work are defined in the Glossary, pp. 225–34; in the introductory material, such terms are given in small-capital letters where they first appear.

3

environments both in this region and in the horse latitudes. Combination of succulent stems and/or leaves, a thick surface covering of waxy material (CUTICLE), a low ratio of surface to volume of the stems or leaves or both—or the reduction or essentially complete elimination of one or the other—and production of SPINES or thorns appear in many plants of deserts or semideserts. These characters have arisen by mutation, and often they have been preserved singly or in combination in response to a dry climate. In these cases evolution has tended to follow parallel paths in producing similar outward appearances in unrelated plants, and this is particularly evident in plants with succulent stems or leaves.

The most distinctive feature occurring in some form throughout the cactus family and in no other is the presence of spines in AREOLES. Areole is the diminutive of area, and it refers to a special, clearly marked area above each leaf or above the normal position for a leaf. The areole produces spines—usually in the mature plant, and always at some juvenile stage.

Most cacti are leafless, but well-developed, PERSISTENT leaves similar to those of most flowering plants occur in the primitive tropical cacti of the genus *Pereskia*. The chollas and prickly pears (*Opuntia*) have fleshy, elongate, EPHEMERAL leaves on the new joints of the stem, but these fall away usually within two or three months, as shown in Figs. 1 and 2. In adult stages most cacti do not have discernible leaves, and commonly the leaf below the areole is represented by a hump of tissue normally overlooked. Since leaves ordinarily are not present at all or are present for only a short time, nearly all food manufacture is carried out by the green cells of the stems.

Internally, the stem has a large, soft CORTEX around a hollow cylinder of wood, which encloses the enlarged pith in the center. The quantity of woody tissue varies, but proportionately it is small. The greatly enlarged cortex and PITH are composed of storage cells adapted especially to water retention (see Fig. 3). The surface of the stem is covered by a waxy surface layer, the EPIDERMIS, which retards or prevents evaporation. The water-retaining power of the surface layers is demonstrated readily by

Fig. 1. Leaves, areoles, spines, and glochids of joints of the stem of a prickly
pear, *Opuntia phaeacantha* var. *discata*. Joints of three ages: the youngest
(two joints at *upper right*) with a leaf subtending each areole (node) of
the stem and with, in some areoles, a single young spine emerging; the next
(*upper left*) with the leaves persistent but ready to fall away and with the
earliest developing spines protruding farther; the mature joint (*below*) without
leaves and with the full complement of spines in each areole strongly barbed
and with glochids (best shown at the top of the joint and at the lower right).
Photograph by David Griffiths.

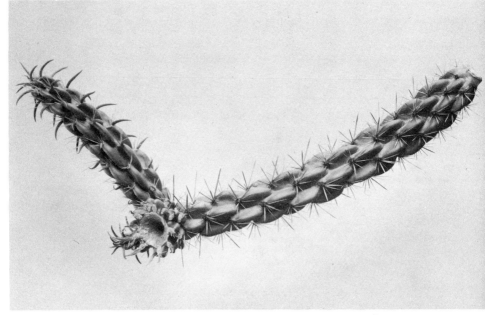

Fig. 2. Tubercles, leaves, areoles, and spines of a mature and an immature joint of the stem of a cholla, *Opuntia imbricata* (Great Plains to Mexico). Both joints have tubercles each of which bears an areole (the prickly pears, Fig. 1, do not have tubercles). The young joint bears a leaf at the base of each areole; the mature joint has no leaves. The glochids are inconspicuous. A still younger joint and a young fruit are at the angle between the longer joints. Photograph by David Griffiths.

cutting a detached joint of a spineless prickly pear in two and peeling one half while leaving the other intact. Within a few hours the peeled half shrivels, and the other part remains unchanged.

Some cacti, such as the desert night-blooming cereus and a few prickly pears, have subterranean TUBEROUS structures formed from the roots or underground stems. These cacti store much water and reserve food underground as well as in the main stems above ground.

Typically, cacti have shallow root systems with many slender, elongated, fleshy roots. Because even the young absorbing portions are resistant to drying for long periods, these roots remain capable of absorbing water whenever it may come during the brief periods of rain in desert or other arid regions. Usually the root systems range widely just under the surface of the soil, and

Fig. 3. Cross section of the stem of a barrel cactus (about 15 inches in diameter), *Ferocactus acanthodes* var. *LeContei*. The relatively small amount of wood (xylem) surrounds the fundamental tissue of the pith at the center; the bulk of the stem is the fundamental tissue of the surrounding cortex. The cortex and the pith are areas of storage of reserve food and large quantities of water. The tubercles of the stem surface are coalescent lengthwise into ribs. The section of each tubercle shows the spine cluster in the apical areole. The areoles at the right show the distinction of central and radial spines.

the plant is capable of making use of even a light rain, which penetrates only a short distance into the ground.

Some species of cacti have downward-directed spines, and water concentrates on the points, which, like the elongated leaf tips of many tropical plants, form "drip-tips." Thus, a light rain or even a dense fog may be converted into large water drops, which fall near the base of the plant. As the young giant cactus or saguaro is developing, the principal spines are directed downward. This promotes concentration of water drops near the base of the plant, as well as providing protection from rodents, which otherwise would climb up and eat the stem to secure food and water (see Fig. 4). After the stem reaches 5 or 6 feet and flowering begins, the saguaro produces a different type of spine, one not directed downward. This is correlated with protection from rodents by the spines on the lower part of the stem and with the wider-spreading root system of the older plant. The water from the downward-directed spines around the base of the plant has become only a minor factor in providing water. The curvature of stems—for example, of the joints of the prickly pear or the "arms" of a saguaro —also promotes concentration of water into large drops or even small "streams."

Characteristic structural features of the members of the cactus family are as follows:

1. *The succulent stem.* The cactus stem ranges from a simple, unbranched, columnar axis, as in the barrel cacti, to a much-branched structure, either at ground level, as in the hedgehog cacti, or well above ground, as in the saguaro or the larger chollas and prickly pears. Branching stems are usually, though not necessarily, jointed, that is, composed of series of segments or JOINTS. The stems of most cacti are cylindroidal, but after a year of growth from seeds the stem joints of prickly pears are flattened (see Fig. 5). The surface may be smooth or there may be a TUBERCLE (mound) under each areole, or the tubercles may be COALESCENT into vertical RIBS on the stem. With respect to each other, regardless of the stem surface, the areoles are arranged spirally, and, as pointed out above, one occurs just above the potential position of each leaf, that is, in the leaf AXIL (the angle between the leaf and the stem). The areole is borne at the apex of the tubercle, or, if the tubercles are joined into ribs, then at the apex of the portion of the tubercle that protrudes above the main rib.

2. *The spines in the areoles.* Fundamentally each spine is a portion of a highly specialized leaf. All the spines in an areole may be alike, or they may differ. Usually the most distinctive ones are in the center of the areole, and they are designated as CENTRAL SPINES, whereas the marginal ones are called RADIAL SPINES. However, the distinction is arbitrary, and classification may depend

Fig. 4. Special functions of the lower spines. *Above*, cactus plants (*left*, prickly pear; *right*, hedgehog cactus) just watered with a light mist. Water drops have become concentrated near the tips of the downward-directed spines. The drops fall to the ground and soak the soil beneath the plant. *Left*, young plant of the saguaro, *Cereus giganteus*. Water concentrates into drops on the downward-directed spines, and after even a light rain the drops soak the ground beneath the plant. The picture was taken during the rainy spring of 1952, when the stem was turgid and the ribs were spread apart by its swelling. In dry periods the plant uses water, and the stem contracts, the furrows between the ribs deepening. This brings the spines closer together and makes the stem less vulnerable to rodents, which would eat it for water during drought. The downward direction of the principal spines makes the stem difficult to climb. When the saguaro is four to six feet tall it begins to flower and to produce finer, spreading spines. In its later life the plant depends upon a more widely spreading root system, but the lower spines still retard the climbing of rodents.

9

Fig. 5. Seedling of a prickly pear, showing the transition from a cylindroidal stem to flattened joints, still far different from those of the adult plant.

upon individual interpretation. The chollas and prickly pears have numerous small or sometimes minute, barbed BRISTLES, as well as spines. These GLOCHIDS ("ch" pronounced like "k") are particularly well developed among the prickly pears, and often they are more troublesome than the spines. Commonly the areole bears hairs as well as spines and sometimes glochids.

3. *The flower structure.* The flowers of all cacti but *Pereskia* are EPIGYNOUS. The SEPALS, PETALS, and STAMENS (see Fig. 6 for

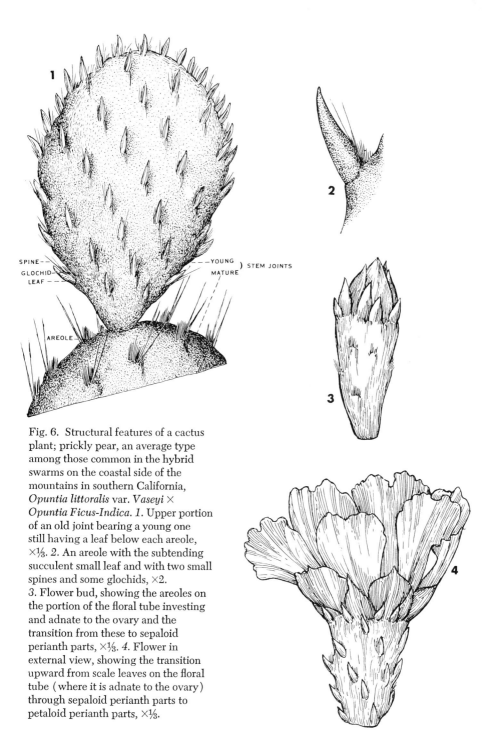

Fig. 6. Structural features of a cactus plant; prickly pear, an average type among those common in the hybrid swarms on the coastal side of the mountains in southern California, *Opuntia littoralis* var. *Vaseyi* × *Opuntia Ficus-Indica*. *1.* Upper portion of an old joint bearing a young one still having a leaf below each areole, ×⅛. *2.* An areole with the subtending succulent small leaf and with two small spines and some glochids, ×2. *3.* Flower bud, showing the areoles on the portion of the floral tube investing and adnate to the ovary and the transition from these to sepaloid perianth parts, ×⅓. *4.* Flower in external view, showing the transition upward from scale leaves on the floral tube (where it is adnate to the ovary) through sepaloid perianth parts to petaloid perianth parts, ×⅓.

SPINE
GLOCHID
LEAF

YOUNG
MATURE) STEM JOINTS

AREOLE

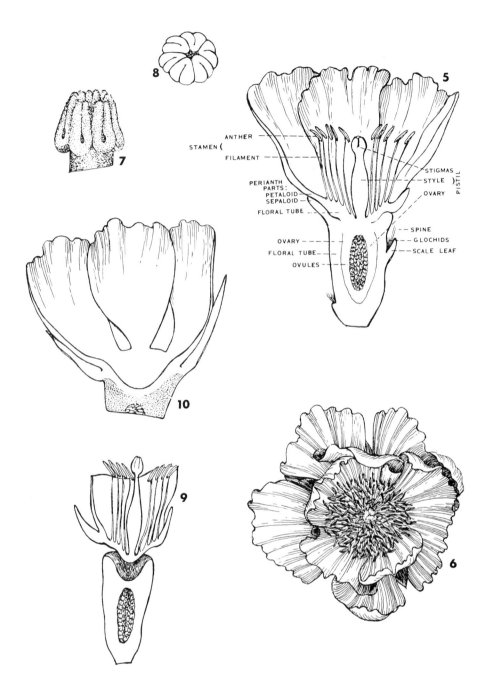

Fig. 6 (*cont.*). *5.* Flower in longitudinal section, ×⅓. *6.* Flower from above, showing the petaloid perianth parts, the numerous stamens, and the stigmas, ×⅓. *7 & 8.* Two views of the stigmas, ×1½. *9.* Flower after anthesis, now beginning to wither, and the upper part of the floral cup separated along a natural line from the lower end of the ovary, ×⅓. *10.* A portion of the floral cup above the ovary; internal view with the stamens removed and the petaloid perianth parts and a part of the upper end of the ovary (in longitudinal section) still present.

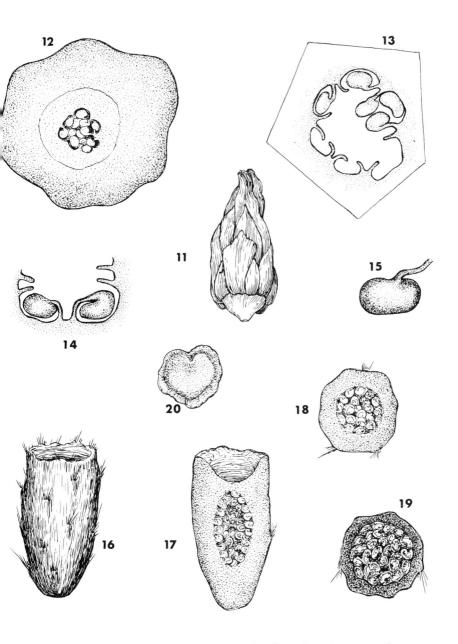

Fig. 6 (*cont.*). *11.* Withered perianth after it is deciduous from the ovary and floral cup, ×⅓. *12.* Cross section of the ovary at flowering time, ×1. *13.* Enlargement of *12*, showing the attachment of the ovules in double rows running vertically on the wall of the single chamber of the ovary (some ovules not appearing in the section and each represented by only the stalk or funiculus), ×3½. *14.* A portion of the section in *12* and *13*, ×70. *15.* A single ovule, ×11. *16.* Fruit, the areoles of the outer layer (floral tube) bearing areoles with glochids and small spines but the leaves having fallen, ×⅓. *17.* Fruit in longitudinal section, showing the seeds, ×⅓. *18, 19.* Fruit in cross section (two ages, *19* mature), ×⅓. *20.* Seed, the outer rim being the area enclosing the curving embryo, ×2. From Lyman Benson, *Plant Classification.* D. C. Heath & Co., Boston, 1957. Used by permission.

flower parts) are supported by a FLORAL TUBE (or FLORAL CUP, depending upon its shape). This is a tube, bowl, or collar of tissue formed partly by an extension of the stem (RECEPTACLE) at the base of the flower and partly by coalescence of the bases of the sepals, petals, and stamens. The lower portion of the floral tube invests the OVARY of the PISTIL closely, and in all the genera but *Pereskia* the two are fused together and are indistinguishable, except through microscopic examination. Inasmuch as the ovary is in a swelling of the stem well below the other flower parts, it is described as an INFERIOR OVARY. In *Pereskia* alone among the cacti, the ovary and the floral cup are free from each other, and the ovary is described as SUPERIOR and the flower as PERIGYNOUS. On the surface of the lower portion of the floral cup covering the ovary, commonly there is a SCALE LEAF (scale) just below each areole. However, often the leaves are deciduous at an early stage, or, in some genera, they are not developed at all, as in *Mammillaria* and nearly all species of *Coryphantha*. The leaves on the floral tube intergrade with the outer sepal-like structures, the SEPALOID PERIANTH PARTS, and in turn these shade off into the petal-like structures, the PETALOID PERIANTH PARTS. This series of intergradations of scale leaves and two kinds of perianth parts is a distinctive feature of the cactus family and one that sets it apart from most others. The petaloid parts of most cacti are highly colored, and the colors may vary between or within species as in other flowering plants. Both sepaloid and petaloid parts are numerous, and the stamens may run into the hundreds. The stamens are arranged spirally along the inside of the floral cup, just inward and downward from the petals. The large number of stamens is also characteristic of the family. As in other flowering plants, each stamen consists of a stalk or FILAMENT and a terminal ANTHER, which is composed of POLLEN SACS. The cactus flower includes a single pistil formed through coalescence of usually from 3 to 20 CARPELS (specialized leaves). At maturity of the FRUIT there is only one SEED CHAMBER, and the numerous ovules (which now have become SEEDS) are borne on the wall of the chamber. At its summit the single STYLE bears STIGMAS, each representing the tip of one of the carpels entering into the compound pistil.

Often young plants differ markedly from the mature plants of the same species. For example, a young barrel cactus one to several inches in diameter may seem quite different from the adult plant because of great differences in the spines. Many species of *Coryphantha* lack central spines when the branches are young. This difference may be observed on the young and other branches of the same individual. However, because young plants may bear flowers and fruits before growing the normal, adult form of spines, numerous supposed species have been based upon what were in fact juvenile plants studied in the absence of mature stems. Also, in *Coryphantha*, ordinarily the flower is developed near the base of the upper side of the tubercle, and it is connected with the spine-bearing areole by a narrow FELTED GROOVE. However, the first-formed flowers on the young stem may be developed much higher on the tubercle, and they may be connected with the spine-bearing portion of the areole by only a short groove, as on the mature stems of related genera.

The discussion in the text and the descriptions and keys are based upon the characters of the adult plants, and they are not necessarily applicable to seedlings (see Fig. 5). The information now available concerning the characters of juvenile plants is too spotty and inconsistent to be of much value in classification. Preparation of a thorough and consistent review of the features of juvenile plants of the species and varieties of cacti is important, but the project remains to be carried out in the future.

IDENTIFICATION OF CACTI

Identification of a cactus requires determining the groups or TAXA* of which it is a member; these categories are the basis for its scientific or botanical name. Plants and animals have names con-

* *Taxon* (plural *taxa*)—a unit of classification, such as a species *or* one of the varieties composing it *or* a larger unit such as a family (composed of genera) or a genus (composed of species).

structed like those of people, but the surname appears first. Thus the name of the California desert barrel cactus is *Ferocactus acanthodes*. *Ferocactus* stands for the genus or general group, *acanthodes* for the species or specific member of the group. The coastal barrel cactus is *Ferocactus viridescens*, occurring near San Diego. Twenty-one species of the genus *Opuntia* occur in California. Among these are chollas like *O. Parryi* and *O. Bigelovii* and prickly pears like *O. basilaris* and *O. littoralis*. In every case the relationship of the parts of the name is the same: the first word is the genus, the second the species, and the combination constitutes the botanical name of the plant. Yet another category, the variety,* may appear. *O. littoralis*, for example, comprises five varieties: *O. littoralis* var. *littoralis*, var. *Vaseyi*, var. *austrocalifornica*, and two others.

The cacti of the world constitute a single order, the Cactales, and a single family, the Cactaceae; the family, in turn, is divided into genera. In California there are nine main groups or genera of cacti. The genus of a particular cactus may be determined from the following synopsis of diagnostic characters:

1. *Opuntia*. Stem jointed, the joints occurring in series and either cylindroidal or flat; areoles with glochids (sharp, barbed bristles). The chollas (pronounced *"choyas"*) with cylindroidal joints and the prickly pears with flattened joints.

2. *Cereus*. Stem with ridges and grooves on the surface; flower produced within a spine-bearing areole on the side of the stem or at least somewhat below the growing point at the apex of a branch; stem 15–100 times as long as its diameter.

3. *Echinocereus*. Stem with ridges and grooves on the surface; fruit with clusters of spines; flower produced just above a mature

---

* An essentially equivalent term is subspecies. In the United States, usage of this term varies with the author, and it has been endowed with several definitions, but essentially it means merely a taxonomic category or taxon with a lower rank than species. On the average its interpretation is about the same as variety in this book. In Europe commonly subspecies is used as a taxon with a rank intermediate between species and variety, and, in this sense, a subspecies is composed of varieties. Individual authors have applied the term freely in some plant families; in others it has not been used.

spine-bearing areole and bursting through the epidermis of the stem as it grows, always below the stem apex; stem length not more than 8 times its diameter. Hedgehog cactus.

4. *Mammillaria*. Stem with tubercles on the surface, these not joined into ridges; fruit bearing no hairs, scales, or spines; flower produced between tubercles and having no surface connection with the spine-bearing areoles, occurring along the side of the stem among the old tubercles.

5. *Ferocactus*. Stem massive, with ridges and grooves on the surface; fruit fleshy at maturity, bearing many scales, opening at the extreme base; flower produced at the upper edge of the spine-bearing areole on a newly forming tubercle composing the APICAL part of a ridge on the stem. Barrel cactus.

6. *Echinocactus*. Stem with ridges and grooves on the surface; fruit fleshy at maturity, with numerous scales; flower produced as in *Ferocactus*, above; sepaloid perianth parts with long, tapering or spiny apices. Barrel cactus.

7. *Sclerocactus*. Stem with ridges and grooves on the surface; tubercles not completely coalescent, their tops protruding above the ridges; fruit dry at maturity, with or without scale leaves and with or without short hairs from the areoles, *either* separating crosswise near the middle or above the base *or* (not in California) splitting lengthwise along 2 or 3 lines; flower produced at the edge of a spine-bearing areole at the summit of a newly forming tubercle on the apical part of a ridge of the stem.

8. *Neolloydia*. Stem with the tubercles prominent but connected basally into ribs; fruit dry at maturity, bearing a few membranous scales; flower produced at the base of a new tubercle at the stem apex, the depression in which it is borne connected with the spine-bearing areole by a narrow ISTHMUS (FELTED groove).

9. *Coryphantha*. Stem with the tubercles on the surface not organized into ridges; fruit fleshy at maturity, with no spines, hairs, or scales; flower produced at the base of the upper side of a new tubercle at the stem apex, the depression in which it is borne connected with the spine-bearing areole by a narrow groove.

By means of the illustrations and the foregoing synopsis, many cacti may be identified and their scientific names determined. However, precision in identification requires use of the keys and the descriptions. Only a small amount of effort is required to learn the proper method of identification of the members of a small group of plants like the cacti. Those who are interested in these plants will be rewarded well for the effort of learning how to use these keys.

To use the key, turn first to the "Key to the Genera" of California cacti (pp. 74–76). The initial lines of the leads on these pages have varying degrees of indention from the lefthand margin. Indention is the same for each member of each pair of leads, i.e., opposed statements, one of which is to be selected as descriptive of the plant being identified. The construction of the key is such that a given plant—let us take the Mojave hedgehog cactus as an example—must fit the description in one or the other of the two leads numbered 1. Upon examining the plant, we find that the areoles do not include sharp, barbed bristles (glochids); even the young stems do not bear leaves; and the floral tube is developed into a funnel-like structure between the ovary and the perianth parts. Obviously, then, the plant fits the lower lead of the pair, that is, the lower number 1; again, obviously, the plant does *not* belong to the genus *Opuntia*. The characters of the seeds and COTYLEDONS bear these conclusions out also, but they are not seen as readily.

The next choice is between the pair of leads numbered 2 and indented slightly from the left margin. These leads are subordinate to the lower lead 1. The flowers of the Mojave hedgehog cactus (as well as, of course, the fruits) are produced on areas of the stem developed at least one and often several years earlier, and they are not on the new growth of the current season. Therefore they appear well below the apex of the stem or branch. The seed is clearly longer than broad, rather than the reverse, and the attachment point scar (HILUM) is obviously at one end. Thus the plant fits the upper of the leads numbered 2 (and we have eliminated from consideration all genera subordinate to the lower lead numbered 2).

Subordinate to upper lead 2 are two leads numbered 3. Close

inspection of the base of the flower or the fruit shows that it does not lie within the spine-bearing areole; rather, it arises from the rib of the stem just above the areole, and it has burst irregularly through the epidermis (surface layer) of the stem. This is shown by irregular fissures in the epidermis above the base of the ovary. The plant is not tall, standing above the ground only a foot or so. Except in young plants, there are usually several stems, and the mature stems are only 1 to 5 or perhaps 10 times as long as their diameter. Although the EMBRYO within the seed is nearly straight, study requires inspection with a dissecting microscope. The choice is clearly the lower lead numbered 3, and at the end of this lead appears the name *Echinocereus*. This is the name of the genus or general group to which the cactus belongs.

Echinocereus is discussed on p. 177, and the reader should now turn to that page. On p. 178 there is a key to the species—that is, the specific kinds—of *Echinocereus* occurring in California. Since there are only two species in this state, the key is simple, and it is composed of only two leads numbered 1. The petaloid perianth parts are clearly red, with perhaps some yellow—not of a color in the magenta series, which ranges from lavender to purple (blue mixed with the red). Furthermore, although this cannot be observed, the pigments that give the flower its color are not water-soluble, and they are deposited on solid bodies (PLASTIDS) within the cells, as opposed to being water-soluble and dissolved in the cell sap. The areoles on the mature parts of the stems bear white felt or soft hairs. At night the flowers do not close, but they remain open for two or three days and nights before the end of flowering. This plant fits the upper lead number 1 above, and it is *Echinocereus triglochidiatus*. On p. 178 there is a description of this species.

After treatment of the species come descriptions of the varieties. The first variety listed is var. *melanacanthus* (p. 179), and the second is var. *mojavensis* (p. 181). Var. *mojavensis* has 1 or 2 central spines, and these are light-colored and usually twisting. The variety *mojavensis* is recognized most readily by this character, and it is the plant known as the Mojave hedgehog cactus.

CLASSIFICATION OF CACTI

Classification rarely is a simple matter. Many individuals in any natural population of plants or animals may have a hodgepodge of characters, some of which appear sometimes also in related taxa. In classifying taxa at any level of rank it is important to discern not only the differences between the taxa but also the degree of association among characters. Classification proceeds not according to single characters, but by the constancy of association of characters in clusters.

Genera, species, and varieties merge gradually and irregularly into each other.* For example, *Echinocereus triglochidiatus* var. *melanacanthus*, the wide-ranging and most common variety of the species, occurs definitely on only the eastern edge of California, though it is common east to Colorado and Texas and south into Mexico. However, in almost any California population of the western *Echinocereus triglochidiatus* var. *mojavensis*, there are at least a few plants that would nearly or completely fit the description of var. *melanacanthus* rather than var. *mojavensis*; and characters at-

---

* The phenomenon involved is intergradation, and it is commonly ascribed to hybridization or formation of hybrids. A HYBRID is an individual derived from parents some of whose hereditary characters differ. Commonly the word is used to describe individuals arising from crosses of different genera, species, or varieties. Since these taxa cannot be limited precisely, intergeneric, interspecific, and intervarietal hybrids cannot be defined in exact terms, either. Crosses involving a limited number of known gene pairs are defined in exact terminology. Individuals who have duplicating genes tending to produce the same characteristic in every pair of genes under consideration are called HOMOZYGOUS (with like genes). For example, a plant having two genes tending to produce red flowers is homozygous for red. If a plant has one gene tending to produce red and one white, it is HETEROZYGOUS (with unlike genes). The gene for red may be dominant to that for white, and, if so, a heterozygous individual will have red flowers. A plant with two recessive genes for white flowers is homozygous, and it will have white flowers. There is another, often correct, explanation for intergradation. This is lack of complete evolutionary separation now or in the past of two or more natural populations or systems of populations. At no time have there ceased to be some individuals with character combinations including features of both or all major populations. Hybridization implies complete separation for some period followed later by resumption of interbreeding.

tributed to var. *mojavensis* are found in some plants of var. *melanacanthus* as far east as Springdale, Utah. Such a breakdown in occurrence of key characters is common between varieties or between species or between higher taxa. The members of a genus, species, or variety vary as do people, and the taxa shade off into one another as do the races of man—though, again as with man, the tendency to a shading off tends to increase as one proceeds to the more subordinate taxonomic levels. The keys designed for segregating taxa can be no more than relatively reliable, because in nature the occurrence of characters in combination is inconsistent.

Because of the complexities of classification, not all published papers and books on the cacti or any other group of plants or animals are in agreement. For example, some authors have considered *Cereus* to include not only the species listed here, but also those of *Echinocereus*. Others have considered these two genera to be distinct. Still others have restricted *Cereus* to a relatively small group of tropical plants and have given other names to the groups of species thus segregated, with the thought that they are different genera. the two species occurring in California have appeared under *Carnegiea* and *Bergerocactus*, the saguaro or giant cactus of the desert in the former, and the thicket-forming cactus along the coast in the latter. These interpretations are based not upon error but upon a difference of opinion concerning classification either of these particular plants or of plants in general. Some botanists include only a narrow range of forms within a genus or a species, whereas others consider it more practical to include a much broader group of variants. Each research worker attempts to classify plants in a uniform manner. No system is necessarily either "right" or "wrong": liberals (favoring few variants) and conservatives (preferring many variants) alike have the goal of a consistent method of classification of the plant kingdom.

A detailed discussion of the philosophy of the writer concerning genera, species, and varieties has appeared in two publications:

The Goal and Methods of Systematic Botany. Cactus and Succulent Journal 15: 99–111. July 1943 (see particularly pp. 101–3).

Plant Taxonomy, Methods and Principles. Ronald Press Co., New York. 1962.

On strictly logical grounds, so long as the populations accorded ranks as genera, species, or varieties are natural, a liberal (few variants) or conservative (many variants) or any intermediate policy for delimiting them must be of equal value. A choice must rest therefore, *first*, upon conformity with prevailing practice through the world as a whole for classifying the entire plant kingdom, insofar as this can be determined, and, *second*, upon practical considerations.

The policy of the writer is conservative, partly because this is most nearly in harmony with worldwide prevailing botanical practice. The work of Britton and Rose on the cactus family represents approximately the high-water mark of a local botanical "liberalism" that flourished in the United States from about 1900 to 1930. Most botanists in this country abandoned or modified this policy in the 1930's.

Britton and Rose's comprehensive review of the Cactaceae has not been matched by a complete, comparable recent treatment based upon research on the natural populations of the family, and there is no comprehensive coverage of the family prepared according to conservative policy. In fact, there has been little botanical research upon classification of the species for half a century. The result is retention in semitechnical works (and even in some technical publications) of microgenera and microspecies at levels recognized currently by few botanists in works on other groups of plants. If the rest of the plant kingdom were to be classified according to the policies often applied to the cacti, millions of changes of plant names would be necessary. The thought of bringing the classification of the rest of the plant kingdom into harmony with some publications on the cacti, expressed by several recent horticultural authors, is beyond comprehension. The policy adopted in *The Native Cacti of California* is about the equivalent of that in such standard botanical books as the eighth edition of Gray's *Manual of Botany* or Jepson's *Manual of the Flowering Plants of California* or his *Flora of California*.

Two practical reasons also underlie the choice of a conservative policy in recognition of genera, species, and varieties:

1. Many natural population systems lack the stability of charac-

ters necessary to make their segregation by means of keys practical. If groups between which the segregating characters are few or in which the clusters of characters are unstable are treated as varieties rather than species, the necessity for attempting to segregate them by keys is removed. This leaves the keys for identification of only the major populations, which have relatively clear and stable diagnostic characters.

The more difficult task of determining varieties is facilitated by comparing them in a table. In this book when a cactus is represented in California by three or more varieties, these are differentiated in a table (e.g., see *Opuntia erinacea*, pp. 120–21). This places the burden of segregation of one variety from another upon the whole complex of characters, rather than upon a single character or upon a few characters, as in a key.

2. If each local element appears as a different species, carrying over knowledge from one geographical region to another is difficult. It gives the flora and its units in each region, state, or lesser area the status of a local independent entity. This obscures its close relationship and its real place in the flora of the continent or the world as a whole. For example, to those whose interest is purely local, use of the trinomial *Prunus virginiana* var. *demissa*, instead of the binomial *Prunus demissa*, for the chokecherry of the Pacific States may seem cumbersome. But for anyone who has known *P. virginiana*, the chokecherry of the East, Middle West, and Southeast, it is helpful to know that the similar plant on the Pacific Coast is related closely to the one known elsewhere, differing only in some unstable characters (that it is so related is immediately apparent from its botanical name). On the other hand, if classification is at the level of species, as *P. demissa* and *P. melanocarpa*, the very close relationship of Pacific Coast chokecherry and Rocky Mountain chokecherry is obscured. Since the character combinations marking each of the three chokecherries are unstable, it is practical to consider all three as varieties of *P. virginiana*. Thus, they appear as var. *virginiana*, var. *melanocarpa*, and var. *demissa*.

If one opens several books written early in the twentieth century by members of the American "liberal" school to see which chokecherries are included, he finds that in some *P. virginiana* appears, in others *P. demissa,* and in others *P. melanocarpa.* In a few areas covered by one or more of the books, two of the chokecherries occur, but there is no indication of the close similarity of the plants or of the instability of their characters. Only if the name chokecherry appears is there evidence of interrelationship of the "species." In most cases all evidence of the transcontinental relationship of chokecherries is lost. Thus, variety may be a strong and useful category of value for improving organization and for coordinating the members of wide-ranging, complex population systems of plants.

To facilitate correlation of the generic and specific designations appearing in this book with those appearing in others, a list of "synonyms" is given in a short paragraph (or in several paragraphs) under each species or variety. This makes possible correlation of the various points of view, and the reader is free, of course, to choose according to his own preference. (The manner of presentation of the synonyms is explained in the next section, under "*Synonymy.*")

In the introduction to an earlier book, *The Cacti of Arizona,* 2d ed., 1950, p. 11), the following statement appears: "It is possible that a better scheme of classification than either [this or Britton and Rose's] may result from further study. This may lie somewhere between the very conservative viewpoint adopted tentatively (but with no hard and fast future commitment) by the writer and the exceedingly liberal one of Britton and Rose. However, since the interrelationships of the subgenera (or microgenera) are amazingly complex, any accurate reevaluation and realignment will require a very long and detailed study of the entire family." In the 19 years since this statement appeared, study of the genera and species of cacti occurring in the United States and Canada has been intensified, and a monograph of these species (to be published about 1970) has been prepared. Progress has been made toward the solution of many problems of classification, and this is reflected in this book, which is based also upon the results of 39 years in the field in all the states and the Canadian provinces and upon visits to about 60 college, university, and museum herbaria for the study of cactus specimens. Many decisions are tentative, and this is inevitable because the data available are still meager. At least, it is hoped a step toward the truth may have been taken. But the truth is an elusive goal, and we never reach it in all particulars.

As stated above, a conservative or liberal viewpoint is tenable on theoretical grounds, but the position of a "lumper" or a "splitter" is not. These terms apply to persons recognizing as "species" or "genera" or other "taxa" groupings of plants or animals that are mere artificial assemblages based upon the presence of some one or two characters to which arbitrary "importance" has been attached. No character is, *per se*, more important than another. *Classification is not according to individual characters, but to the tendency of groups of characters to be consistent in association.* Application of this criterion brings about recognition of natural taxa composed of related plants or animals. One or more characters commonly in the association may not be present in any particular instance; therefore a single character, by itself, means little.

"Splitting" of taxa, especially at the generic and specific levels, has been the rule rather than the exception in treatments of the cactus family. Commonly this has been associated with choice of some one character, designated as the "mark" of the taxon and as being so "important" as to eliminate all other considerations. This, of course, is a fallacy, and it leads to formulation of an artificial system of classification.

NAMES OF CACTI

Botanical names. The plant chosen for illustration of the use of keys in classification was the Mojave hedgehog cactus, *Echinocereus triglochidiatus* var. *mojavensis.* The major portion of the name, *Echinocereus triglochidiatus,* consists of the designations of the genus and species. The first word is a noun, meaning spiny torch cactus or cereus. The second word is an adjective reflecting the presence of 3 spines (glochid being used not in the modern technical sense but to mean spine), the originally collected type specimen of var. *triglochidiatus* having had only 3 or 4 spines per areole. The third word, *mojavensis,* refers to the place of occurrence of the variety. Var. *melanacanthus,* also mentioned above, received a name indicating "black-spined," but, although the type specimen had black spines, most members of the variety do not.

This was a point unknown when the name was applied in 1849, but under the International Code of Botanical Nomenclature names are not later changed merely because they are found or are thought to be inappropriate.

In other cases, there may be no division of the species into varieties. This is true, for example, of *Opuntia chlorotica*, the pancake prickly pear.

The word designating a particular species within a genus is an EPITHET. Commonly it may be an adjective, referring to some quality of the plant, as in *Cereus giganteus*. Often it is a name in the Latin genitive (the same as the possessive in English), as with *Cereus Emoryi* or *Opuntia Wigginsii*.

The plural of genus is genera; each genus stands for a general grouping. The plural of species is species; each species stands for a specific population or system of related populations characteristic of one segment of the genus.

Commonly, if the name of a plant differs from one book to another, this reflects underlying changes in classification, but not necessarily so. Once the classification of a genus, species, or variety is worked out to the best of an author's ability, the application of names to taxa follows a set of rules adopted at an International Botanical Congress. These have been published in the International Code of Botanical Nomenclature, the latest published version of which was adopted by the Tenth International Botanical Congress at Edinburgh in August 1964 (published in Utrecht, 1966). The code is based upon relatively simple principles, as follows: (1) any taxon may have only one valid name; (2) two or more taxa may not have the same name; (3) if the first two points are not in agreement, then the decision is based upon priority in publication of names, that is, the proper name is the earliest one published in the proper rank (e.g. species); (4) determination of which plant was given a name is according to the type specimen designated by its author. In practice, of course, the application and use of the code are much more complex than this. For a full explanation, refer to the following work: Benson, Lyman, *Plant Taxonomy, Methods and Principles*. Ronald Press Co., New York. 1962.

Following *Echinocereus triglochidiatus*, the abbreviation "Engelm." appears. This stands for the name of the person who in 1848 applied this name combination to the species: George Engelmann, a St. Louis physician, and the foremost student of the cactus family. The original plants of this species were brought to Engelmann by Wislizenus, who explored large areas of New Mexico and northern Mexico. The abbreviation of the name of the author of the species is not included so much to honor him as to provide precision in naming. Sometimes more than one author may give different plants the same name, and the abbreviation constitutes a distinction and at the same time a reference to the original place of publication of the name, and therefore to the description supplied by the author and to the type specimen. The full reference is found by consulting the *Gray Herbarium Card Index, being a Catalog of American Plants . . .* , Harvard University, or the *Index Kewensis: An Enumeration of the Genera and Species of Flowering Plants,* Royal Botanic Gardens, Kew, England.

Following the name of the variety, var. *mojavensis*, three names appear, the first two in parentheses, "(Engelm. & Bigelow)." In this instance, Engelmann, studying the specimens collected by J. M. Bigelow on the survey to determine the feasibility of a railway route to the Pacific Ocean (approximately that of the Santa Fé), decided, with Bigelow, that specimens of the Mojave hedgehog cactus represented a new species. They named it *Echinocereus mojavensis* Engelm. & Bigelow. In later studies, with the advantage of better transportation and the possibility of study of the entire intergrading complex ranging from California to Utah and Texas and deep into Mexico, the taxon was reduced in status to variety *mojavensis* by L. Benson.

Synonymy. With the treatment of each species or variety in the text there is a paragraph or a series of paragraphs listing the "synonomy" for that taxon. This is simply a chronological list of the scientific names that have been applied at one time or another to the taxon since the time it was first named. All the names in a given paragraph are based upon a single TYPE SPECIMEN (see next paragraph), and by their multiplicity they indicate that the original name of the taxon has gone through a series of recombinations. For example, *Rosa alba* may have appeared also as *Rosa flava* var. *alba*, or it may have been considered to be of another genus and have been recombined as *Fragaria alba*. All these combinations appear in the paragraph, and they are followed by the TYPE LOCALITY at which the original or type specimen was collected. The implication where the synonymy comprises several paragraphs is that the several type specimens thus represented are thought by the writer to be properly included within the single taxon.

The classification of any group of plants or animals is always in a state of flux; periodic revision is to be expected. Progress is made in the direction of learning the truth, either as new information becomes available or in the light of new interpretations of the data, but the whole truth is never ascertained. Thus the classification of the cactus family in this book into genera, species, and varieties represents a great many tentative conclusions based upon the data available, conclusions subject to later revision by the author or by others. And of course the underlying changes in classification usually result in name changes or shifts in taxonomic rank. Synonymy is thus seen to be an essential part of each description.

The scientific name of a plant taxon applies to a broad range of more or less differing individuals; but at the time the name is applied to the taxon a particular preserved specimen is chosen by the author of the taxon to illustrate the basis for the combination of characters appearing in the description of the species or variety he is naming. This specimen, the TYPE SPECIMEN, is the permanent record with which the name is associated. Regardless of how great or small a range of other plants may then or later be considered to be included in the same taxon (as for example the same species), the type specimen is always included among those to which the name is applied. The specimen, which must be preserved permanently in a herbarium, serves as a sort of "least common denominator" for the plants that are to bear the name. Later, if by chance the species or other taxon is given one or more new names (and there are many reasons why this may be found appropriate), then each new name is based upon a new type specimen.

Presumably, in the field, plants similar to a given type specimen may be found at the given type locality. It should be possible, by visiting the area, to determine the relationship of these plants to others of the same natural population. Such an investigation may yield characters in living plants that were either not represented or were obscure in the type specimen. It may permit establishing the relationship of the type plant to the others with which it grew, these together having formed a natural population. The type specimen may prove to have a combination of characters in harmony with the rest of the population or one unusual and representing a transition between taxa. For example, the type specimen may represent only one of many character combinations among the members of a hybrid swarm resulting from interbreeding of two or more taxa (e.g., species), followed by crossing of the progeny with both parents and with each other and their own descendants. Two or more plants growing at the same place may have received names indicating them to be different taxa. Investigation at their mutual type locality may confirm this or may show their differing character combinations to appear, along with many others, in the populations of a single taxon. Thus, field study at the type locality may yield either information confirming the identity of a proposed taxon or a basis for accepting or rejecting it. To put it another way, field study may indicate whether the taxon is a valid one maintaining itself as a population apart from others or whether the individual forming the type specimen represented merely one of many genetic combinations occurring sporadically in the field.

The paragraphs of synonyms are arranged in order of date of publication of the epithet (adjective used as a noun) appearing in one or more name combinations in each. An example of an epithet forming part of a scientific name is *alba* in *Rosa alba*. Within each paragraph the combinations in which the epithet has appeared—for example, *Rosa alba* and *Rosa flava* var. *alba*—would be listed in order of priority in publication. The choice of the name for the taxon as a whole is based upon time of publication; i.e., the epithet used for a part of the name of a species is the one first published in that rank, provided there is no special obstacle to its use, and the name for a variety includes the first epithet published in that rank.

Popular names. The application of common or vernacular names of plants is far more confused than the use of scientific names. Popular names are merely common language designations that follow no established rules. Often the same name may be applied, especially in different areas, to different plants, or a single plant may be given several popular names. In some regions fairly common plants may have been given no popular names at all.

In *The Native Cacti of California*, English, Spanish, and Indian names for cacti are included when they are available. However, the vast majority of cactus species do not have special popular names other than those applied to relatively large groups of species, such as the chollas and prickly pears or the hedgehog cacti. In general I have made no attempt to achieve artificial convenience or consistency by fabricating popular names where none exist. But I have followed no fixed policy concerning popular names, since none is possible.

Geographical Distribution of Cacti

The cactus family is characteristic of the Western Hemisphere, where it ranges from at least northern British Columbia and Peace River, Alberta, Canada, to southern South America. A few members of the specialized genus *Rhipsalis* (largely EPIPHYTIC, i.e., growing on trees) occur in Africa and Ceylon; they may be either native or introduced, and the point has been the subject for much argument. Primarily, members of the cactus family are desert plants occurring in both Northern and Southern hemispheres in the New World; however, some species occur in tropical rain forests, and, as in southern Florida, they may grow where the water table is within a few inches of the surface of the soil. Other species are native in the relatively moist areas of the United States east of the Mississippi River. Cacti are native in all the adjacent 48 states except Vermont, New Hampshire, and Maine. In Canada they occur in British Columbia, Alberta, Saskatchewan, Manitoba, and Ontario.

The cacti of the United States are most abundant in the desert or arid regions ranging from southern California to central and southern Texas. They are most spectacular on the low hills and mountain ranges in the deserts of southern Arizona. The number of native taxa (species and varieties) occurring in Arizona is almost identical to that occurring in Texas. The third-ranking cactus state is New Mexico, and California is fourth. The family is less important but significant in the floras of Florida, Nevada, Utah, and Colorado. In other states the number of species is relatively small, but one or more may be locally abundant. In Hawaii there are no native cacti, but introduced species have escaped from cultivation, and they are conspicuous on the dry sides of the islands. The common cactus there is the spiny form of *Opuntia Ficus-Indica*.

In northern California, cacti are confined to the relatively narrow zone of Sagebrush Desert and Juniper-Pinyon Woodland east of the Cascade Mountains and the Sierra Nevada, extending intermittently and rarely to grassy areas west of the main mountain crest from San Luis Obispo County and Tulare County south. Cacti occur throughout southern California. The dots, asterisks, etc., used on the distribution maps indicate places where the plants are known to occur naturally. Because actual plant distributions are inadequately known, ranges cannot reasonably be delimited simply by cross-hatching some presumed range or by using a line to describe its supposed periphery.

THE EFFECT OF GLOBAL WINDS AND CALMS

The global or planetary winds and calms largely determine the zones of climate and consequently the primary zones of vegetation of the earth. The principal zones of the global winds in the Northern Hemisphere are as follows, from north to south (in reverse order in the Southern Hemisphere):

1. The zone of the polar winds—the arctic and subarctic region.

2. The zone of the prevailing westerlies—the north temperate region.

3. The horse latitudes—the belt of calms in the vicinity of the 30th parallel of latitude (roughly from the 23d to the 34th parallel).

4. The zone of the trade winds and the belt of tropical calms (in the vicinity of the equator)—the tropics.

The pattern of the planetary or global winds is produced chiefly by unequal heating of the atmosphere at different latitudes and altitudes. The direction of the winds is altered by the rotation of the earth.

In the vicinity of the 30th parallel, in either the Northern or the Southern Hemisphere, the air mass is descending. As the air reaches lower altitudes, it is under greater pressure from the air above, becoming compressed and warmer and increasing in moisture-holding capacity. Any large land mass near the 30th parallel tends to become a desert, because mostly the air takes up moisture rather than depositing it. In the Northern Hemisphere the 30th parallel runs through the deserts of the United States and Mexico, the Sahara Desert, the deserts of the Middle East, and the Arabian Desert (eastward as far as India). In the Southern Hemisphere it lies across the deserts of Chile, South and South West Africa, and Australia. However, some areas near the 30th parallel are not deserts. A small land mass such as Florida may be moist because the descending warm air comes into contact with warm seas on both sides of a narrow peninsula. The air absorbs moisture, which is deposited on the adjacent strip of land.

Because a descending air mass is under relatively high pressure, it spreads in all directions over the land surface. Because the horse latitudes encircle the earth, the spread of air is to the north and south. Consequently, in either hemisphere, one current of air moves from the horse latitudes toward the low-pressure area at the equator, and another current moves toward the pole.

The air mass leaving the horse latitudes does not move directly south or north. In either hemisphere, air moving away from the horse latitudes toward the equator or the pole is deflected to the west or east because the relative speed of revolution of the earth varies according to latitude. At the equator the earth's surface moves at an easily calculated rate. The circumference of the earth is about 24,000 miles, and the planet rotates once in 24 hours. Therefore, any point on the equator moves eastward at about 1,000 miles per hour. If the air along the surface of the earth were not moving and the ground moved at 1,000 miles an hour, the effect would be catastrophic. A 130-mile-per-hour wind is sufficient to blow slate shingles off a roof; a 1,000-mile-per-hour wind would devastate the landscape. However, such an extreme wind does not occur, because after a time the air assumes approximately the same speed as the ground beneath it. As the earth's diameter decreases toward the poles, the rotation speed decreases proportionately. Near the pole the ground speed tends toward zero. The air descending in the horse latitudes assumes the rotation speed at that level of latitude—approximately 900 miles per hour. In the Northern Hemisphere the air mass moving toward the equator tends to be left behind to the west as the eastward motion of the land becomes more rapid. Consequently, the trade winds in the Northern Hemisphere blow more or less from northeast to southwest (in the Southern Hemisphere from southeast to northwest). Toward 40° North Latitude the air moving north from the horse latitudes encounters ground speed of only 800 miles per hour, and at 48° only 700. Thus, the air mass has a relative eastward movement faster than that of the earth's surface. Because the air moves east faster than does the ground beneath it, the prevailing westerly winds blow east as well as north. As the air mass moves north, the wind velocity increases; thus sailors call the latitudes between 40 and 50 degrees the "roaring forties."

Movement of air from the high-pressure areas at the poles toward the equator produces the polar winds. As air moves south from the Arctic, it is deflected westward because it is moving from an area of less to one of greater ground speed. Because of inertia the air lags, and is therefore deflected westward. In the Northern Hemisphere, the polar winds blow from northeast to southwest, in the Southern from southeast to northwest, as with the trade winds.

The climatic and vegetational areas correspond to those of the global or planetary winds and calms, as follows:

1. The Arctic regions (polar winds) and their extensions at high altitudes into the mountains to the south. These areas are cold in winter and cold or cool in summer. There are no cacti.

2. The temperate regions (prevailing westerlies). In both hemi-

spheres these regions form zones of mild climate, except for winter cold. Winter freezing is a major factor limiting distribution of many plants, and only a few hardy species of cacti are able to survive temperatures more than a few degrees below freezing. In temperate regions cacti are restricted also by the competition of species better adapted to the moist ground or the temperature.

3. The horse latitudes (calms). The large land areas are predisposed to desert formation at these latitudes. In summer, southern California is on the border zone between the prevailing westerlies and the horse latitudes, but in winter it is in the zone of prevailing westerlies. In such a border zone, desert formation depends upon local conditions, as described below.

4. The tropical regions (including both the trade winds and the doldrums or tropical calms). The climate is mostly warm and humid, but it may be locally dry. Some cacti may occur in even the tropical rain forests. They are common near the sea on the dry sides of islands or continents.

Within each major climatic and vegetational zone, local conditions induce variability of both climate and vegetation. The prevailing westerly winds are moisture-laden when they encounter the Pacific coast of North America. In the summer the coastal land is warmer than the ocean, because the radiant energy from the sun is distributed to greater depths into the water than into the ground and because on the ocean more heat is lost through evaporation of water. In summer, when the prevailing westerlies strike the warmer coast, there is little or no precipitation. In winter, the ocean is commonly warmer than the land, because, although the surface water is chilled, warmer water from beneath is constantly mixed with it. Consequently, as it moves east, the air may lose moisture along the lowlands, which frequently may be colder than the ocean.

As the air moves inland, it is deflected upward over the hills and mountains. As it rises it expands, cools, and loses moisture, depositing rain or snow on the western slopes and the summits. As the air mass descends on the leeward side of the mountains, it is compressed and it becomes warmer. Consequently, it may absorb moisture, creating a desert on the leeward side of the range. Because southern California is on the edge of the horse latitudes, it is predisposed to formation of deserts if local conditions shift the balance toward aridity. Thus, there are deserts or arid lands in the "rain shadows" on the inland (eastern) side of each mountain axis.

HISTORICAL DEVELOPMENT OF THE NATURAL VEGETATION

CALIFORNIA IN THE EOCENE

In Eocene time, about 50 to 70 million years ago, the lowlands of California were occupied by a tropical or subtropical rain forest. The rest of the Pacific Coast and the higher ground of the interior were covered by warm temperate floras. See the Scale of Geologic Time below.

Since Tertiary times the earth has cooled, and the climate has become gradually drier. For the most part, the tropical and subtropical plants once occurring in California and other temperate regions in the Northern Hemisphere have moved southward or perished. Now there are few relics of the Eocene flora. A possible example is the bay tree, pepperwood, or mountain laurel (*Umbellularia californica*). In southwestern Oregon the same plant is called "myrtle." This plant is the only member of the laurel family (LAURACEAE) native in or anywhere near the western United States. Inasmuch as the family is common in tropical and subtropical regions, probably the single California species is a relic of the flora of Eocene time. If so, the species must have become gradually adapted to the changing conditions, and probably it is modified considerably from its forerunners, which occurred in California when the area was tropical or subtropical. The plant must have adapted to survive drought, especially in summer, and to withstand cold, because it is native now in dry areas where the temperature is not uncommonly below 20° F.

CALIFORNIA IN OLIGOCENE AND MIOCENE TIMES

In Oligocene and Miocene times the area now forming the entire western United States was essentially a region of plains, rolling hills, and low mountains. In California there was no major mountain system until the close of the Tertiary Period. The entire

SCALE OF GEOLOGIC TIME
(Emphasis upon Mesozoic and Cenozoic Time)

Era	Period	Epoch	Plants	Animals
CENOZOIC (began about 60 or 80 million years ago)	Quaternary	Recent and Pleistocene (glacial)	Dominance of flowering plants	Passing of large mammals
	Tertiary	Pliocene Miocene Oligocene Eocene Paleocene		Dominance of mammals and insects
MESOZOIC (began about 200 million years ago)	Cretaceous		Ascendancy of flowering plants	Rise of insects; end of dinosaurs
	Jurassic		Climax of cone-bearing trees, including cycads	Age of reptiles, including dinosaurs
	Triassic			
PALEOZOIC (began about 500 million years ago)	Several		Age of pteridophytes (ferns, etc.)	Ages of invertebrates, then chordates, fish, amphibians, reptiles
PRECAMBRIAN	Few organisms left fossils, and the record is meager.			

area from the Pacific Coast eastward through the Great Basin region was of low relief. According to Chaney, in middle Miocene the region from approximately the latitude of San Francisco and Salt Lake City north was occupied by forest, various versions of which were present in the areas around the temperate portions of the Northern Hemisphere. Its fossil remains are the Arctotertiary geoflora. This forest flora included many species that ranged widely in north temperate regions, and among them were trees still living in some parts of the world. The more prominent survivors include the California coast redwood, *Sequoia sempervirens*, and a near relative, the Chinese (or "dawn") redwood, *Metasequoia glyptostroboides*. During Miocene times in many areas these two trees occurred together. Their appearance is similar, and the fossil specimens were not distinguished until 1928. The branchlets and leaves on the twigs of *Metasequoia* appear to be in pairs, that is, opposite each other, whereas those of the coast redwood are arranged alternately (spirally) on the branchlets. This difference can be made out readily in fossils. Living trees of the Chinese redwood were discovered in 1944. The two redwoods are making a last stand on the two sides of the Pacific Ocean. The Chinese redwood has been found in only one small area in the interior of China in adjacent portions of Szechwan and Hupeh provinces. The coast redwood occurs only in coastal northern California as far south as the Big Sur and barely within the border of coastal Oregon. Associated with these trees in middle Tertiary times were various others, among them the maidenhair tree (*Ginkgo biloba*), the Chinese tree of heaven (*Ailanthus altissima*), and the Chinese wing nuts (*Pterocarya* ssp.). These plants lived together in a temperate climate, with considerable precipitation distributed throughout the year.

According to Axelrod, in middle Miocene times south of the sites of San Francisco and Salt Lake City the countryside was occupied largely by an oak woodland flora that had migrated northwestward from the area now occupied by the Sierra Madre Occidental in northwestern Mexico. The oak woodland flora, like the forest flora, was adapted to year-round rainfall but to a warmer temperate climate with lower total precipitation than the forest flora to the north.

There must have been many local forms of both vegetation types. These minor variations are difficult to reconstruct in detail, but, in view of the low relief of the entire area, probably the degree of differentiation within either flora was not great. The zone at the latitude of San Francisco and Salt Lake City included areas of intergradation, and in accordance with local conditions there were numerous extensions of one type southward and the other northward.

Since the middle of Miocene time, and especially in Pliocene and Pleistocene times, there were three major changes (which we shall take up in the following pages):

1. *Disappearance of summer rainfall* along the entire Pacific Coast and in the Great Basin region.

2. *Uplift of the great mountain axis,* which included the Cascades to the north in Washington and Oregon and as far south as Mount Lassen, California, the Sierra Nevada continuing on the same axis south to Kern County, California, and extensions southward through other mountains in southern California and Baja California. Two important effects of the uplift, which we shall also take up, were the formation of a *rain shadow* and the development of *new habitats in the new mountain ranges.*

3. *Onset of four glacial periods in Pleistocene time,* which included glaciation to the north and along the mountain chains to the south, accompanied by heavy rainfall or winter snowfall to the south and at lower levels.

Disappearance of summer rainfall. Since middle Tertiary time winter rainfall has dwindled, and summer rainfall has essentially disappeared. Probably this has accompanied the cooling of the ocean and the lowering of the uptake of water by the air mass of the prevailing westerlies moving across the Pacific Ocean toward North America. Rainfall on the Pacific Coast is associated partly with the interrelationship of temperatures of the ocean and land. For this reason the area, especially California, now receives little or no summer rain through the agency of the prevailing westerlies. Exceptional summer rains are due to tropical storms (hurricanes or typhoons) that have traveled north beyond their usual limits on the western coast of Mexico. Occasionally in the late summer or early fall these storms appear as far up the coast as San Diego and in the deserts of California. Less frequently they may continue north even beyond San Francisco. Sometimes in the areas near the Mexican border the storms may cause seed germination and growth of desert species ordinarily dormant for lack of a warm, moist period. This is not provided by the rains of winter, but once in several years it may result from a series of tropical storms. Thus some trees and shrubs in the deserts of southern California tend to be in age classes correlated with the infrequent years of germination and growth of their seeds.

Uplift of the mountain axis. The Cascade Mountains, the Sierra Nevada, and the mountains of southern California (San Gabriel, San Bernardino, San Jacinto, Palomar, and Cuyamaca mountains) form a "great stone wall." This wall is continuous with mountain ranges from central and southern Alaska through British Columbia, the Pacific States, and Baja California. The Cascade Mountains form a wall from just north of the Canadian boundary southward across Washington and Oregon and to the area just south of Mount Lassen in California. The Cascades are a recently formed volcanic range with high peaks along the axis. This upthrust dates primarily from the Pliocene and Pleistocene. The Sierra Nevada is continuous with the Cascades but of different origin. The major uplift, which also occurred during the Pliocene and Pleistocene, was due to the tilting of a gigantic fault block of granite underlying sedimentary rock. This sunk gradually in the Sacramento and San Joaquin valleys and rose in the Sierra Nevada, dropping off abruptly along a fault from the summit into the Great Basin and Owens Valley. Most of the original sedimentary rocks have been worn away, thus exposing the underlying granite. The axis continues through the granite mountain ranges of southern California into the Peninsular Ranges, which include the granitic mountains from Riverside County south to the tip of Baja California.

The uplift of the Cascade–Sierra Nevada axis has had two major effects on floral development: formation of a rain shadow on the lee side of the mountain axis, and development of new habitats at various altitudes in the new mountain ranges.

The rain shadow. When the great stone wall between coastal California and the present desert regions was elevated, rainfall in the lee of the mountains was reduced markedly. California as a whole has a Mediterranean climate; that is, it is relatively dry and warm, and essentially precipitation is limited to winter. Rainfall results from cooling of the air mass of the prevailing westerly winds blowing toward the coast across the Pacific Ocean. In winter the land is often colder than the ocean, and since Tertiary times this temperature relationship has brought about precipitation in the lowlands along the coast. Since uplift of the mountain ranges, as the air mass moved inland it has been forced upward over the crests, which in the Sierra Nevada extend to elevations of 14,500 feet. Under lower atmospheric pressure, the rising air mass has expanded and cooled, depositing rain or snow on the mountains. Descending on the eastern or lee side of the cordillera, the air mass has become compressed and warmed. The result has been a rain shadow in the lee of the mountains, with formation of either a dry area or a desert on the inland side of each mountain axis.

The following examples illustrate the magnitude of the climatic effect of uplifting of the great stone wall. At Snoqualmie Falls, east of Seattle, Washington, the average rainfall is about 8.5 feet per year. Near Wenatchee, only 65 air miles to the east, the average rainfall is about 8.5 inches. The intervening Cascade Mountains, which at this point are only about 4,000 to 5,000 feet in altitude, are responsible for the difference. In southern California the average rainfall on the western side of the mountains in the vicinity of Claremont is 17 or 18 inches per year, but across the mountain range at Palm Springs the average is only 2 or 3 inches. In California the mountain barriers toward the ocean are the principal factor determining local climate, and this is responsible for the great differences of the western and eastern portions of the state. All along the great stone wall the differences in the climate and the vegetation on the west and east sides of the mountain axis parallel these two examples.

Other mountain ranges may produce additional rain shadows. For example, in northern California the moist area of the redwood belt is on the western side of the North Coast Ranges, and the drier Sacramento Valley lies inland. Farther to the east the Sierra Nevada takes more moisture from the air mass, and the Sagebrush Desert lies beyond it. Similar contrasts occur in numerous areas, as, for example, on the seaward and San Joaquin Valley sides of the South Coast Ranges. Near the coast in San Luis Obispo

County, the rainfall may average 15 or 20 inches per year, whereas in the lee of the Coast Ranges near Taft it is 1 or 2 inches. Death Valley (average rainfall 1 inch) is in the lee of four successive mountain systems—the Coast Ranges, the Sierra Nevada, the Argus Mountains, and the Panamint Mountains.

Although evolution of the California deserts has been recent and rapid, many species had already adapted or partly adapted themselves to similar local conditions, and were waiting in the wings for the opportunity to play on just such a stage. Evolution of plants suited to dry conditions had in fact been stimulated long before the principal uplift of the mountain axis in Pliocene and Pleistocene. According to Axelrod, for more than one hundred million years the general, though erratic, trend of climate on the Pacific Coast has been toward dryness. Although until recently there were only small or discontinuous mountain ranges, there were local rain shadows, and in the dry leeward pockets xerophytic species had evolved. As the mountain axis became higher and continuous, these species spread out over the newly formed deserts to leeward. In addition, there were invasions by species adapted to similar conditions in dry portions of the Rocky Mountain region or of Mexico. In the northern or sagebrush type of desert, many species were drawn from the Miocene oak woodland and fewer from the Miocene forest and Rocky Mountain area. In the southern or creosote bush type of desert, some species evolved on the spot; others were modified from migrants from drier parts of northwestern Mexico. The climate east of the mountain axis not only has become drier, but also, for lack of the stabilizing effect of water upon temperature, has become hotter in summer and colder in winter. Water restricts fluctuations of temperature because it absorbs more heat accompanying a change of a given number of degrees than does any other substance. The interior area of rain shadow has been deprived of the temperature-stability characteristic of moist areas and particularly of those areas adjacent to large bodies of water like the Pacific Ocean.

New habitats in the new mountain ranges. Uplift of the mountain axis created new habitats, because temperature decreases 4° F. with each 1,000 feet of altitude and because the rising air mass of the prevailing westerlies deposits much water and snow on the western slopes and crests. This has resulted in two new types of forest habitats below timberline, the Sierran Montane Forest and the Sierran Subalpine Forest.

The Sierran Montane Forest habitat occurs at middle altitudes along the great stone wall and in adjacent ranges. The species have been derived largely from ancestral types in the Miocene forest. Some species are identical with those in the present forests along the Pacific Coast (Pacific Forest), and others are related closely to coastal forest species. A smaller number must represent invasions from other sources.

The Sierran Subalpine Forest habitat forms the upper half of the timber belt. It includes many elements derived from species occurring in the Miocene forest, but there are species related closely to those in the American Northern Forest, which extends from Alaska to Labrador.

The flora of the Alpine Tundra, which occurs above timberline in the mountains, is not related to that of the forests. It is composed largely of floral elements derived from those in the Arctic, but some arrived from various floras from other regions, including even the deserts. Derivatives of desert species tend to occupy the dry inland-facing slopes at high elevations. Here the evaporation of water is rapid, because the wind velocity is high and the atmospheric pressure at upper altitudes is low.

Onset of glacial periods. Four segments of Pleistocene time favored formation of ice sheets, which covered much of North America. These ranged as far south as Olympia, Washington; Flathead Lake, Montana; Cincinnati, Ohio; and Long Island, New York. In the time of glaciation, temperatures were low not only in the glacial regions themselves but also south of the ice, and were associated with heavy rain- and snowfall.

The magnitude of Pleistocene precipitation is illustrated by the Grand Coulee in eastern Washington and ancient Lake Bonneville in Utah. On the site in the Columbia River now occupied by the Grand Coulee Dam, a tremendous ice jam diverted the river into a new course remaining today as the dry Grand Coulee, recently partly converted into a reservoir. In this great Pleistocene watercourse there was a waterfall about 60 times the size of Niagara. This remains as the Dry Falls. In Pleistocene time, gigantic Lake Bonneville extended from southern Idaho almost to the southern boundary of Utah and from the eastern edge of Nevada to the Wasatch Mountains above Salt Lake City and Utah Lake. The old beachlines of Lake Bonneville form terraces on the mountainsides above Salt Lake City, and from an airplane the full outline of the old lake bed is evident.

In the glacial and interglacial intervals the climate fluctuated from colder and wetter to warmer and drier, and with these changes the floras were on the move. In colder times all the types of vegetation were pushed to lower latitudes or altitudes, only to return north or up the mountains between glaciations. The relatively rapid changes required exploitation of new locations, and, in the changing ecology of each locality, mutants and hybrids were able to survive because there was as a weakening of competition from established species that had adapted to disappearing conditions. The resulting new gene combinations gave rise to altered species, then new varieties, and ultimately new species. Many older species were exterminated by climate or competition, and were replaced by others as climatic factors were reversed from time to time.

THE RESULTING ECOLOGIC MOSAIC

The result of these changes is a mosaic of plant and animal species derived primarily from the original sources but with invasions from more northern floras, from the floras of the Rocky Mountain region, and from floras in the horse latitudes in Mexico. The recognizable elements of this mosaic and their derivatives are discussed on pp. 45–63.

The floras and their subdivisions* are based upon association of species most of whose ancestral types have been together in space through long periods of geologic history—perhaps 25 to 60 million years. However, floras do not necessarily persist as wholly

* Lyman Benson, *Plant Classification* (Heath [Div. Raytheon Educational Co.], Boston, 1957), pp. 563–647; *Plant Taxonomy, Methods and Principles* (Ronald, New York, 1962).

consistent units through long segments of geologic time. They are subject to modification in the association of species. The ecological requirements of no two taxa are exactly the same, and each phase of every flora has undergone some dissociation of its members. Some of these have taken up new alliances, with even a minor change of climate. Each vegetation type gains and loses some members from time to time, as illustrated above by the changes during the Pleistocene glaciations. Nevertheless, even though associations are not wholly stable, many species or their modified descendants remain together for long periods, and historic floras are a valid part of the basis for classification of natural vegetation.

Through its history each flora tends to retain its earlier ecological formation, such as forest, grassland, or desert, but it may give rise to other formations. For example, under local forest conditions some herbaceous plants or their evolutionary derivatives may become adapted to open, often dry, places surrounded by forest. If conditions change, for example, to a somewhat drier climate, the open areas may become larger, until they constitute considerable regions of grassland, as in the local prairies occurring in the Pacific Forest from Puget Sound to Mendocino County, California. If this process is carried far enough, a new grassland vegetation type, like the Palouse Prairie of the Pacific Northwest, may evolve. However, except for invasion by some species from other sources, the grassland was derived from the same ancestral flora as the forest, and its primary relationship is to the forest rather than to other grasslands.

Furthermore, plants of similar formations are not necessarily derived from the same historic sources. The vegetation of the deserts or grasslands of southern Africa and that of the corresponding ecological formations in other parts of the world, such as southwestern North America, appear at first glance so much alike as to be indistinguishable. However, not one native species is the same, and many of the plants are of different genera or families. Not even the desert regions east of the great stone wall of the American Pacific coast are coherent in their floras. As shown above, the desert vegetation that developed in the rain shadow of the mountain axis was from two origins.

The ecologist has a primary interest in formations and life forms of plants growing together, in the physical and chemical factors affecting them and their association, and in the interrelationships of all the plants and animals forming the natural community. Consequently, his classification system for living vegetation may be altered, according to his purpose, in one direction or another, and it may be different from that of the taxonomist. Since the taxonomic or systematic botanist is concerned primarily with classification of taxa of all ranks in the light of their evolutionary development, the origin and development of the species associated in floras are fundamental knowledge for his purpose. To him historic floras are of first importance, because their development explains and clarifies the classification of some of their included species and varieties.

THE FLORAS OF CALIFORNIA

The species and varieties not only of cacti but of all types of plants and animals are associated with vegetation types. Understanding the natural communities of living organisms is necessary to interpreting their distribution, and it is basic to working out the interrelationships of genera, species, and varieties.

The floras discussed in the following pages are those that are clearly Californian, at least in part, plus a few others significant in the preceding discussions of floras and their history. Those that are clearly Californian are indicated by asterisks in the table on p. 46. Maps of the topography of California are given on pp. 48 and 50, and maps of the natural floras, or vegetation types, are given on pp. 49 and 51. The occurrence of cactus species and varieties in these floras is indicated in the endsheet table.

A great many educated guesses have had to go into the making of the vegetation map. I have been up and down the state again and again studying these matters, but one person cannot possibly know at first hand every mountain range occurring through a

The North American Floras and Their Subdivisions
(North America north of Mexico)

*THE BOREAL FLORA (Boreal–Alpine Region)
    1. The Arctic Tundra
  *2. The West American Alpine Tundra

THE NORTHERN FOREST FLORA
    1. The American Northern Forest

*THE ROCKY MOUNTAIN FOREST FLORA
  *1. The Rocky Mountain Subalpine Forest†
  *2. The Rocky Mountain Montane Forest†

*THE PACIFIC NORTHWESTERN FLORA
  *1. The Pacific Forest
  *2. The Sierran Subalpine Forest
  *3. The Sierran Montane Forest
    4. The Palouse Prairie

*THE SIERRA MADREAN FLORA
    1. The Southwestern Oak Woodland and Chaparral
  *2. The California Oak Woodland
  *3. The California Chaparral
  *4. The Pacific Grassland
  *5. The Juniper-Pinyon Woodland
  *6. The Sagebrush Desert
    7. The Navajoan Desert

*THE MEXICAN DESERT FLORA
  *1. The Mojavean Desert
  2. The Sonoran (Colorado and Arizona) Deserts
    3. The Chihuahuan Desert

THE PLAINS AND PRAIRIE FLORA
    1. The Great Plains Grassland
    2. The Desert Grassland
    3. The Prairie

THE EASTERN FOREST FLORA
    1. The Deciduous Forests

THE AMERICAN TROPICAL FLORA
    1. The Caribbean Tropical Flora

* Vegetation types occurring in California.
† Approached in character by forests in desert mountains in Inyo County.

thousand miles. Fortunately, most of them are known and in most cases well enough to allow extrapolation to the rest. But the question of just how far up each canyon in the Sierra Nevada there is a change from oak woodland to montane forest requires interpretation based upon the canyons one has seen, whether from the ground or from the air. Likewise, whether a particular mountain range or valley would be high enough to support Sagebrush Desert as opposed to Mojavean Desert or low enough to support Sagebrush Desert as opposed to Juniper-Pinyon Woodland can be a matter of conjecture, because altitude is not the only factor involved. It is quite likely, therefore, that I have misinterpreted some areas, and more precise information concerning the extent of vegetation types would be appreciated.

THE BOREAL FLORA

The West American Alpine Tundra. This vegetation type occurs above timberline in the high mountains. Most of its elements came from the Arctic, but some came from other sources, including the deserts. There are no cacti. Except for a few mat-forming species such as dwarf willows, the characteristic species are herbs, usually perennials.

THE NORTHERN FOREST FLORA

The American Northern Forest. This forest is not represented directly in California, but historically it contributed species to the cooler forests, especially the Sierran Subalpine Forest, and particularly its phase just below timberline. The fluctuations of climate during the Pleistocene doubtless facilitated this migration as well as the stranding of species, often with modification, in the mountains of the Pacific Coast.

THE ROCKY MOUNTAIN FOREST FLORA

This forest flora is not represented clearly in California. Some elements of the subalpine and montane forests of the Rocky Mountain system occur in the southern Sierra Nevada and in the higher Great Basin and desert ranges of Mono and Inyo counties. These include *Pinus flexilis*, limber pine (subalpine and to some

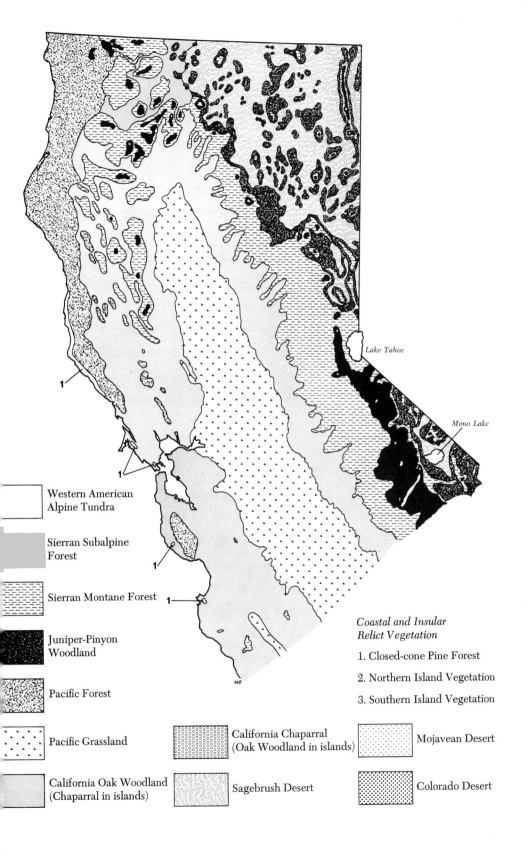

Western American
Alpine Tundra

Sierran Subalpine
Forest

Sierran Montane Forest

Juniper-Pinyon
Woodland

Pacific Forest

Pacific Grassland

California Oak Woodland
(Chaparral in islands)

California Chaparral
(Oak Woodland in islands)

Sagebrush Desert

Mojavean Desert

Colorado Desert

*Coastal and Insular
Relict Vegetation*

1. Closed-cone Pine Forest

2. Northern Island Vegetation

3. Southern Island Vegetation

Lake Tahoe

Mono Lake

NF

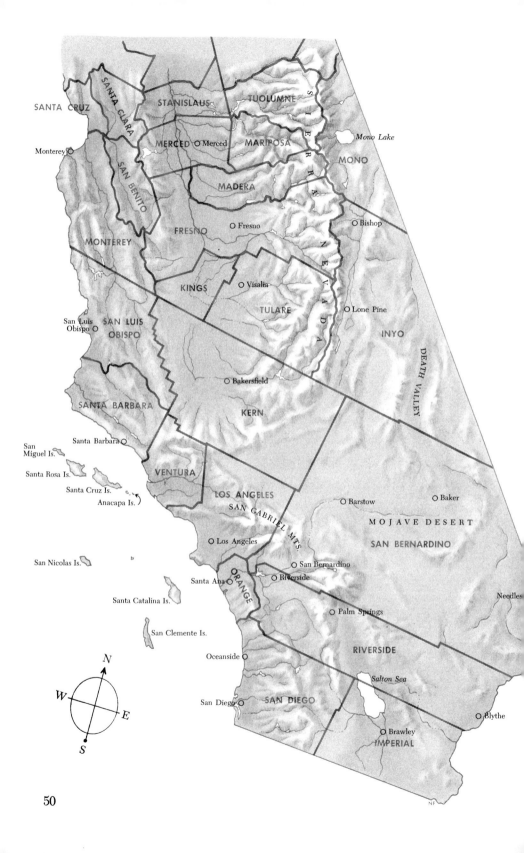

SANTA CRUZ

SANTA CLARA

STANISLAUS

TUOLUMNE

S
I
E
R
R
A

SAN BENITO

MERCED O Merced

MARIPOSA

Mono Lake

Monterey O

MONO

MADERA

O Bishop

MONTEREY

FRESNO

O Fresno

N
E
V
A
D
A

KINGS

O Visalia

San Luis
Obispo O

SAN LUIS
OBISPO

TULARE

O Lone Pine

INYO

DEATH VALLEY

O Bakersfield

SANTA BARBARA

KERN

San
Miguel Is.

Santa Barbara O

Santa Rosa Is.

Santa Cruz Is.

VENTURA

Anacapa Is.

LOS ANGELES

O Barstow

O Baker

SAN GABRIEL MTS.

MOJAVE DESERT

SAN BERNARDINO

San Nicolas Is.

O Los Angeles

b

O San Bernardino

Santa Ana O

O
R
A
N
G
E

O Riverside

Santa Catalina Is.

Needles

San Clemente Is.

O Palm Springs

N

RIVERSIDE

Oceanside O

W

E

Salton Sea

S

O Blythe

San Diego O

SAN DIEGO

O Brawley

IMPERIAL

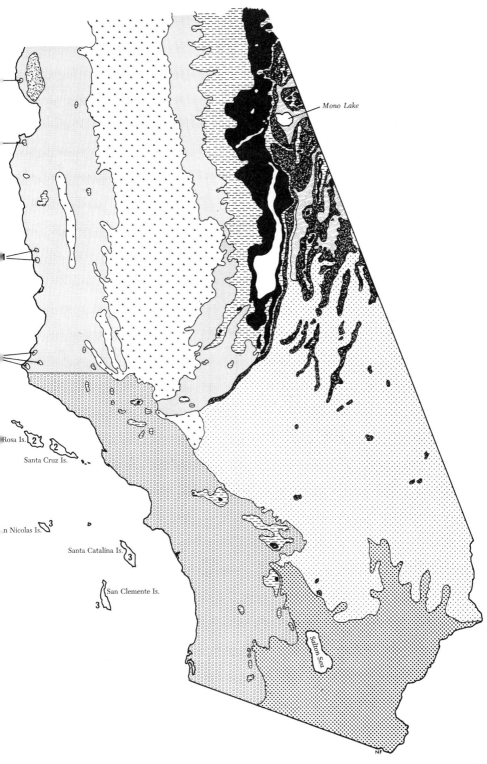

Mono Lake

Rosa Is.

Santa Cruz Is.

n Nicolas Is.

Santa Catalina Is.

San Clemente Is.

Salton Sea

extent montane); and *Pinus aristata,* the bristlecone pine (subalpine). In California the Rocky Mountain Subalpine Forest and the Rocky Mountain Montane Forest are not enough differentiated from the Sierran forests to be discussed independently. Several species of cacti occurring more or less characteristically in the lower part of the Rocky Mountain Montane Forest to the east are listed in the endsheet table under that forest, but none of these is restricted to it. Their association with this forest in California is not necessarily clear, although in the states to the east it is.

THE PACIFIC NORTHWESTERN FLORA

This flora has been derived largely from the ancient Miocene forest. In the forest belt west of the mountains and on the forests of the main mountain axis there has been modification from the wide-ranging temperate forest of middle Tertiary. When summer rainfall disappeared and the climate of the forest regions from Washington to California changed toward dryness, there was a general sorting out of the more drought-resistant species. The emphasis shifted from summer-drought-sensitive, broad-leaved deciduous trees to the more xerophytic evergreen, coniferous trees. The following subdivisions are the modified remnants of the ancient forest flora; the coastal Douglas fir, *Pseudotsuga Menziesii* var. *Menziesii,* is characteristic of the first two forest types.

The Pacific Forest. This is the least modified of the present forests. It extends as a fringe along the west coast of Alaska and thence west of the mountain axis to northern California as far south as the Big Sur in Monterey County. The forests near Seattle and Portland and the coastal redwood forests of California are of this type. Disjunct areas of Pacific Forest occur inland in patches along the storm track across southern British Columbia to the Rocky Mountains in northern Idaho and northwestern Montana. Except in the rain shadow of the Olympic Mountains on the islands and northern shore of Puget Sound, there are no cacti in the Pacific Forest. Characteristic trees include *Arbutus Menziesii,* madrone; *Quercus Garryana,* Garry oak; *Abies grandis,* lowland fir; *Pinus contorta* var. *contorta,* beach pine; *Picea sitchensis,* tideland spruce; *Tsuga heterophylla,* western hemlock; *Sequoia sem-*

pervirens, coast redwood; *Thuja plicata,* giant or white cedar; and *Chamaecyparis Lawsoniana,* Lawson cypress.

The Sierran Subalpine Forest. This forest occurs at high altitudes in the mountains, extending upward to timberline. Some species are highly modified derivatives of those in the Miocene forest, but there is a strong element from the American Northern Forest. Characteristic trees include *Tsuga Mertensiana,* mountain hemlock; *Pinus monticola,* western white pine; *P. albicaulis,* white bark pine; *P. ponderosa* var. *Jeffreyi,* Jeffrey pine; *Abies magnifica,* red fir; *A. nobilis; Juniperus occidentalis,* western juniper; *Chamaecyparis nootkatensis,* Alaska cedar. There are no cacti, but on the dry eastern side of the Sierra Nevada desert-type species have joined the assemblage.

The Sierran Montane Forest. This forest is restricted to middle altitudes in the mountains. It resembles strongly the Pacific Forest, to which it is related. Cacti are rare, occurring only just above the edge of the deserts on the eastern side of the southern Sierra Nevada. Characteristic trees include *Quercus Kelloggii,* California black oak; *Pinus Lambertiana,* sugar pine; *P. ponderosa,* western yellow pine; *Abies concolor* var. *Lowiana,* white fir; *Sequoiadendron giganteum,* big tree or Sierra redwood; *Libocedrus decurrens,* incense cedar. (See Fig. 7.)

The Palouse Prairie. This grassland occurs on plains east of the northern part of the Cascade–Sierra Nevada axis. It is not represented in California. In the Columbia River Basin the drier areas of Palouse Prairie include a few cacti. The characteristic species are herbs, including such grasses as *Festuca idahoensis,* Idaho fescue, and *Agropyron spicatum,* wheat grass or bunch grass.

THE SIERRA MADREAN FLORA

This flora was derived from the Miocene oak woodland. In California it has been modified by loss of summer rainfall.

The Southwestern Oak Woodland and Chaparral. This vegetation occurs in Arizona and Sonora, but is not represented in California. It is the nearest remaining approach to the Miocene oak woodland, and it survives in an area retaining summer rainfall. There are some species of cacti. Characteristic trees include *Arbu-*

Fig. 7. *Left*, Sierran Montane Forest near Hat Creek, Shasta County. The characteristic tree is the western yellow pine, *Pinus ponderosa*, the older trees having large platelike segments of bark. *Right*, closeup view of the trunk, showing the bark; cones on the ground beneath the tree. *Left*, from Lyman Benson, *Plant Taxonomy, Methods and Principles*. Copyright © 1962. The Ronald Press Company, New York. Used by permission. *Right*, from Lyman Benson, *Plant Classification*. D. C. Heath & Co., Boston, 1957. Used by permission.

tus arizonica, Arizona madrone; *Quercus diversicolor*, netleaf oak; *Q. oblongifolia*, Mexican blue oak; *Q. Emoryi*, Emory oak or bellota; *Q. hypoleucoides*, white-leaf oak; *Q. arizonica*, Arizona oak; *Pinus leiophylla* var. *chihuahuana*, Chihuahua pine; *P. cembroides* var. *cembroides*, three-leaf pinyon; *Cupressus arizonica* vars. *arizonica* and *glabra*, Arizona cypresses.

The California Oak Woodland. This woodland occurs west of the main mountain axis in northern California and continuously as far south as Ventura County and Kern County. In northern California it is the predominant lowland vegetation (see Fig. 8), sometimes enclosing "islands" of California Chaparral, but in southern California it occurs in "islands" in the chaparral. In northern

Fig. 8. The California Oak Woodland, on the hills near Upper Lake, Lake County. The trees here are the blue (or white) oak, *Quercus Douglasii*. Characteristically this is an open, parklike woodland, the dominant lowland vegetation of northern California. Cacti are rare. From Lyman Benson, *Plant Taxonomy, Methods and Principles.* Copyright © 1962. The Ronald Press Company, New York. Used by permission.

California, cacti are absent, except rarely from San Luis Obispo and Tulare counties south. Characteristic trees include *Aesculus californica*, California buckeye (sometimes also in the chaparral); *Quercus Engelmannii*, Engelmann oak; *Q. lobata*, valley oak; *Q. Douglasii*, blue oak (for its bluish-green leaves, more commonly known as white oak, for its bark); *Juglans californica* var. *californica*, southern California black walnut; *J. californica* var. *Hindsii*, northern California black walnut.

The California Chaparral. This is the characteristic brushland of low elevations in southern California, where it is the predominant vegetation type (see Fig. 9). It occurs in "islands" in the oak woodland in northern California. Usually no cacti grow within the dense parts of the chaparral of the coastal side of the mountains,

Fig. 9. The California Chaparral, on hills near the site of Highland Springs, Mayacamas Range, Lake County. In the middle foreground the leather oak, *Quercus durata*, and at the left the chamise brush, *Adenostoma fasciculatum*. This thick growth of numerous species of fire-resistant shrubs is the original dominant vegetation of the lowlands as well as the low mountains of southern California. Cacti are usually excluded from the dense brushland by the hot fires, but they abound in the more open areas. From Lyman Benson, *Plant Taxonomy, Methods and Principles*. Copyright © 1962. The Ronald Press Company, New York. Used by permission.

which are burned over every few years by fires too intense to be withstood by any cactus. However, cacti occur where the brush is not too dense, as in the dry desert-edge phase of the chaparral, and they are abundant in the more open grassy coastal areas. They abound in southern California in the areas disturbed by man, where grass fires have affected their evolution but not eliminated them. Characteristic shrubs include *Dendromecon rigida*, bush poppy; *Rhus laurina*, laurel sumac; *Rhus integrifolia*, lemonade berry; *Rhamnus crocea* var. *crocea*, redberry; *Ceanothus*, numerous species of mountain lilac; *Eriogonum fasciculatum* var. *foliolosum*, wild buckwheat; *Arctostaphylos*, numerous species of manzanita;

Fraxinus dipetala, foothill ash; *Eriodictyon*, three species of yerba santa; *Salvia apiana*, bee or white sage; *S. mellifera*, black sage; *Pickeringia montana*, chaparral pea; *Cercocarpus montanus* vars. *glaber* and *minutiflorus*, mountain mahogany; *Adenostoma fasciculatum*, chamise brush; *A. sparsifolium*, red shank; *Lonicera subspicata*, moronel; *L. interrupta*, chaparral honeysuckle; *Artemisia californica*, coastal sagebrush; *Quercus dumosa*, coastal scrub oak; *Q. durata*, leather oak; *Garrya*, three species of silk-tassel bush; *Pinus attenuata*, knobcone pine; *Cupressus Sargentii*, Sargent cypress; *C. MacNabiana*, McNab cypress.

The Pacific Grassland. This vegetation type has developed in the rain shadow of the Coast Ranges in the Great Valley of California and especially around the southern end of the San Joaquin Valley. It also occurs near the Mojave Desert in Antelope Valley. Nearly all the species are herbs. Most were derived from elements in the Miocene oak woodland. One variety of the beavertail cactus, *Opuntia basilaris* var. *Treleasii*, occurring near Bakersfield, is the only cactus native in this grassland. Woody plants are few, and they are bushes rather than trees or shrubs. (See Fig. 10.)

The Juniper-Pinyon Woodland. This woodland is common east of the Cascade–Sierra Nevada axis, especially in the disconnected mountain ranges of the Great Basin. In southern California the upper parts of the desert-edge phase of the chaparral often have the aspect of Juniper-Pinyon Woodland because of the presence of pinyons and juniper. However, the associated species are not those of the Juniper-Pinyon Woodland in the Great Basin, and the juniper (*Juniperus californica*) is one that is characteristic of chaparral, not of the Great Basin region. From southern Riverside County south the pinyon is different, too. The true Juniper-Pinyon Woodland of the Great Basin includes a number of native species of cacti, some of which occur in California. Characteristic woody species include *Chrysothamnus nauseosus* (several varieties), rabbit brush; *Pinus cembroides* vars. *monophylla* and *edulis*, one- and two-leaf pinyons; *Juniperus californica* var. *utahensis* (*J. osteosperma*), Utah juniper. (See Fig. 11.)

The Sagebrush Desert. The Sagebrush Desert occupies low areas in the Columbia River Basin, and it is dominant through the lower

Fig. 10. Pacific Grassland. *Above*, in summer east of Simmler, San Luis Obispo County, in a dry area near Carissa Plains west of the southern San Joaquin valley. *Below*, in spring, near Bakersfield, Kern County. Such areas are dry in summer but like flower gardens in the spring after a rainy winter. The California poppy, *Eschscholtzia californica*, is conspicuous. Photograph (*below*) by Burton Frasher, Sr., Frasher Fotos; courtesy of Burton Frasher, Jr., and the Pomona Public Library.

Fig. 11. Juniper-Pinyon Woodland and Sagebrush Desert and their interrelationship; near St. George, Utah. Characteristically the woodland is on the hills, and the desert is in the valleys, as shown. In part this is a function of altitude and in part one of soil, the soils of the valleys being deeper. Sorting of species follows these lines, but it is not exclusive. From Lyman Benson, *Plant Classification*. D. C. Heath & Co., Boston, 1957. Used by permission.

parts of the Great Basin. The plants are derivatives of various temperate floral elements, with emphasis upon the Miocene oak woodland. Many, though by no means all, of the species are related to those of the less modified oak woodlands and chaparrals of California and southeastern Arizona. Characteristic woody species include *Atriplex Nuttallii*, salt sage; *Salvia carnosa*, purple sage; *Purshia tridentata*, antelope brush; *Tetradymia spinosa*, spiny horsebrush; *Artemisia tridentata*, sagebrush; *A. arbuscula*, black sagebrush. In California the Sagebrush Desert occurs along the eastern side of the Sierra Nevada and on the adjacent plains of the Great Basin. There are a few species of native cacti.

The Mexican Desert Flora occupies almost exactly the same area as the creosote bush, *Larrea divaricata*. This plant is ubiquitous from the Mojave Desert in California to the Rio Grande region in Texas and south to Zacatecas in Mexico. It occurs also in Chile. The plants occurring in this flora are derivatives primarily of elements of the dry regions of northern Mexico and of plants that occupied pockets on the dry sides of whatever mountains existed formerly as discontinuous ranges near the areas of the present deserts. These communities are a part of the great desert system of the southwestern United States and northern and central Mexico. The creosote bush desert (see Fig. 12) is the principal cactus area of the United States, and there are numerous species. The best markers of the Sonoran Deserts are the desert ironwood, *Olneya Tesota*, and the ocotillo, *Fouquieria splendens*. The subdivisions occurring in California are as follows:

The Mojavean Desert. The upper parts of this desert are characterized by the Joshua tree, *Yucca brevifolia*, which forms an outline around it. The flora of the Mojave Desert in California extends east to the vicinity of St. George, Utah, and just beyond the Bill Williams River in Arizona. This desert lies at higher elevations than the Colorado Desert, mostly at 2,000 to 4,000 feet elevation, but up to 5,000 feet directly in the rain shadows of the higher mountains. The average rainfall in most areas is about 10 or 12 inches. The winter temperatures are relatively low, and freezing is much more common than in the Colorado Desert to the south. Characteristic woody species include *Yucca brevifolia*, the Joshua tree; *Atriplex Parryi*, Parry saltbush; *Salvia mohavensis*, Mojave sage; *Cassia armata*, spiny senna; *Dalea arborescens* and *D. Fremontii* vars. *pubescens*, *Saundersii*, and *minutifolia*, indigo bushes; *Haplopappus linearifolius* var. *interior*; *Tetradymia stenolepis*, horsebrush; *Ephedra viridis*, green ephedra; *E. californica* var. *funerea*, Death Valley ephedra. (See Fig. 13.)

The Sonoran Deserts. This complex of deserts has only one representative in California—the low-lying Colorado Desert, which is mostly at an elevation of 2,000 feet or less, though sometimes

Fig. 12. The desert floor, with large areas of desert pavement and sometimes
with areas of sand, as in the foreground (*above*). The dominant plant is the
creosote bush, *Larrea divaricata* (*above*, right foreground, and *below*), the
distribution of which almost exactly outlines the occurrence of Mexican Desert
Flora. Photograph, *above*, by Frank B. Salisbury. From Lyman Benson, *Plant
Taxonomy, Methods and Principles.* Copyright © 1962. The Ronald Press
Company, New York. Used by permission. *Below*, from Lyman Benson, *Plant
Classification.* D. C. Heath & Co., Boston, 1957. Used by permission.

Fig. 13. The Mojavean Desert. *Above,* the upper portion of the desert (above 3,000 feet elevation) marked by occurrence of the Joshua tree, *Yucca brevifolia;* near Morongo Valley, Riverside County. Photograph by Burton Frasher, Sr., Frasher Fotos; courtesy of Burton Frasher, Jr., and the Pomona Public Library. *Below,* the lower portion (below about 3,000 feet), where the Joshua tree seldom occurs; Valley of Fire, Clark County, Nevada. The darker, taller shrubs are creosote bush, *Larrea divaricata;* the lighter, lower ones are bur sage, *Franseria dumosa.* From Lyman Benson, *Plant Classification.* D. C. Heath & Co., Boston, 1957. Used by permission.

higher in the immediate lee of high mountains. The desert (named for the Colorado River) occupies the areas along the Colorado River and in the Salton Sea basin. Characteristic woody species include *Holacantha Emoryi*, crucifixion thorn; *Condalia Parryi*, California lotebush; *Asclepias subulata* and *A. candicans*, desert milkweeds; *Tetracoccus Hallii*; *Ayenia compacta*; *Salvia Greatai* and *eremostachya*, sages; *Beloperone californica*; *Hoffmanseggia microphylla*; *Dalea spinosa*, smoke tree (the best marker of the Colorado Desert); *D. Schottii*; *D. Emoryi*; *Prunus Fremontii*, desert apricot; *Franseria ilicifolia*, bur sage; *Washingtonia filifera*, California fan palm (a marker of the Colorado Desert); *Agave desertii*, desert century plant. (See Figs. 14 and 15.)

The dominant feature of southern Arizona is the Arizona Desert, another of the Sonoran group. The saguaro or giant cactus, *Cereus giganteus*, is the characteristic tree.

In Baja California an extremely dry type, the Viscaino Desert, lies in the rain shadow of the coastal mountains of the northern portion of the state; it is the prevailing vegetation type along the western edge of the Gulf of California. *Idria columnaris*, the cirio or boogum tree, is characteristic, as are many species of chollas.

Early Study of the California Cacti*

Cacti along the coast of southern California were reported first by the surgeon-naturalist Archibald Menzies in 1793 (Menzies, 1793). He accompanied the British navigator George Vancouver around the world from 1791 to 1795 aboard the *Discovery*. On November 10, 1793, the party landed in Santa Barbara, California, and a few days later it was visited by "Padri Vincenti" of the Buena Ventura Mission. He presented the crew with various gifts "such as sweet and common Potatoes, Onions, Maize, Wheat, some Baskets of Figs and what are called prickly pears &c." On November 29, 1793, the *Discovery* landed in San Diego, California. Menzies ascended a ridge from which there was an extensive view of

* For this section, I am indebted to David L. Walkington, Department of Botany, California State College at Fullerton. The references cited are listed at the end of the section.

Fig. 14. The Colorado Desert. Hills, alluvial fan, and broad sandy wash near Palm Springs. The chollas in the foreground are *Opuntia echinocarpa* var. *echinocarpa*. Photograph by Burton Frasher, Sr., Frasher Fotos; courtesy of Burton Frasher, Jr., and the Pomona Public Library.

Fig. 15. The Colorado Desert (*opposite*). *Above*, the smoke tree, *Dalea spinosa*, one of the best markers of the Colorado Desert, as is the California fan palm, *Washingtonia filifera*. Both plants are confined to areas of extra water, the smoke tree in sandy washes, the palm in canyons or at springs or other points where there is subsurface water. A species characteristic of dry ground and marking only this desert is the diamond cholla, *Opuntia ramosissima*, Fig. 30 and Color Plate 1. *Below*, the desert floor in bloom; sandy area near Palm Springs, with the San Jacinto Mountains in the background. Photographs by Burton Frasher, Sr., Frasher Fotos; courtesy of Burton Frasher, Jr., and the Pomona Public Library.

the San Diego Presidio. "Five or six species of the Genus Cactus" were observed and reported from this exploration.

The prickly pears presented by the padre may have been fruits gathered from the local native flat-jointed opuntias. However, when the Franciscan fathers established their various missions along coastal southern and central California from 1769 to 1782, they brought with them seeds and cuttings of fruit-bearing plants from Mexico and Spain. These included horticultural forms of the large cultivated fruit-tree prickly pear of Mexico, *Opuntia Ficus-*

Indica (L.) Miller. Most likely they were well established by the time of Menzies's visit. It is also possible that some of the cacti observed in the San Diego Presidio may have been these introduced types.

The second report of cacti in southern California was in 1836 by the English botanist Thomas Nuttall (Coville, 1899). Nuttall traveled by ship south from Monterey, California, and put into port at a number of places along the coast. While in San Diego, in May 1836 Nuttall wrote the following description of a cactus that is believed to have been *Opuntia Parryi* var. *serpentina*: "Erect and shrubby, with numerous clusters of long and short spines; the branches somewhat cylindric, repandly grooved, reticulated; flowers small, yellow; fruit dry and spiney. Arid hills and denuded tracts near St. Diego, California, common." This description, with the name *Cactus californicus*, was sent to John Torrey and Asa Gray. According to Coville, Nuttall apparently preserved no specimens of the plant, and Torrey and Gray (in their *Flora of North America*, 1840), having only this meager description as a guide, placed the species doubtfully in the genus *Cereus*. Another cactus observed and described by Nuttall on this visit was *Ferocactus viridescens* (Nutt.) Britton & Rose (*Echinocactus viridescens* Nutt. in Torrey and Gray, 1840), which was named *Melocactus viridescens* in the unpublished manuscript.

The next record of coastal cacti was written by Richard Brinsley Hinds, the surgeon and botanist on the British exploring ship *H.M.S. Sulphur* from 1836 to 1842. During the year 1839, observations were made along the coast of southern California. In the report entitled "The Botany of the Voyage of *H.M.S. Sulphur* (Hinds and Bentham, 1844, part 1, p. 3), Hinds states, "My attention has been directed to the distribution of *Cacteae*, by meeting with two species for the first time at San Pedro, as we are descending the coast. Their limit here then may be stated at 34° N." On p. 4 of the same report Hinds continues, "San Diego, 32° 29′ N. lat. . . . Cacteae are now common, and three species have been noticed."

The first reported collections and taxonomic treatments of the southern California prickly pear complex were made in connection with the United States and Mexican Boundary Survey, which was conducted following the Gadsden Purchase. Dr. George Engelmann, a physician of St. Louis, Missouri, published a paper entitled "*Notes on the Cereus Giganteus of Southeastern California, and Some Other California Cactaceae*" in 1852. In this report he lists a number of cacti collected by Dr. C. C. Parry, a surgeon on the Boundary Survey expedition. Engelmann states, "Dr. Parry has, in the years 1849 and 1850, when he was also attached to Colonel Emory's corps in the survey of the Mexican Boundary, examined and described ten or eleven distinct species of Cactaceae, all found along the southern boundary of California, from the seacoast to the mouth of the Gila." Among this list of species the following were included: "6. OPUNTIA ENGELMANNI, Salm. San Diego, on dry hillsides in patches, 4 to 6 feet high. Originally discovered about Chihuahua, this species appears to extend westward to the Pacific. 7. O. TUNA, Mill. [actually *Opuntia Ficus-Indica* (L.) Miller] is cultivated for fences, and naturalized about the missions; called 'Tuña.' It is 10–15 ft. high; the fruit large and edible."

The next reported collections were those made on the Whipple Expedition, 1852 to 1854 (Engelmann and Bigelow, 1857). This was an exploration on horseback for a railroad route to the Pacific Ocean that is now followed by the Santa Fe Railroad from Arkansas to Los Angeles. Accompanying the expedition as surgeon and botanist, John M. Bigelow collected cacti and sent them to Engelmann, who later described the material. In his "Synopsis of the Cactaceae of the Territory of the United States and Adjacent Regions (1856), Engelmann named the prickly pear sent him "*Opuntia engelmanni* subspecies *occidentalis*." His description and comments about this new taxon were as follows: "Flowers in June. Plant 4 feet high, forming large thickets, the joints 9–12 inches long, pulvilli with very fine closely set bristles, spines about 1 inch long. Larger seeds [than *O. Engelmannii*, a name he had applied to a plant from New Mexico, Texas, and Chihuahua].

"Another form grows on hills and plains near San Diego and neighboring sea-beach with higher and upright growth and coarser bristles on the pulvilli. I cannot well distinguish it from *O. engelmanni* as I have seen no fruit or seed of it." The citation of plants growing on the neighboring beach was in reference to collections reported by Arthur Schott, a botanist working under Major Emory on the Boundary Survey expedition in 1854 (Engelmann and Bigelow, 1859). Schott reported another *Opuntia* in the mountain valleys of San Pasqual and Santa Ysabel.

In a report of the botany of the Whipple Expedition (1857), Engelmann and Bigelow elevated the subspecies *occidentalis* to the species level, describing its distribution as follows (cf. p. 164): "On the western slopes of the California mountains, from Quilqual Gungo, east of Los Angeles, to San Pasquale and San Isabel, northeast of San Diego (A. Schott), at an elevation of 1,000 to 2,000 feet, in immense patches, often as large as half an acre." A qualifying note followed this description, which stated: "The plant mentioned in Sillimans Journal [*American Journal of Science and Arts,* Engelmann, 1852], November, 1852 (Dr. Parry's collections), as being common 'on the hill-sides and plains near San Diego,' and which Mr. Schott seems to have also found 'on the sea-beach near San Diego,' may be a form of *O. Engelmanni,* as suggested in the above publication; or it may be a naturalized wild state of *O. Tuni* [later corrected to be *O. Ficus-Indica,* introduced in California], which is cultivated about the missions there." On p. 16, in a different section of the same report referring to one of the above collection sites, Dr. Bigelow (1857) states: "At Cocomungo [evidently a different transliteration of the Indian place name Quiqual Gungo, which in modern usage must be Cucamonga] in this valley [Cajon Valley], we found vast and dense patches of an Opuntia, nearly akin to *O. engelmanni,* which had the appearance of having been introduced; but whether it really is so, cannot be determined. The Spanish *Tuna* [*Opuntia Tuna*], which is cultivated for its fruit, forms hedges fifteen or twenty feet high. The Indians and Mexicans are very fond of the fruit, which serves them for food during its season."

Bigelow, J. M. 1857. General description of the botanical character of the country, p. 16. *In* Report of the botany of the expedition, U.S. Senate Rept. Expl. & Surv. R.R. Route Mississippi River to Pacific Ocean.
Coville, F. V. 1899. The botanical explorations of Thomas Nuttall in California. Proc. Bio. Soc. Wash. 13: 109–21.

Engelmann, G. 1852. Notes on the *Cereus Giganteus* of southeastern California, and some other Californian Cactaceae, American Journal of Science and Arts. II. 14: 335–39. Also in W. Trelease and A. Gray, eds. 1887. The Botanical Works of the late George Engelmann, John Wilson and Son, Cambridge, Mass., p. 123.

Engelmann, G. 1856. Synopsis of the Cactaceae of the territory of the United States and adjacent regions. Proc. American Academy of Arts and Sciences 3: 259–314.

Engelmann, G., and J. M. Bigelow. 1857. Description of the Cactaceae, p. 38. *In* Report of the botany of the expedition, U.S. Senate Rept. Expl. & Surv. R.R. Route Mississippi River to Pacific Ocean.

Hinds, R. B., and G. Bentham. 1844. The botany of the voyage of *H.M.S. Sulphur*, under the command of Captain Sir Edward Belcher, R.N., F.R., G.S., etc., during the years 1836–42.

Menzies, A. 1793. Journal of Vancouver's voyage along the Pacific Coast of North America, published by the Quarterly of the California Historical Society, Jan. 1924. *In* S. D. McKelvey, 1955, Botanical exploration of the Trans-Mississippi West, 1790–1850. The Arnold Arboretum of Harvard Univ., Jamaica Plain, Mass. 1,144 pp.

Torrey, J., and A. Gray. 1838–40. A Flora of North America. 2 vols. New York.

The Cacti

The Cacti

The family Cactaceae (cactus family) shows relationships to each of several other families of flowering plants, notably but remotely to the Aizoaceae, the family to which the ice plant belongs. In the view of the writer the Cactaceae stand as the lone family in the order Cactales. The following description uniquely characterizes all the genera and species of the Cactaceae.

Stems simple or branching, strongly succulent, up to 50 feet long and more than 3 feet in diameter, the ribs none to many, the tubercles coalescent through various heights or separate. Leaves usually not discernible but, when visible, from persistent, large, and flat to ephemeral, small, and conical to cylindroidal. Areoles in the leaf axils or the equivalents, producing spines during at least the juvenile stages. Spines variable. Flower on the new or old growth and located near or below the apex of the stem, its position correlated with that of a tubercle or a spine-bearing areole, usually epigynous but in *Pereskia* perigynous; floral tube a hypanthium or the superior portion a perianth tube, bearing areoles and usually small leaves, but sometimes bare, above the junction with the ovary almost obsolete to elongate and tubular, the leaves or scale leaves of the floral tube shading into the sepaloid outer perianth parts and these into the petaloid inner parts; stamens numerous, sometimes more than 1,000, arranged spirally; carpels cyclic, 3 to about 20; stigmas separate; style 1; ovary with a single seed chamber and numerous ovules on (as seen at maturity) parietal placentae (on the ovary wall); ovules usually campylotropous (curved between the hilum and the micropyle) or sometimes amphitropous (half-inverted) or orthotropous (straight). Fruit fleshy or dry at maturity, bearing tubercles, scales, spines, hairs or glochids or without appendages. Seeds black, brown, white, reddish, gray, or bone-white, of many shapes, longer than broad to broader than long (length being hilum to opposite side); hilum* either obviously basal or appearing "lateral"; embryo with the cotyledons lying either parallel or at right angles to the flat faces of the seed as a whole and with either the edges of both cotyledons or the back of only one cotyledon toward the hypocotyl (root), i.e., accumbent or incumbent or sometimes oblique.

Perhaps 800 or 1,000 or more valid species occurring from Canada to southern South America; 33 species, as well as 22 varieties beyond the nomenclaturally typical ones, occurring as native or, in a few cases, introduced plants in California.

KEY TO THE GENERA

1. Areoles bearing glochids (small or minute, sharp-pointed, barbed bristles) and usually longer and stouter spines; new stem bearing a fleshy leaf just below each areole; floral tube *not* developed above the ovary; seeds bony, often discoid; cotyledons large, leaflike, usually incumbent, i.e., with the back of one turned or turning somewhat toward the hypocotyl (root) and both lying at right angles to the flat faces of the seed, rarely oblique or accumbent; stems of series of cylindroidal or flattened joints; flower on a joint grown the preceding year; flower within or on the edge of the spine-bearing aerole; stems *not* ribbed; fruit *not* bearing scale leaves, *not* splitting open . . . . *Opuntia*, p. 77
1. Areoles *not* bearing glochids; stem leafless or with only minute bulges or scales representing leaves; floral tube often developed into a deep cup or tube above the ovary and below the perianth parts; seeds *not* bony; cotyledons *not* leaflike:
    2. Flower on an area of the stem developed one to several years earlier, *not* on the new growth of the current season, therefore

---

* In common cactus parlance the hilum is spoken of as "basal" or "lateral," but the real point is whether the seed is longer than broad or broader than long. By definition the hilum is the attachment point, therefore the base, of the seed. It cannot be lateral.

clearly below the apex of the stem or branch; seed longer than broad, and the hilum therefore obviously basal or rarely oblique:

3. Stems ribbed by coalescence of the tubercles; flower bud developing within the spiniferous areole *or* bursting through the epidermis just above it; ovary bearing scale leaves or spines; embryo with the usually minute cotyledons incumbent:

   4. Flower bud within at least the edge of a mature spine-bearing areole; stem 15 to 100 times as long as its diameter; plant never depressed or caespitose, the mature stem(s) 1 to 50 feet long—when shorter than 2 feet, less than 1 inch in diameter; embryo curved . . . . *Cereus*, p. 172

   4. Flower bud bursting through the epidermis of the stem above a mature spine-bearing areole; plant depressed or caespitose, the stems solitary to (in older plants of some species) often numerous and forming a mound, the mature stems 2 to 12(24) inches long, those of maximum length 2 to 4 inches in diameter; embryo nearly straight . . . . *Echinocereus*, p. 177

3. Stems *not* ribbed, with separate tubercles; flower bud in a special areole between one tubercle and the next one above it, *not* associated with the spine-bearing areole on the tubercle or with any evident extension of it; embryo with the cotyledons accumbent, i.e., lying parallel to the flat faces of the seed and with the edges of both cotyledons toward the hypocotyl (root); superior floral tube deciduous at fruiting time . . . . *Mammillaria*, p. 188

2. Flower on the new growth of the current season and therefore near the apex of the stem or branch, developing on the rib or on the side of the tubercle toward the growing apex of the stem, either in a felted area adjacent to and merging with the new spine-bearing areole or in a remote similar area on the side or at the base of the tubercle but then connected with the areole by a felted groove (isthmus), the flowering portion of the areole and the groove (if any) persisting for many years as a circular to jagged scar either just ventral (toward the stem apex) to the spine-bearing areole or extending down the ventral side of the tubercle; embryo with the cotyledons accumbent (cf. lower lead 3, above):

   3¹. Flower-bearing portion of the areole adjacent to and merging into the spine-bearing portion, the flower or fruit crowded against the edge of the spine cluster, the scar left on the tubercle (after the fruit has fallen) merging into the spine-bearing portion of the areole, not separated by an isthmus:

4¹. Mature fruit not releasing the seeds by separating crosswise at the middle or above the base; flower-bearing portion of the areole nearly circular, the scar marking the former position of the fruit circular to rectangular or irregular:

    5. Fruit fleshy for several months after reaching maturity; areoles of the ovary *not* bearing long wool; sepaloid perianth parts *not* spinose or aristate; seed longer than broad, the hilum therefore either obviously basal or "subbasal" or sometimes "diagonal" .... *Ferocactus*, p. 196

    5. Fruit becoming dry soon after maturity; areoles of the ovary bearing long woolly hairs that obscure the fruit; sepaloid perianth parts with spinose or aristate tips; seed broader than long, the hilum therefore appearing "lateral" .... *Echinocactus*, p. 201

4¹. Mature (dry) fruit releasing the seeds by (in the California species) separating crosswise at some level from *above* the base to near the middle; ovary *either* without scales *or* with only a few, the areoles axillary to these with inconspicuous tufts of short hairs; seed broader than long, the hilum therefore appearing "lateral" .... *Sclerocactus*, p. 205

3¹. Flower-bearing portion of the areole (except on juvenile stems) distant from the spine-bearing portion, the flower or fruit standing apart from the spine cluster, the scar marking the former position of the fruit on the old tubercle or rib segment at the end of a narrow, felted, usually linelike groove extending to the base of the tubercle:*

    4². Tubercles of the stems of *mature plants* coalescent basally into ribs, the tops remaining free; ovary bearing one to many scale leaves; fruit dry at maturity, opening (in the California species) lengthwise ...... *Neolloydia*, p. 207

    4². Tubercles of the stems remaining separate, *not* coalescent into ribs; ovary *not* bearing scale leaves; fruit green or red, fleshy but very thin-walled at maturity, indehiscent .... *Coryphantha*, p. 208

---

* The earliest flowers on the young stem of *Coryphantha* and perhaps *Neolloydia* are produced high on the tubercle (which is separate and not part of a rib). From then on, as flowers appear on new crops of tubercles, they emerge lower and lower on the ventral surface of the tubercle and farther and farther from the area of spines, and the connecting grooves become longer and longer. Ultimately the flower emerges from the base of the tubercle, and the groove extends full length.

Opuntia Miller (Prickly Pear, Cholla)

Stems of series of cylindroidal or flattened joints, these 2 to 12(24) inches long, if cylindroidal, ¼ to 2 inches in diameter, or, if flattened, broad; ribs none, the tubercles separate. Leaves cylindroidal, narrowly conical or subulate, ¼ to 1(2) inches long. Areoles circular. Spines smooth, white, gray, yellow, brown, red, pink, or purplish, commonly 1 to 10(15) per areole, sometimes lacking, straight or curved, ¼ to 2(4) inches long, ⅟₉₆ to ⅟₂₄ inch in diameter, acicular or subulate; glochids in the areoles with the longer spines. Flowers and fruits subapical on the joints grown the preceding season, each within a spine-bearing areole. Flower ½ to 4 inches in diameter; floral tube above the ovary very short, deciduous, bearing stamens just above the ovary. Fruit fleshy or dry at maturity, with or without spines or hairs from the areoles, spheroidal to obovoid or elongate, ½ to 2 inches long, indehiscent. Seeds gray, tan, brown, white, or tinged with other colors, flat and bony, smooth to irregularly angled, longer than broad (hilum to opposite side) or discoid, ⅟₁₆ to ¼ inch long, the hilum usually appearing "lateral."

Many species in the Western Hemisphere, the number uncertain and commonly overestimated; 21 species in California, 19 of these native.

Key to the Species

1. Joints of the stem cylindroidal; spine with the epidermis separating into a thin paperlike sheath, sometimes (in low mat-forming species) the sheath separating at only the tip; glochids *usually* small and inconsequential, except on the underground stems and the fruits of the mat-forming species (lower lead 2, below): Subgenus 1. Cylindropuntia:
    2. Spine with a full-length thin and paperlike sheath, slender, not papillate or striate; glochids usually all small and harmless; joints cylindroidal, usually uniformly spiny, of varying lengths, developing from any areole of an older joint, the terminal bud continuing to grow and the joint to elongate for an indefinite period, the plant therefore shrubby, arborescent, or treelike:
    3. Stem either smooth or with simple tubercles:

4. Fruit *dry* at maturity, *spiny* (sometimes only sparsely so), *the spines of the fruit* (in all but one very rare species) *strongly barbed*; terminal joints ⅝ to 1 (1½) inches in diameter, elongate, attached firmly:

    5. Spines of the fruit few, mostly solitary in the areoles of the two uppermost nearly horizontal series; main trunk none, the branches prostrate to erect; chaparral areas nearly always west of the mountain axis of southern California, reaching the edge of the Colorado Desert in northeastern San Diego County .... 1. *O. Parryi*

    5. Spines of the fruit numerous, several per areole in the upper nearly horizontal series; deserts:

        6. Terminal joints ¼ to ⅜ inch in diameter; central spine 1 (or sometimes also 1 to 2 shorter upper ones); radial spines 6 to 8 and much smaller; fruit with several spines per areole, these weakly barbed ....
.... 2. *O. Wigginsii*

        6. Terminal joints (some of them) at least ⅝ inch in diameter; central and radial spines indistinguishable; spines of the fruit strongly barbed:

            7. Tubercles 1 to 2 times as long as broad; longer terminal joints 4 to 6 inches long; main trunk one-third to one-half the height of the plant .. 3. *O. echinocarpa*

            7. Tubercles 3 to several times as long as broad; larger joints 6 to 18 inches long; main trunk, when present, rarely more than one-fifth the height of the plant ...
.... 4. *O. acanthocarpa*

4. Fruit *fleshy* at maturity, sometimes drying after long persistence on the plant, *spineless* or rarely slightly spiny; terminal joints (1¼) 1½ to 2 inches in diameter, usually short, readily detached and abundantly vegetatively reproductive; spines usually straw-colored:

    5¹. Fruit smooth or slightly tuberculate, with the apical cuplike depression shallow, long-persistent, with new flowers and fruits formed from the areoles of some of the persistent old usually sterile fruits; tubercles of the terminal joints longer than broad; stem branched below and rebranched above, some main branches as long as the short main stem; spines barbed but not strongly so; coastal ...
.... 5. *O. prolifera*

    5¹. Fruits tuberculate, with the apical cuplike depression deep, persisting only one season; tubercles of the terminal joints nearly as broad as long; stem erect, forming a column, branching on only the upper portion, the branches either not rebranched or much shorter than the main stem; spines effectively and strongly barbed; deserts:

    6¹. Tree 6 to 14 feet high, the trunk less than half the height of the plant; major branches elongate, rebranched several times; terminal joints 1 inch in diameter; tubercles about twice as long as broad, ½ to ⅝ inch long, markedly raised above the stem surface . . . . . .
. . . . 6. *O. Munzii*

    6¹. Tree 3 to 5(9) feet high, the stout trunk bearing above usually much shorter branches, which usually are only once to twice rebranched; terminal joints (1¼)1½ to 2 inches in diameter; tubercles 1 to 1½ times as long as broad, ¼ to ⅜ inch long, only slightly raised from the stem surface . . . . 7. *O. Bigelovii*

3. Stem nearly covered with low, flattened, platelike, diamond-shaped to obovate tubercles; areole in an apical notch or groove of the tubercle; fruit dry at maturity, spiny or spineless, brown; joints becoming woody the first year; spines with strong barbs . . . . 8. *O. ramosissima*

2. Spine with a sheath at only the extreme apex, the larger spines at least basally flattened and with either rough crossbands of papillae or longitudinal ridges and grooves (striate); glochids on underground stems and often on fruits large and strongly barbed; joints enlarged upward like clubs, all about the same length, developing from the basal areoles of older joints, the plant therefore tending to form a mat, the terminal bud ceasing to grow when the joint reaches a particular size:

    3¹. Petals yellow; spines rigid, papillate and rough to the touch . . .
. . . . 9. *O. Stanlyi*

    3¹. Petals reddish-purple; spines flexible, not papillate or rough to the touch, usually with longitudinal basal ridges and grooves
. . . . 10. *O. pulchella*

1. Joints of the stem flattened after the first year of seedling growth (see Fig. 5); spine with *no* sheath; glochids usually large, well developed, barbed, and effective: Subgenus 2. OPUNTIA:

    2¹. Fruit green but becoming tan and *dry* as the seeds mature; seeds usually ⅛ to ⁵⁄₁₆ inch in diameter, rough and irregular:

        3². Fruit with at least an apical rim of horizontally spreading, strongly barbed spines, often spiny all over; joints glabrous, nearly always spiny:

        4¹. Spines all circular to broadly elliptic in cross section, none markedly even basally flattened (though hybridization sometimes obliterates this distinction in and east of the southern Sierra Nevada):

5². Larger joints 2 to 4(5) inches long, 1½ to 4 inches broad, broadly obovate to orbiculate, up to about ½ inch thick, less than one-quarter as thick as broad; spines not strongly barbed except on the fruits; joints not readily detached .... 11. *O. polyacantha*

5². Larger joints 1 to 1½ inches long, 1 inch or less broad, flattened-obovoid or flattened-ovoid, ½ to ¾ inch thick, at least one-half as thick as broad; spines nearly always present, strongly barbed; joints readily detached, clinging by the barbed spines .... 12. *O. fragilis*

4¹. Spines *or some of them* elliptic or narrowly elliptic in cross section, being flattened at least basally; joints mostly 4 to 6 inches long and 2½ to 3½ inches broad, elliptic-oblong to obovate-oblong .... 13. *O. erinacea*

3². Fruit *not* with an apical rim of horizontally spreading, strongly barbed spines, spineless or essentially so; joints often pubescent, spineless except in some plants of the San Joaquin Valley and of mountains near the lower Colorado River ......
.... 14. *O. basilaris*

2¹. Fruit *fleshy and juicy* as the seeds mature, usually red or reddish-purple, sometimes yellowish-orange, nearly always spineless but with glochids; seeds ⅛ to 3⁄16(¼) inch in diameter, usually smooth and regular in outline:

3³. Spines present:

4². Plant not more than 6 to 8 feet high (usually much less), rarely with a main trunk, the trunk, if any, rarely more than 1 foot long; joints rarely more than 8 inches to 1 foot long; fruit red to purple at maturity; native species:

5³. Spines needlelike, elliptic to nearly circular in cross section (sometimes an occasional spine flattened basally), only 1 to 3 per areole (except in *O. littoralis* vars.), not *all* yellow, at least some of the spines obviously of other colors:

6². Plants low and mat-forming, usually prostrate; largest joints 2 to 3(4) inches long, 1½ to 3 inches broad; spines white, gray, or brownish .. 15. *O. macrorhiza*

6². Plants rising the height of several joints, commonly 2 to 3(7) feet high; largest joints usually 4 to 7(12) inches long, usually 3 to 6(8) inches broad; spines tan, brown, pink, gray, reddish-brown, or sometimes white or some of them yellow .... 16. *O. littoralis*

5³. Spines (at least some of the larger but not necessarily the smaller) flattened at least basally, like shoemakers' awls, tapering to the apices, usually 3 or more per areole:

  6³. Spines not all deflexed, spreading in various directions:

    7¹. Spines *not all* yellow: some gray, tan, brown, reddish, or white; *or,* if spines are yellowish, with at least reddish or brownish bases:

      8. Fruit purple or reddish-purple (with betacyanin pigments, a mixture of red and blue), obovoid to elongate; areoles of the flower bud and fruit small and inconspicuous; spines 1 to 6(11) per areole, straight or nearly so; seed ⅛ to ⅕ inch long or in diameter, the margin enclosing the embryo *usually* broad and irregular:

        9. Mature spines *not* (or only a few of them) white or pale gray, spreading:

          10. Spines all brown or brownish-red or sometimes with lighter tips, the longest ones (1¼) 1½ to 2½(3½) inches long; almost wholly on desert sides of mountains . . . .
. . . . 17. *O. phaeacantha* var. *major*

          10. Spines not necessarily all the same color: gray, red, brown, or mixtures of these or with yellow, the longest ½ to 1⅜(1⅞) inches long; seeds sometimes each with a smooth, narrow margin enclosing the embryo; coastal region
. . . . Hybrid population *"occidentalis"*

        9. Mature spines white or pale gray, or younger ones sometimes brownish, 1 in each areole deflexed; mountains of desert margins, rare on the coast . . . . 17. *O. phaeacantha* var. *discata*

      8. Fruit red, subglobose; areoles of the flower bud, including those on the inferior ovary, bearing yellow glochids up to ⅛ to ½ inch long, these persisting on the fruit; spines (4)8 to 16 per areole, the lower ones curving and twisting gently; seed discoid, ⅛ inch in diameter, the margin enclosing the embryo narrow and smooth; coastal . . . .
. . . . 18. *O. oricola*

    7¹. Spines *all* yellow, turning dirty gray or black in age and often so in pressed specimens; seed discoid, about ⅛ inch in diameter, the margin enclosing the embryo narrow and smooth; coastal . . . .
. . . . Hybrid population *"demissa"*

6³. Spines *all*—1 to 6(8) per areole—*deflexed*, clearly yellow, changing (often through white first) to black in age or in herbarium specimens; fruit grayish, subglobose to ellipsoid, tinged with purple, 1 to 1½ inches long; plant 3 to 6 feet high, with a definite short trunk
.... 19. *O. chlorotica*

4². Plant at maturity 10 to 20 feet high, usually a tree or sometimes arborescent, the trunk commonly a yard or more high; cultivated species sometimes escaped about old dwelling sites or in deep soils with extra water:

5⁴. Joints glabrous, green, (¾)1 to 2 feet long; fruit (in the plants introduced in this area) commonly yellowish or tannish-orange (purple or reddish in some other forms), glabrous, 2 to 3 inches long, about 2 inches in diameter
.... 20. *O. Ficus-Indica*

5⁴. Joints densely short-tomentose (woolly), velvety to the touch, green or with a whitish sheen because of the hairs, mostly 5–9 inches long; fruit red, tomentose, 1¼ to 1½ inches long, 1 inch in diameter ..... 21. *O. tomentosa*

3³. Spines none:

4³. Plant creeping or sprawling, up to 1 or rarely 2 feet high; joints 3 to 4 inches long, 2 to 2½(3¼) inches broad, strongly glaucous (blue-green); fruit reddish (with a tint of blue) to reddish-purple, about 1½ inches long, 1 to 1½ inches in diameter; native ....
.... 16. *O. littoralis* var. *austrocalifornica*

4³. Plant a tree or arborescent, 10 to 20 feet high, the trunk commonly a yard or more high; joints ¾ to 2 feet long, not blue-green; fruit (in the plants introduced in this area) yellowish, orange, or pure red (with no tint of blue); cultivated species, sometimes escaped about old dwelling sites or in deep soils of valleys or at canyon mouths:

5⁵. Joints glabrous, green, (¾)1 to 2 feet long; fruit (in the plants introduced in this area) commonly yellowish or tannish-orange (purple or reddish in some other forms), glabrous, 2 to 3 inches long, about 2 inches in diameter
.... 20. *O. Ficus-Indica*

5⁵. Joints densely short-tomentose (woolly), velvety to the touch, green or with a whitish sheen because of the hairs, mostly 5 to 9 inches long; fruit red, tomentose, 1¼ to 1½ inches long, 1 inch in diameter ....
.... 21. *O. tomentosa*

LIST OF SPECIES, *Opuntia*

Subgenus 1. CYLINDROPUNTIA

Section 1. CYLINDROPUNTIA

Series 1. ECHINOCARPAE
 1. *O. Parryi*
 1a. var. *Parryi*
 1b. var. *serpentina*
 2. *O. Wigginsii*
 3. *O. echinocarpa*
 3a. var. *echinocarpa*
 3b. var. *Wolfii*
 4. *O. acanthocarpa*
 4a. var. *coloradensis*
 4b. var. *major*
 4c. var. *Ganderi*

Series 2. BIGELOVIANAE
 5. *O. prolifera*
 6. *O. Munzii*
 7. *O. Bigelovii*
 7a. var. *Hoffmannii*
 7b. var. *Bigelovii*

Series 3. RAMOSISSIMAE
 8. *O. ramosissima*

Section 2. CORYNOPUNTIA
 9. *O. Stanlyi*
 9a. var. *Parishii*
 9b. var. *Kunzei*
 10. *O. pulchella*

Subgenus 2. OPUNTIA

Section 1. OPUNTIA

Series 1. POLYACANTHAE
 11. *O. polyacantha*
 11a. var. *rufispina*
 12. *O. fragilis*
 13. *O. erinacea*
 13a. var. *erinacea*
 13b. var. *ursina*
 13c. var. *utahensis*

Series 2. BASILARES
 14. *O. basilaris*
 14a. var. *basilaris*
 14b. var. *brachyclada*
 14c. var. *Treleasei*

Series 3. OPUNTIAE
 15. *O. macrorhiza*
 16. *O. littoralis*
 16a. var. *littoralis*
 16b. var. *Vaseyi*
 16c. var. *austrocalifornica*
 16d. var. *Piercei*
 16e. var. *Martiniana*
 17. *O. phaeacantha*
 17a. var. *major*
 17b. var. *discata*
 18. *O. oricola*
 19. *O. chlorotica*
 20. *O. Ficus-Indica*
 Hybrid population *"occidentalis"*
 Hybrid population *"demissa"*
 21. *O. tomentosa*

1. Opuntia Parryi Engelm.   CANE CHOLLA

Prostrate or upright; trunk none; joints 3 to 6(15) inches long, ¾ to 1 inch in diameter; tubercles two and one-half to seven times as long as broad, ½ to ¾(1) inch long; spines distributed uniformly on the joint, grayish- to reddish-brown or brown (the sheaths the same or a lighter color), 7 to 20 per areole, ⅜ to ⅝ (1¼) inches long, ¹⁄₃₂ inch broad, subulate, barbed; flower 1¼ to 1½ inches in diameter; petaloid perianth parts yellow or greenish-yellow, the outer with a purplish to reddish tinge; fruit greenish, but turning to tan or brown, dry at maturity, with prominent

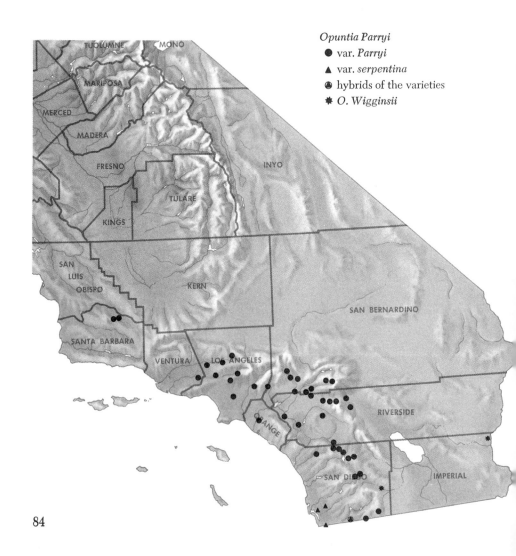

Opuntia Parryi
- ● var. *Parryi*
- ▲ var. *serpentina*
- ◉ hybrids of the varieties
- ✳ *O. Wigginsii*

Fig. 16. A thicket of a cane cholla, *Opuntia Parryi* var. *Parryi*, in flower, near Claremont, Los Angeles County. The cacti of the chaparral belt occur on disturbed areas similar to this one. The fires of the climax chaparral are too hot for them, and the competing shrubs are too dense.

tubercles and relatively few spines, which are about ¼ inch long, obovoid-turbinate, ½ inch long; seed whitish-tan, ¼ inch long.

1a. Opuntia Parryi var. Parryi

Erect bush or shrub; joints ⅝ to ¾(1) inch in diameter; tubercles raised and compressed from side to side, 4 to 7 times as long as broad.

Gravel or sand or alluvial fans in canyons or valleys; mostly on the coastal side of the mountain axis; 500 to 3,000 feet elevation. Disturbed areas normally covered by California Chaparral. California from Cuyama Valley on the northern edge of Santa Barbara County to Los Angeles County and the vicinity of San Bernardino and south through the interior valleys to San Diego County; edge of the Mojave Desert at Rock Creek and of the Colorado

Fig. 17. Snake cholla, *Opuntia Parryi* var. *serpentina*, sprawling through shrubs in disturbed chaparral; near Chula Vista, San Diego County.

Fig. 18. (*Opposite.*) Snake cholla, *Opuntia Parryi* var. *serpentina*. *Above,* flower and young fruits. *Below,* flower buds and young fruits.

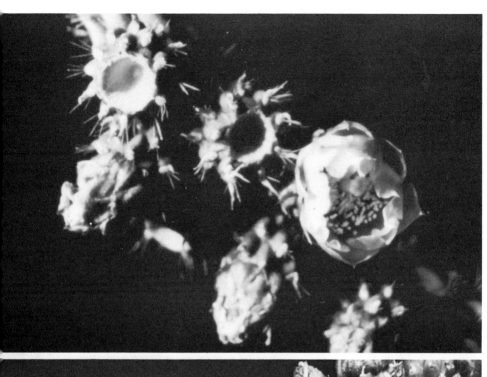

Desert east of Banning and in San Felipe Valley. Mexico, probably in northwestern Baja California.

Opuntia Parryi Engelm.; Cylindropuntia Parryi F. M. Knuth. San Felipe, San Diego County.

O. Parkeri Engelm.; O. echinocarpa Engelm. & Bigelow var. Parkeri Coulter. Campo, San Diego County.

O. bernardina Engelm. ex Parish. San Bernardino.

FIG. 16; PLATE 1; DISTRIBUTION MAP, p. 84.

1b. Opuntia Parryi var. serpentina (Engelm.) L. Benson

SNAKE CHOLLA

Prostrate or suberect; joints ¾ to 1 inch in diameter; tubercles raised but typically not compressed from side to side, 3(2½ to 4) times as long as broad.

Sandy soils of valleys and of coastal bluffs and hills; usually at less than 500 feet elevation. Open, disturbed places in the California Chaparral. California near San Diego and eastward to the Tecate region. Mexico on the Pacific coast of northern Baja California.

Opuntia serpentina Engelm. San Diego.

Cereus californicus Torrey & Gray. O. californica Cov., not Engelm.; Cylindropuntia californica F. M. Knuth. San Diego.

FIGS. 17, 18; PLATE 1; DISTRIBUTION MAP, p. 84.

2. Opuntia Wigginsii L. Benson

Shrub, 1 to 2 feet high; trunk ¾ to 1½ inches in diameter; joints somewhat expanded upward, 2 to 4 inches long, apically ⅜ inch in diameter; tubercles one and a half times as long as broad, up to 3⁄16 inch long; spines red or pink but with straw-colored sheaths, 6–8 per areole, those on the terminal part of the joint much larger, central spine far larger than the others, ¾ to 1¾ inches long, about 1⁄96 to ⅛₈ inch in diameter, straight; radial spines almost hairlike, up to ¼ inch long, perhaps 1⁄256 inch in diameter, spines not markedly barbed; flower (judging by a dried one) about 1 to 1½ inches in diameter; fruit green, dry at maturity, ⅝ to ¾ inch long, with all the spines of each areole well developed, barbed, and rather flexible, the longer ones ⅜ to ¾ inch long; seed tan, 3⁄16 inch long.

Sandy soils in the lower desert; 1,000 feet or less elevation. Colorado Desert. California in the Carrizo Desert in eastern San Diego

Fig. 19. *Opuntia Wigginsii.* The type plant from the Colorado Desert near Quartzite, Arizona.

County and in northeastern Imperial County. Arizona from the Quartzite area in Yuma County to the Gila River as far east as the edge of Maricopa County.

Opuntia Wigginsii L. Benson. Quartzite, Yuma County, Arizona.

Fig. 19; Distribution Map, p. 84.

3. Opuntia echinocarpa Engelm. & Bigelow

Silver or Golden Cholla

Intricately branched shrub or a miniature tree, the trunk often forming one-third to one-half the height of the plant, usually 2 to 3 inches in diameter; joints 2 to 6 (or rarely, along the western edge of the Colorado Desert, 10 to 15) inches long, ¾ (1¼ to 1½) inches in diameter; tubercles 1 to 2 times as long as broad, ¼ to ⅜ (¾) inch long; spines straw-colored, silvery, or golden or pinkish below, the sheaths being similar in color and persistent, about 3 to 12 per areole, spreading in all directions, ¾ to 1½ inches long; flower usually 1¼ to 2½ inches in diameter; petaloid perianth parts greenish yellow; fruit green, turning to light tan or straw-colored, dry at maturity, with dense spreading barbed spines on the upper half, obovoid-turbinate or nearly hemispherical, ¾ to 1(1¼) inches long; seeds light tan, ¼ inch in diameter.

3*a*. Opuntia echinocarpa var. **echinocarpa**

Silver or Golden Cholla

Intricately branched; joints 2 to 3(6) inches long, ⅝ to ¾(1) inch in diameter; tubercles ¼ to ⅜ inch long, about ⅛ to ¼ inch broad and high; flower 1¼ to 1½(2½) inches in diameter; fruits ½ to 1 inch long, weakly tuberculate.

Sand or gravelly soil in the desert; 1,000 to 4,000(5,600) feet elevation. The Mojavean Desert and (less commonly) the Colo-

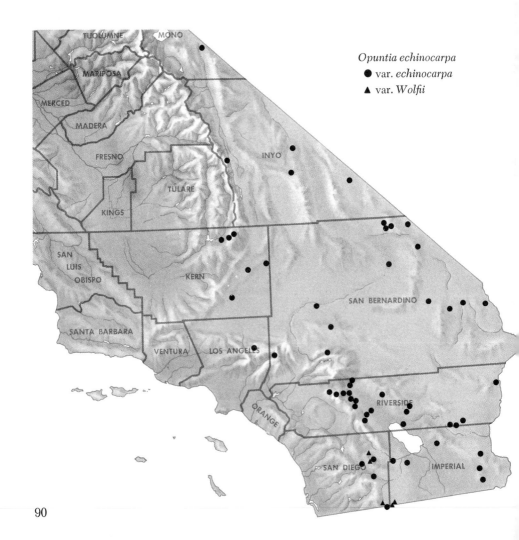

Opuntia echinocarpa
● var. *echinocarpa*
▲ var. *Wolfii*

Fig. 20. Silver cholla or golden cholla, *Opuntia echinocarpa* var. *echinocarpa*, in the southeasternmost Mojavean Desert near Aguila, Arizona. Commonly the plant is a miniature tree.

rado Desert. California from Benton Station, Mono County, to the Mojave and Colorado Deserts and South Fork Valley, Kern County. Nevada from Esmeralda and Nye counties south; southwestern Utah near Milford, Beaver County, and in Washington County; Arizona in Mojave, northernmost Coconino, Yuma, southwestern Yavapai, and northwestern Maricopa counties. Mexico in northeastern Baja California and northwestern Sonora.

Opuntia echinocarpa Engelm. & Bigelow; *Cylindropuntia echinocarpa* F. M. Knuth. Mouth of the Bill Williams River, Arizona.
O. deserta Griffiths. Searchlight, Nevada.

Figs. 14, 20, 21; Plate 2; Distribution Map, p. 90.

Fig. 22. A robust cholla, *Opuntia echinocarpa* var. *Wolfii*, in the Colorado Desert near Mountain Springs, westernmost Imperial County. The joints are much stouter than in var. *echinocarpa*.

Fig. 21. (*Opposite.*) Silver cholla or golden cholla, *Opuntia echincocarpa* var. *echinocarpa*. *Above, left and right,* young and old joints, the young ones with leaves. *Middle,* older branch with fruits just maturing, and in this species becoming dry. *Below,* six views of the mature, dry fruits. Photographs by David Griffiths.

3*b*. Opuntia echinocarpa var. Wolfii L. Benson

Simply branched robust plants; joints 4 to 10 inches long, 1¼ to 1½ inches in diameter; tubercles up to ¾ inch long and ⅜ inch broad and high; flower 1½ to 2 inches in diameter; fruits 1 to 1¼ inches long, strongly tuberculate.

Sand or gravel or rocky hillsides in or sometimes above the desert; 1,000 to 4,000 feet elevation. Western edge of the Colorado Desert. California in San Diego and Imperial counties. Mexico probably in adjacent Baja California.

Opuntia echinocarpa Engelm. & Bigelow var. *Wolfii* L. Benson. Mountain Springs Grade, Imperial County.

Fig. 22; Distribution Map, p. 90.

4. Opuntia acanthocarpa Engelm. & Bigelow   BUCKHORN CHOLLA

Shrub or arborescent plant or small tree; trunk usually much less than one-fifth the height of the plant, up to 4 or 6 inches in diameter; joints 6 to 12(24) inches long, (⅝)¾ to 1¼(1½) inches in diameter; tubercles conspicuous, sharply raised and compressed from side to side, 3 to several times as long as broad, ¾ to 1(2) inches long; spines tan to reddish-tan or straw-colored or whitish, turning to brown, then to black in age (the sheaths conspicuous, papery, and straw-colored or rarely silvery), 7(20) to 25 per areole, ½ to 1(1½) inches long, ¹⁄₃₂ to ¹⁄₂₀ inch broad, flattened, not strongly barbed; flower 1½ to 2¼ inches in diameter; petaloid perianth parts variable in color, usually purplish or red or yellow; fruit turning to tan or brown, dry at maturity, with numerous spreading spines except at the very base, obovoid-turbinate, 1 to 1½ inches long; seeds pale tan, less than ¼ inch long.

Fig. 24. Buckhorn cholla, *Opuntia acanthocarpa* var. *coloradensis*. Joints
in three stages of maturity, showing the ephemeral character of the leaves
and (*left*) an immature fruit that is still green and fleshy. Mature fruits are
dry, and they resemble those of *O. echinocarpa* (Fig. 21, *lower photograph*).
Photograph by David Griffiths.

Fig. 23. (*Opposite.*) Buckhorn cholla, *Opuntia acanthocarpa* var.
coloradensis; in the southeasternmost Mojavean Desert near Aguila, Arizona.
This species tends to become arborescent and up to about 9 feet high.

4a. Opuntia acanthocarpa var. coloradensis L. Benson

BUCKHORN CHOLLA

Treelike or sometimes shrubby, 4 to 6(9) feet high, the relatively few joints forming acute angles; joints 6 to 12 inches long, 1 to 1¼ inches in diameter; spines 1 to 1½ inches long.

Sand or gravelly soils in the desert; 2,000 to 4,300 feet elevation. Mojavean and Sonoran deserts. California, occasional in the eastern Mojave Desert from the road between Baker and Las Vegas south to the area west of Needles and to the eastern Colorado Desert near the Colorado River. Nevada in western Clark County; southwestern Utah in Washington County; Arizona from western Mohave County to northern Yuma County and east through the desert mountains to Yavapai and Gila counties.

The variety is named for the basin of the lower Colorado River.

Opuntia acanthocarpa Engelm. & Bigelow var. *coloradensis* L. Benson. Near South Pass, west of Needles, San Bernardino County.

FIGS. 23, 24; DISTRIBUTION MAP, p. 97.

4b. Opuntia acanthocarpa var. major (Engelm. & Bigelow) L. Benson

Shrub, sprawling or diffuse, 3 to 5 feet high, the numerous joints forming acute and obtuse angles; joints 5 to 10 inches long, ¾ to 1 inch in diameter; spines 1 inch long.

Sandy soils in the desert; 1,000 to 3,000 feet elevation. Arizona Desert. California near Vidal Junction, Riverside County. Arizona from Yuma County to Maricopa, Gila, western Graham, and western Pima counties. Mexico in northern Sonora.

Opuntia echinocarpa Engelm. & Bigelow var. *major* Engelm. & Bigelow; *O. echinocarpa* var. *robustior* Coulter; *O. acanthocarpa* Engelm. & Bigelow var. *major* L. Benson. Deserts on both sides of the Colorado River.

O. acanthocarpa Engelm. & Bigelow var. *ramosa* Peebles; *Cylindropuntia acanthocarpa* (Engelm. & Bigelow) F. M. Knuth var. *ramosa* Backeberg. Sacaton, Pinal County, Arizona.

PLATE 2; DISTRIBUTION MAP, p. 97.

4c. Opuntia acanthocarpa var. Ganderi (C. B. Wolf) L. Benson

GANDER CHOLLA

Shrubby to more or less treelike, robust, 3 to 4 feet high, the numerous joints ascending, 8 to 20 inches long, 1¼ to 1½ inches in diameter; spines 15–25 per areole (10–15 in the other varieties), ⅝ to 1¼ inches long.

Sand and gravelly soils in the desert; 1,000 to 3,000 feet elevation. Colorado Desert and the desert-edge version of the California Chaparral. California on the western edge of the Colorado Desert from Riverside County to San Diego and Imperial counties. Possibly continuing south into Mexico in Baja California.

Opuntia acanthocarpa Engelm. & Bigelow subsp. *Ganderi* C. B. Wolf. *O. acanthocarpa* var. *Ganderi* L. Benson. Vallecito, San Diego County.

FIG. 25; DISTRIBUTION MAP, this page.

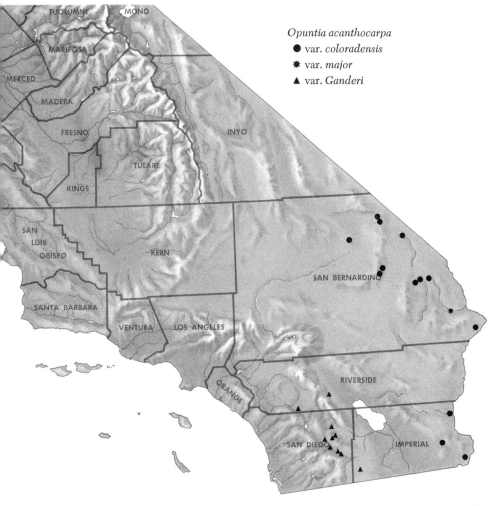

Opuntia acanthocarpa
● var. *coloradensis*
✳ var. *major*
▲ var. *Ganderi*

Fig. 25. Gander cholla, *Opuntia acanthocarpa* var. *Ganderi*, a robust variety; growing in the Rancho Santa Ana Botanic Garden, Claremont.

5. Opuntia prolifera Engelm.   COASTAL CHOLLA

Small trees or arborescent plants, 3 to 8 feet high; trunk 1 to 2 feet long, 2 to 4 inches in diameter, branched and rebranched several times, the branches longer than the trunk; terminal joints elongate-ellipsoid, 3 to 5½ inches long, (1¼)1½ to 2 inches in diameter, readily detached, rooting (the principal method of reproduction); tubercles mammillate, remarkably large, ½ to ¾ inch long, ³⁄₁₆ to ¼ inch broad; spines reddish-brown or in age dark gray with yellowish tips (the sheaths yellowish to tannish or rust-colored), about 6 to 12 per areole, spreading, ½ to 1⅛ inch long, ¹⁄₄₈ inch in diameter, acicular, not barbed; flower about 1 inch in diameter; petaloid perianth parts magenta to reddish-purple; fruit green, usually sterile, fleshy, smooth or somewhat tuberculate, globose or broadly obovoid, ¾ to 1¼ inches long, in later years obovoid and up to 2¼ inches long, persistent for two to several years, forming branched chains 2 to 4 fruits long; seeds formed rarely, ellipsoid, about ⅕ inch long.

Fine soils on hills and flats; coastal at low elevations. Grasslands and California Chaparral. California on Santa Rosa, Santa Cruz, San Nicolas, Santa Catalina, San Clemente, and Anacapa islands; on the mainland from Ventura south; inland rarely as far as Fallbrook. Mexico in Baja California southward to Rosario and on Guadalupe Island.

In 1876 J. C. Parker found only 2 seeds in 100 fruits, both in one fruit.

Opuntia prolifera Engelm.; *Cylindropuntia prolifera* F. M. Knuth. San Diego.

Figs. 26, 27; Plate 1; Distribution Map, p. 102.

6. Opuntia Munzii C. B. Wolf   Munz Cholla

Tree, 6 to 15 feet high; major branches elongate, rebranched several times; terminal joints often pendulous, mostly 4 to 10 inches long, about 1 inch in diameter; older joints often 1½ inches in diameter; tubercles about twice as long as broad, markedly raised above the surface, ½ to ⅝ inch long, ¼ to ⅜ inch broad; spines light yellow or straw-colored (the sheaths the same color), 9 to 12 per areole, spreading, ½ to ¾ inch long, ¹⁄₂₄ inch in diameter, acicular, markedly barbed; flower 1½ to 2 inches in diameter; petaloid perianth parts yellowish-green with a tinge of red or lavender; fruit yellow or green (usually sterile and drying without maturing), fleshy, tuberculate, spineless, about ¾ inch long, not persistent or proliferous; seeds light tan, nearly globose, very hard, about ⅛ inch in diameter.

Gravel or sand of washes and canyons in the desert; 500 to 1,000 feet elevation. Colorado Desert. California, in the Chuckawalla Mountains, Riverside County, and the Chocolate Mountains, Imperial County.

Opuntia Munzii has been suggested as a hybrid between *O. Bigelovii* and *O. acanthocarpa* var. *coloradensis*. This may or may not be correct; the evidence is not strong. It is not known whether *O. Munzii*, maintained chiefly through sexual reproduction, is highly heterozygous and is not capable of maintaining sexually

"STUDY NATURE NOT BOOKS"

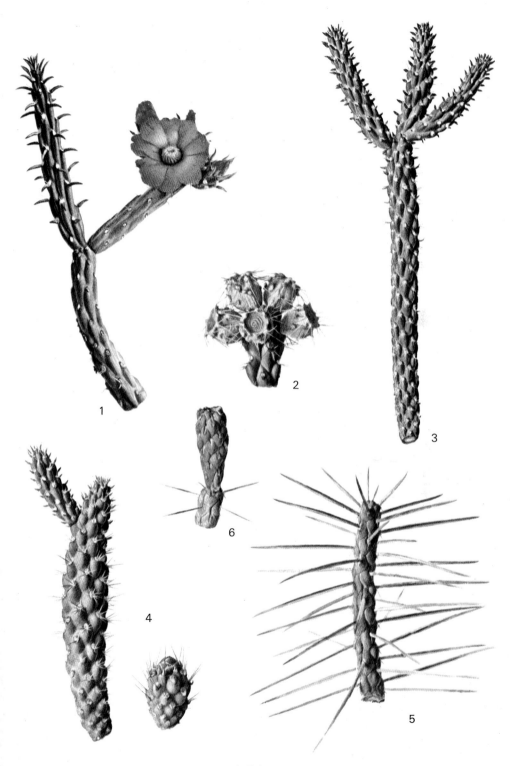

PLATE 1. 1 & 2. *Opuntia Parryi* var. *Parryi* (cane cholla). 3. *O. Parryi* var. *serpentina* (snake cholla). 4. *O. prolifera* (coastal cholla). 5 & 6. *O. ramosissima* (diamond cholla). Detailed legends for all color plates follow Contents page.

PLATE 2. 1 & 2. *Opuntia echinocarpa* var. *echinocarpa* (silver cholla). 3 & 4. *O. Bigelovii* var. *Bigelovii* (teddy bear cholla). 5. *O. acanthocarpa* var. *major* (buckhorn cholla).

1

2

PLATE 3. 1. *Opuntia basilaris* var. *basilaris* (beavertail cactus).
2. *O. polyacantha* var. *rufispina* (plains prickly pear).

1

2

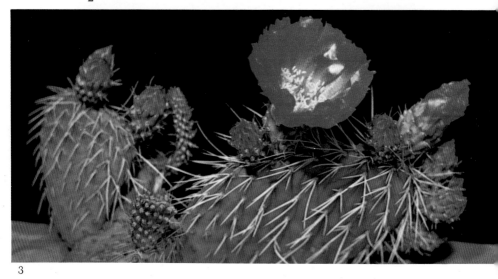

3

PLATE 4. *Opuntia erinacea* var. *utahensis* (Mojave prickly pear). 1. Natural habitat.
2. Sectioned flower. 3. Joints, spines, flower buds, and a flower.

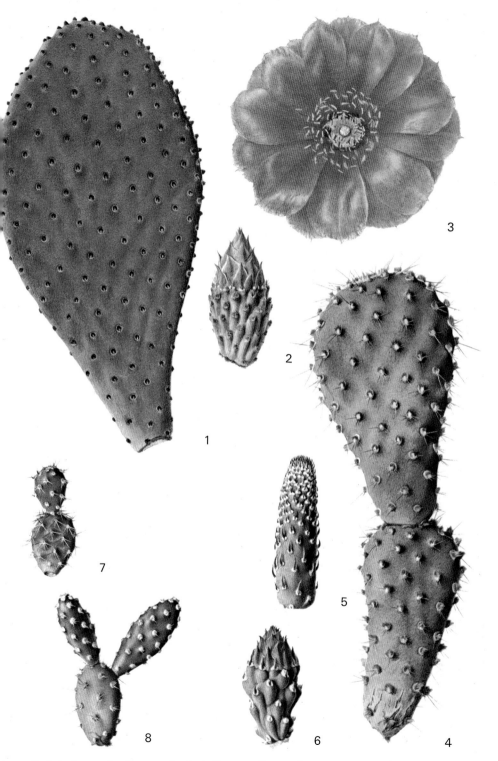

PLATE 5. 1–3. *Opuntia basilaris* var. *basilaris* (beavertail cactus).
4–6. *O. basilaris* var. *Treleasei* (Kern cactus). 7 & 8. *O. fragilis* (little prickly pear).

1

2

PLATE 6. 1. *Opuntia littoralis* var. *austrocalifornica*, a prickly pear. 2. *O. littoralis* var. *Vaseyi*, a prickly pear.

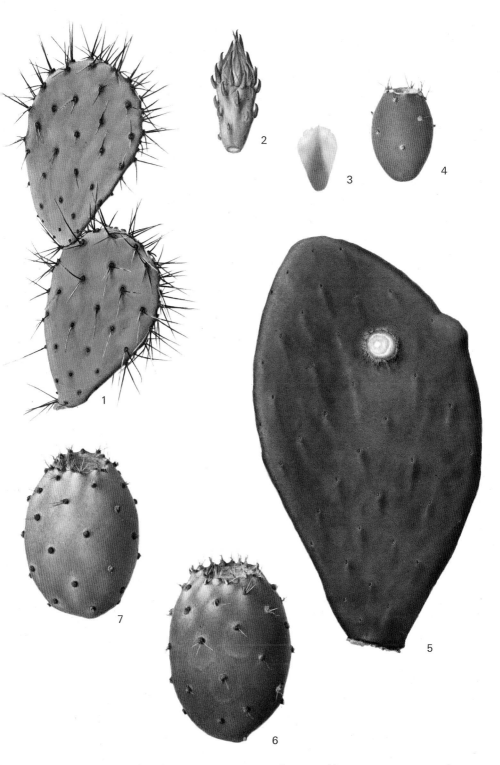

PLATE 7. 1–4. *Opuntia phaeacantha* var. *major,* a common desert prickly pear.
5–7. *O. Ficus-Indica* (Indian fig or mission cactus).

1

2

3

PLATE 8. 1. *Opuntia Ficus-Indica* (Indian fig or mission cactus, spiny form), large plant at left with prickly pears of several other types. 2 & 3. *O. Ficus-Indica* (spineless form).

Fig. 27. Coastal cholla, *Opuntia prolifera*, with mature and young joints, the latter bearing the ephemeral leaves; top views of two flowers showing the petaloid perianth parts, the stamens, and the eight to ten stigmas. Photograph by David Griffiths.

Fig. 26. (*Opposite.*) Coastal cholla, *Opuntia prolifera. Above,* large plant in fruit; growing in disturbed soil on low hills near the ocean in San Diego County. *Below,* joints (two young ones small and with leaves) and the proliferous fruits. The fruits, nearly all sterile, persist on the plant, new flowers being developed from their areoles; fruits falling to the ground produce roots and develop vegetatively into new plants. Photographs by David Griffiths.

101

a natural population not overlapping the character combinations of related species. See discussion under *O. Bigelovii* var. *Hoffmannii*.

> *Opuntia Munzii* C. B. Wolf. Chocolate Mountains, Imperial County.
> FIG. 28; DISTRIBUTION MAP, p. 102.

7. Opuntia Bigelovii Engelm.   TEDDY BEAR CHOLLA

Miniature tree, 3 to 5(9) feet high; trunk usually the height of the plant, becoming black as the spines turn dark; branches short, usually rebranched only once or twice, joints narrowly ellipsoid, 3 to 5(10) inches long, (1¼)1½ to 2½ inches in diameter, readily detached, mostly deciduous (rooting and reproducing the plant),

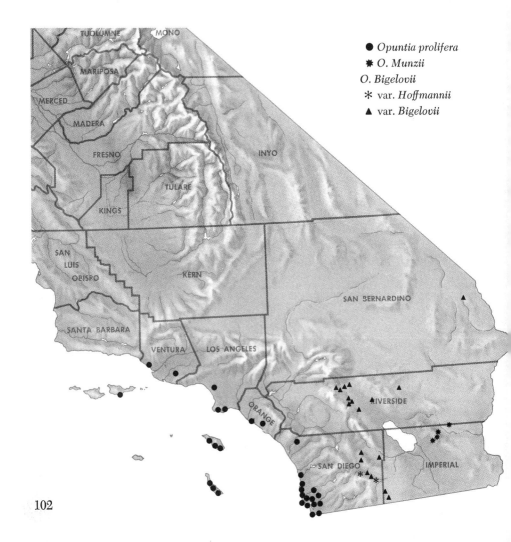

- ● *Opuntia prolifera*
- ✻ *O. Munzii*
- *O. Bigelovii*
- ✳ var. *Hoffmannii*
- ▲ var. *Bigelovii*

Fig. 28. Munz cholla, *Opuntia Munzii*. The very stout joints and dense
spines are characteristic of the species.

103

leaving the main trunk with the appearance of a post; tubercles one to one and a half times as long as broad, six-sided, ¼ to ⅜ inch long; spines conspicuous, obscuring the branch (except in var. *Hoffmannii*), pinkish-tan or reddish-brown (the sheaths straw-colored, conspicuous and persistent), 6 to 10 per areole, spreading, ⅝ to 1 inch long, ¹⁄₂₄ inch broad, subulate, with many backward-directed microscopic scabrous projections and so exceedingly strongly barbed, persistent and turning black; flower 1 to 1½ inches in diameter; petaloid perianth parts pale green or yellow streaked with lavender; fruit yellow or greenish-yellow (usually sterile), fleshy, strongly tuberculate, with no appendages, ½ to ¾ inch long, not proliferous; seeds (when present) broadly obovate, ⅛ inch long.

7a. Opuntia Bigelovii var. Hoffmannii Fosberg

Branching usually more diffuse than in var. *Bigelovii*; main branches longer and more rebranched; joints about 1¼ inches in diameter; tubercles about ⅜ inch long, about one and a half times as long as broad, six-sided but elongate rather than hexagonal; spines forming only a moderately dense mass, not obscuring the stem, barbed, pinkish-tan, the sheaths lighter tan or straw-colored.

Gravelly soils in the desert; 1,000 to 1,500 feet elevation. Colorado Desert. California in the Anza Desert in eastern San Diego County from Mason Valley and Vallecito to Canebrake Canyon.

The population is maintained by vegetative reproduction. A hybrid origin from var. *Bigelovii* and *Opuntia echinocarpa* var. *coloradensis* has been suggested. The plants may be sufficiently heterozygous (variable in their hereditary makeup, the members of gene pairs differing) not to be able to maintain their identity by sexual reproduction. Flowering and fruiting and setting of viable seeds are rare, as in many hybrids, but completion of sexual reproduction is rare also in var. *Bigelovii*, and it is uncommon in *O. fulgida* and *O. prolifera*, as well as various other species of *Opuntia*. Hybrid origin is a ready explanation for any plant intermediate be-

Fig. 29. Teddy bear cholla, *Opuntia Bigelovii* var. *Bigelovii*. Stem joints with the dangerous barbed spines and several fruits. The fruits are tuberculate, yellow, and rather fleshy at maturity. Photograph by David Griffiths.

tween two population systems; so is divergent evolution from an original intermediate population to the extremes. So also is origin of all three from a common ancestor. By itself, even a proved explanation of origin does not necessarily solve the question of classification.

Opuntia fulgida Engelm. var. *Hoffmannii* Fosberg, not *O. Hoffmannii* Bravo; *O. Fosbergii* C. B. Wolf. Canebrake Canyon, San Diego County.

Distribution Map, p. 102.

7*b*. Opuntia Bigelovii var. Bigelovii

Branches much shorter than main trunk, rebranched only once or twice; joints 1½ to 2½ inches in diameter; tubercles ¼ inch long, of equal width, hexagonal, but the sides of irregular length; spines densely covering the stem and obscuring it, strongly barbed, straw-colored, the sheaths the same color.

Rocky or gravelly areas of south-facing slopes or flats in the desert; 100 to 2,000(3,000) feet elevation. Colorado Desert and Arizona Desert. California throughout the Colorado Desert. Arizona from Mohave and Maricopa counties to Yuma and Pima counties. Mexico in Baja California and Sonora.

The weird appearance and the effectiveness of the spines make this cholla never to be forgotten. The spines are numerous, sharp, and strongly barbed, and they are difficult to remove from human flesh. Each spine may have to be clipped with scissors.

Opuntia Bigelovii Engelm.; *Cylindropuntia Bigelovii* F. M. Knuth. Bill Williams River, Arizona.

Fig. 29; Plates 2, 15; Distribution Map, p. 102.

8. Opuntia ramosissima Engelm.   Diamond Cholla

Bushy, matted, shrubby, or arborescent plants, ½ to 2(5) feet high; trunk seldom present; main branches rebranched profusely

Fig. 30. Diamond cholla, *Opuntia ramosissima. Above,* large plant in the Colorado Desert. Rarely the plant becomes a miniature tree up to 5 feet high; usually it is a bush or is decumbent. *Below,* branches, showing the diamond-shaped tubercles each with an areole in the groove, the areole bearing a solitary long spine. Usually the fruits bear spines, but sometimes (*middle*) they are spineless. Ordinarily the dry fruit is a densely spiny bur. Photographs by David Griffiths.

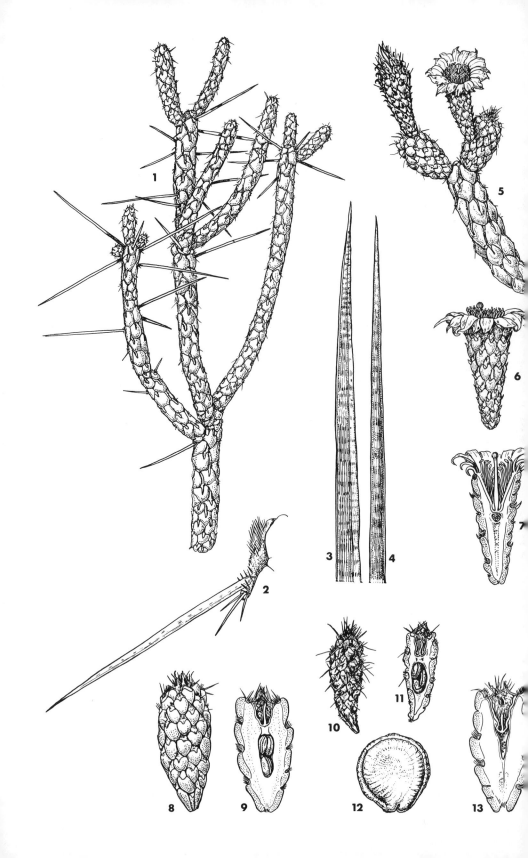

1
2
3
4
5
6
7
8
9
10
11
12
13

at or above ground level; joints grayish-green, slender, 2 to 4 inches long, up to about ¼ inch in diameter; woody core of the joint nearly solid; tubercle flattened, platelike, diamond-shaped on mature branches, bearing the areole in an apical notch or groove, 3/16 to 5/16 inch long, about 3/16 inch broad, only 1/24 inch high; spines tan (the sheath light tan, apically reddish-tan, thin, membranous, conspicuous), in only the upper areoles of the joint, at first 1–3 per areole but only 1 developing, spreading 1½ to 2¼ inches long, 1/48 to 1/32 inch in diameter, acicular, with many minute strong barbs; flower ½ inch in diameter; petaloid perianth parts apricot to brown with some lavender or red; fruit brown or tan, dry, densely spiny and burlike (the spines up to ¾ inch long) or sometimes spineless, tuberculate, ellipsoid, up to ¾ inch long; seed creamy white or light tannish-gray, nearly circular but irregular, about ⅛ inch in diameter.

Fine or sandy soils in the desert; 100 to 2,000(3,000) feet elevation. Colorado Desert. California in the southern Mojave Desert from Death Valley to the Mojave River and the Colorado Desert. Southern Nevada near the Colorado River; Arizona from western Mohave County to Yuma, western Maricopa, and western Pima counties. Mexico in northwestern Sonora.

In areas along the edge of the Mojavean Desert in the Joshua

Fig. 31. Diamond cholla, *Opuntia ramosissima*, drawn from a plant from Pierce's Ferry, Colorado River, Mohave County, Arizona. *1.* Vegetative branch showing the diamond-shaped tubercles each with an areole depressed in a groove, the areole bearing one conspicuous long spine, ×¼. *2.* Areole with one long spine, three short spines, and glochids, ×1. *3.* Spine, enlarged, enclosed by and visible through the paperlike sheath typical of cholla spines but lacking in those of prickly pears, ×2½. *4.* Spine with the sheath removed, 2½. *5.* Joint bearing two sterile fruits of the previous season, which, being proliferous, have produced a flower bud and a flower from areoles of the floral cup, forming in each the outer layer of the ovary, ×⅜. *6.* Flower, ×½. *7.* Flower in section, showing, in ascending order, the inferior ovary with the seed chamber enclosing ovules, the style and stigmas, the stamens, the scale leaves subtending the areoles of the floral cup, and the transition of scales into sepaloid then petaloid perianth parts, ×½. *8 & 9.* Fruit, without spines (most, but not all fruits being densely long-spiny, Fig. 30), ×½. *10 & 11.* Fruit after drying, this one with short spines, ×½. *12.* Seed, the marginal portion enclosing the curved embryo, ×2½. *13.* Sterile fruit in section, showing the abortive ovules, ×½.

Tree National Monument, California, and sometimes in southern Nevada the plants are treelike.

Opuntia ramosissima Engelm.; *O. tessellata* Engelm., *nom. nov.* (*O. ramosissima* having been considered inappropriate because many species branch profusely); *Cylindropuntia ramosissima* F. M. Knuth. "Gravelly soil near the Colorado . . . ," California.

FIGS. 30, 31; PLATE 1; DISTRIBUTION MAP, this page.

9. Opuntia Stanlyi Engelm.   DEVIL CHOLLA

Plants forming mats or clumps 6 inches or rarely 1 foot high, the mats up to several yards in diameter; joints subcylindroid to mostly narrowly obovoid, (2)3 to 6(8) inches long, ⅝ to 1½ inches

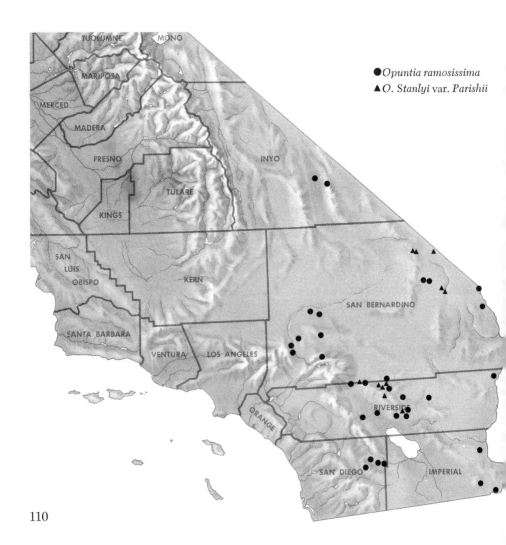

●*Opuntia ramosissima*
▲*O. Stanlyi* var. *Parishii*

Fig. 32. Parish cholla, *Opuntia Stanlyi* var. *Parishii*. *Above*, in the
Mojavean Desert. *Below*, in cultivation, with a large, mature fruit.
Photographs by David Griffiths.

111

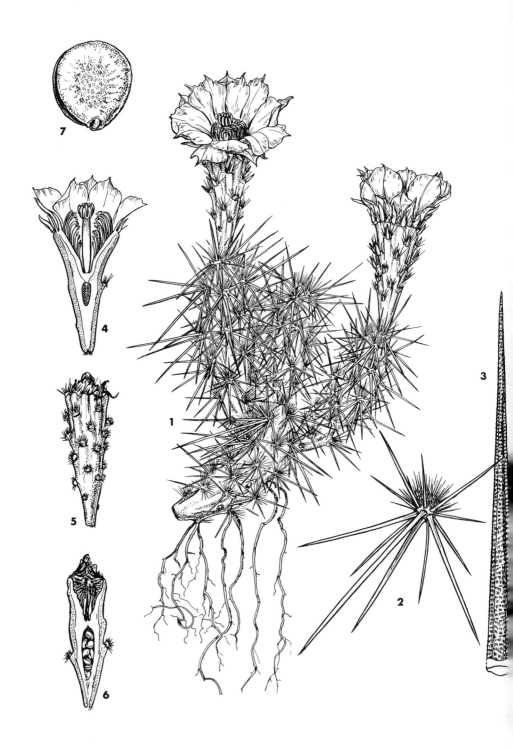

Fig. 34. Parish cholla, *Opuntia Stanlyi* var. *Parishii*. Plant with sterile, proliferous fruits, each new one growing from an areole of the floral tube forming the outer layer of an older one. Photograph by David Griffiths.

Fig. 33. (*Opposite.*) Parish cholla. *Opuntia Stanlyi* var. *Parishii*, drawn from a plant from Pierce's Ferry, Colorado River, Mohave County, Arizona. *1.* Plant in flower, ×¼. *2.* Areole with spines and glochids, ×1½. *3.* Spine enlarged, showing the papillae, which roughen the surface, ×10. In the species of this group of chollas the sheath of the spine ultimately separates into only an apical cap. *4.* Flower in section, showing the ovary and ovules, style and stigmas, stamens, and sepaloid and petaloid perianth parts, ×¼. *5.* Fruit, ×¼. *6.* Fruit in section, showing the seeds, ×¼. *7.* Seed, ×2½.

in diameter, enlarged upward (clavate or clublike), attached firmly; tubercles large and conspicuous, mammillate, ½ to 1¼ inches long, ¼ to ½ inch broad; spines chiefly on the upper part of the joint, tan or straw-colored to brown or red (the sheath on only the apex of the spine), with rough papillae in crosswise ranks, not longitudinally ribbed or grooved, 10 to 18 per areole, the longest turned downward, up to 2 inches long, ½₄ to ³⁄₁₆ inch broad, subulate, not barbed; flowers 1 to 2 inches in diameter; petaloid perianth parts yellow or (in var. *Parishii*) sometimes reddish; fruit yellow, fleshy, smooth, usually densely spiny, with large glochids, slender, enlarged upward, 1½ to 3¼ inches long; seed light gray, tan, or yellow, obovate to nearly circular, ⅛ to ¼ inch long.

9a. Opuntia Stanlyi var. Parishii (Orcutt) L. Benson

PARISH CHOLLA

Joints 2 to 3 inches long, ¾ to 1¼ inches in diameter, obovoid or narrowly so, gradually narrowed basally; tubercles separate, ½ to 1 inch long; flowers red or yellow; fruit usually not spiny or only weakly so; seed ⅛ to ³⁄₁₆ inch long.

Sandy soils in valleys or on plains in the desert; 3,000 to 4,000 feet elevation. Mojavean Desert. California in San Bernardino and northern Riverside counties (Joshua Tree National Monument) and in the mountains northeastward across the eastern Mojave Desert. Nevada in Clark County from the Charleston Mountains south; Arizona, rare in Mohave County.

Opuntia Parishii Orcutt; *Corynopuntia Parishii* F. M. Knuth; *O. Stanlyi* Engelm. var. *Parishii* L. Benson; *C. Stanlyi* (Engelm.) F. M. Knuth var. *Parishii* Backeberg. Mojave River.

FIGS. 32, 33, 34; DISTRIBUTION MAP, p. 110.

9b. Opuntia Stanlyi var. Kunzei (Rose) L. Benson

This variety is stated by Baxter (*California Cactus* 58–59. 1935) to occur in California near the Colorado River opposite the Petrified Forest north of Yuma, Arizona, but no specimens have been found. The plant has stout stems usually rising several joints above ground level; these are 4 to 8 inches long, cylindroidal, abruptly narrowed basally, and with the tubercles (in older plants) basally coalescent into ribs and each ¾ to 1¼ inches long. The flowers are yellow and the fruits spiny.

Opuntia Kunzei Rose; *Corynopuntia Kunzei* (Rose) F. M. Knuth. *O. Stanlyi* Engelm. var. *Kunzei* L. Benson. Gunsight Mine, southeast of Ajo, Arizona.

Grusonia Wrightiana Baxter; *O. Wrightiana* Peebles; *O. Stanlyi* Engelm. var. *Wrightiana* L. Benson; *C. Stanlyi* (Engelm.) F. M. Knuth var. *Wrightiana* Backeberg. Petrified Forest, north of Yuma, Arizona.

10. Opuntia pulchella Engelm.   SAND CHOLLA

Plants clump-forming, inconspicuous, the clumps usually only a few inches in diameter; stems arising from a glochid-covered tuber about 2 or 3 inches in diameter; the entire areole bearing the glochids ultimately deciduous; joints variable, especially so in young plants or after browsing by animals or following disease, gradually expanded upward or narrowly ellipsoid or cylindroid, (1) 1½ to 2½(4) inches long, (³⁄₁₆)½ to 1 inch in diameter; ribs none; tubercles low and inconspicuous or projecting and mammillate, ¼ to ⅜ inch long, about ⅙ inch broad, ¹⁄₁₆ inch or less high; longer spines toward the top of the joint, white to gray, brown, or pink, basally with ridges and grooves, not papillate, with the sheaths apical, about 8 to 15 per areole, somewhat deflexed, flexible, the longest one light-colored, up to 2½ inches long, up to ¹⁄₁₆ inch broad, flattened, not barbed (*in juvenile plants* the spines all alike, white with tan bases, ¹⁄₁₆ to ⅛ inch long, slender and acicular, not ridged); glochids of the tubers yellow to brown, ⅜ to 1 inch long; flower ¾ to 1¼(1½) inches in diameter; petaloid perianth parts purple to rose; fruit reddish, fleshy, smooth, the areoles each bearing 20 or more purplish or brownish soft and bristlelike spines ½ to ⅝ inch long, about ¾ to 1⅛ inches long; seed bone-white, elliptic to irregular, ³⁄₁₆ to ¼ inch long.

Sand of dry lake borders, dunes, river bottoms, washes, valleys, and plains in the desert; 4,000 to 5,000 feet elevation. Sagebrush Desert. Reported to occur in California but the locality not given and the statement undocumented; occurring near the state line in Nevada. Nevada from east-central Washoe County, Lyon County, and Esmeralda County east; western Utah; northwestern Arizona.

Fig. 35. Sand cholla, *Opuntia pulchella. Above,* mature plant about 4 inches high and with long spines; Walker River, Nevada. *Below,* juvenile plant with short spines and with branches about the diameter of a lead pencil; as with some other cacti, flowering occurs before development of the mature types of spines; near Tonopah, Nevada. Photographs by Homer G. Rush. From Lyman Benson, *The Opuntia pulchella Complex,* Cactus and Succulent Journal 29: 20. 1957. Used by permission.

O. pulchella includes several minor forms or abnormal types. These have been named as species under the proposed genus "*Micropuntia*," which is based upon (1) absence of glochids on the tubers (these, however, being deciduous in age with the areoles), (2) special spine types (these being actually highly variable in all populations, the small types being produced after injury or disease or desiccation), and (3) small joints (these varying as do the spine types). (See L. Benson, *The Opuntia pulchella Complex*. Cactus & Succulent Journal 29: 19–31. 1957.) Because the plants flower and fruit while they are still in juvenile stages, there is confusion.

Opuntia pulchella Engelm.; *Corynopuntia pulchella* F. M. Knuth. Walker River, Nevada.

Micropuntia brachyrhopalica Daston; *O. brachyrhopalica* Rowley; *M. Barkleyana* Daston; *O. Barkleyana* Rowley; *M. spectatissima* Daston; *O. spectatissima* Rowley. U.S. Desert Experimental Range, west of Milford, Utah.

M. tuberculosirhopalica Wiegand & Backeberg; *O. tuberculosirhopalica* Rowley. "USA (Utah, Arizona)."

M. pygmaea Wiegand & Backeberg; *O. pygmaea* Rowley. "USA (Idaho australis, Nevada)."

M. gracilicylindrica Wiegand & Backeberg; *O. gracilocylindrica* Rowley. "USA (Nevada)."

M. Wiegandii Backeberg; *M. gigantea* Wiegand ex Backeberg, *pro syn.*; *O. Wiegandii* Rowley. "USA (Nevada, California)."

Fig. 35.

11. Opuntia polyacantha Haw.   Plains Prickly Pear

Plants mat-forming; clumps 3 to 6 inches high and 1 to several feet in diameter; joints orbiculate to broadly obovate, 2 to 4 inches long, (1)2 to 4 inches broad, about ⅜ inch thick, glabrous, not readily detached; spines distributed variously in the varieties, white to brown or reddish-brown or in age gray, about 6 to 10 per areole, mostly deflexed, 1 to 3¼ inches long, ⅟₆₆ to ⅟₄₈ inch in diameter, not flattened, not strongly barbed; flower 1¾ to 3¼ inches in diameter; petaloid perianth parts yellow or occasionally pale or tinged with pink or rarely red (in some varieties); fruit dull tan or brown, dry, spiny (with barbed spines) over the entire surface, obovoid, ¾ to 1½ inches long; seed light tan to nearly white, irregular in outline, flattened, the margin usually conspicuous, ⅛ to ¼ inch long.

11a. Opuntia polyacantha var. rufispina (Engelm. & Bigelow)
    L. Benson

Spines in all the areoles of the joint, those of the lower areoles rigid, straight, short, ½ to 1¼ inches long, the longest ones in the upper areoles usually 1¾ to 3¼ inches long, white, gray, or sometimes reddish brown, ¹⁄₂₄ to ¹⁄₃₂ inch in diameter; fruit densely spiny.

Sandy areas in deserts and woodlands; 4,000 to 7,000(10,000) feet elevation. Juniper-Pinyon Woodland; Sagebrush Desert; Chihuahuan Desert. California along the eastern edge and slopes of the Sierra Nevada and in the mountains in Mono and Inyo counties and the New York Mountains in San Bernardino County. Higher parts of Nevada and Utah (less commonly); Wyoming near Green River; western Colorado; northern Arizona; New Mexico; Texas west of the Pecos.

Opuntia missouriensis DC. var. *rufispina* Engelm. & Bigelow; *O. polyacantha* var. *rufispina* L. Benson. Pecos River, New Mexico.

PLATE 3; DISTRIBUTION MAP, p. 124.

12. Opuntia fragilis (Nutt.) Haw.   LITTLE PRICKLY PEAR

Plants mat-forming, usually 2 to 4 inches high, the clumps 1 foot or more in diameter; joints flattened-obovoid or flattened-ovoid, elliptic, orbiculate, ¾ to 1¾ inches long, ½ to 1(1½) inches broad, ½ to ¾ inch thick, at least one-half as thick as broad and sometimes almost as thick as broad, readily detached, clinging by the barbed spines; spines on most of the joints, the longest in the upper areoles, white or pale gray, 1 to 6(9) per areole, spreading, ½ to 1 (1¼) inches long, ¹⁄₃₂ inch in diameter, nearly circular to elliptic in cross section, strongly barbed; flower 1½ to 2 inches in diameter; petaloid perianth parts yellow or greenish or reportedly magenta; fruit at first green or reddish-green but becoming dry and tan at maturity, nearly always spiny, obovoid, ½ to ⅝ inch long; seed bone-colored, very irregularly discoid, with the margin conspicuous, about ¼ inch long.

Sandy, gravelly, or rocky soils of valleys, low hills, or mountains mostly in the desert; sea level to 2,000 feet elevation or (southward) 3,000 to 5,000(8,000) feet. Sagebrush Desert but also sparingly in the Pacific Forest, Rocky Mountain Montane Forest, Juni-

Fig. 36. Little prickly pear, *Opuntia fragilis*, characteristic primarily of the Sagebrush Desert; growing under sagebrush (partly removed) near Glenwood Springs, Colorado. The joints of the stem are relatively very thick and mostly only an inch to an inch and one-half long.

per-Pinyon Woodland, Navajoan Desert, Great Plains Grassland, and Prairie. Northeastern corner of California. British Columbia to western Manitoba. Washington along northern Puget Sound; Columbia Basin and eastward through the Rocky Mountain System, Great Plains, and Great Lakes region to southern Michigan and Illinois and to northeastern Nevada, northern Arizona, northern New Mexico, Kansas, and the panhandles of Oklahoma and Texas.

Cactus fragilis Nutt.; *Opuntia fragilis* Haw.; *Tunas fragilis* Nieuwl. & Lunell. Upper Missouri River.

O. Sabinii Pfeiffer, *pro syn.* for *C. fragilis* Nutt.

O. Schweriniana K. Schum.; *O. polyacantha* Haw. var. *Schweriniana* Backeberg. Sapinero, Colorado.

O. fragilis (Nutt.) Haw. var. *caespitosa* Hort. ex Bailey. "Colo."

O. fragilis (Nutt.) Haw. var. *tuberiformis* Hort. ex Bailey. "Colo."

O. fragilis (Nutt.) Haw. var. *parviconspicua* Backeberg. "Hab.?"

O. fragilis (Nutt.) Haw. var. *denudata* Wiegand & Backeberg. "USA (Utah australis)."

Fig. 36; Plate 5.

119

Var. *erinacea*

JOINT SHAPE	Elliptic- to obovate-oblong, commonly 4 to 5 inches long, 1 to 1½ or 2 inches broad
DISTRIBUTION OF SPINES ON THE JOINT	In all areoles, the apical longest, reduced gradually down the joint, usually recurved or deflexed, somewhat flexuous, the longest 1¼(2) to 3¾ inches long, ⅛s inch broad
SPINES OF THE FRUIT	Abundant above
GEOGRAPHICAL DISTRIBUTION	Deserts from California to southwestern Colorado, northern Arizona, and New Mexico (rare)

13. Opuntia erinacea Engelm. & Bigelow

Plant forming clumps mostly 6 inches to 1 foot high and 1 yard or more in diameter; joints elongate, elliptic-oblong to obovate-oblong, (2)4 to 6(8) inches long, 2½ to 3½ inches broad, less than ½ inch thick, not more than one-fourth as thick as broad; spines over the entire joint or (in var. *utahensis*) restricted to the upper areoles, white or pale gray, 4 to 7(9) per areole, deflexed, somewhat twisted, flexible and curving irregularly, (½)2 to 4 inches long, ⅛s inch broad, almost filiform but subulate, at least some basally flattened, not markedly barbed; flower about 1¾ to 3⅝ inches in diameter; petaloid perianth parts rose to deep pink or yellow; fruit tan to brownish, dry at maturity, densely spiny with the spines (especially in a ring at the apex) spreading and strongly barbed, obovoid-cylindroid, 1 to 1¼ inches long; seeds bone-white, irregularly discoid, ⅙ to ¼ inch long.

Var. *ursina*	Var. *utahensis*
As in var. *erinacea*	Broadly to narrowly obovate or elliptic, mostly 2 to 3½ inches long, 2 to 3 inches broad
In all areoles, the longest ones above, but those in the lower areoles also long and more slender, being deflexed, curving and remarkably flexuous, the longest spines 3 to 4 inches long, ⅟₉₆ inch broad	In only the upper areoles, spreading or (if long) deflexed, straight or sometimes recurving, not flexuous, 1 to 1½(2¼) inches long, usually about ⅟₃₂ inch broad
Abundant on the entire fruit	Above, few and short
Mojavean Desert. California to southwestern Utah and northwestern Arizona	Southern Idaho to California (southern Sierra Nevada), western Colorado, northern Arizona, and New Mexico

13a. Opuntia erinacea var. erinacea   MOJAVE PRICKLY PEAR

Sandy or gravelly soils in the desert or woodland; 1,500 to 5,000 (7,500) feet elevation. Mojavean Desert or Juniper-Pinyon Woodland or sometimes adjacent parts of the Sagebrush Desert or Colorado Desert. California from the White Mountain region to the Mojave Desert and on the inland sides of the San Gabriel, San Bernardino, San Jacinto, and Santa Rosa mountains. Nevada from Esmeralda County to White Pine County and southward; Utah from Millard and Emery counties south; Colorado (Montrose); northern Arizona; western New Mexico.

The distinction of the varieties of *Opuntia erinacea* from those of *O. polyacantha* is not strictly clear-cut on the basis of the flattening of at least the basal portions of the larger spines in *O. erinacea*. Examples of hybridizing are found occasionally along the zone of geographical contact of var. *erinacea* and *O. polyacantha*

Fig. 37. Mojave prickly pear, *Opuntia erinacea* var. *erinacea*, in the Mojavean Desert near Kingman, Arizona. Photograph by A. A. Nichol.

Fig. 38. (*Opposite.*) Mojave prickly pear, *Opuntia erinacea* var. *erinacea*; drawn from a plant from Steamboat Springs, Arizona. *1.* Joint with the characteristic flattened, downward-directed spines, this joint atypically narrower at the top, ×¼. *2.* Areole with spines and glochids, ×½. *3.* Apical portion of a spine, showing the minute barbs, and (in this part, as opposed to the base) the elliptic cross section, ×3¾. *4.* Flower, ×¼. *5.* Flower in section, showing the ovary with ovules, the stigma and styles, the stamens on the floral tube above the ovary, the sepaloid and petaloid perianth parts, and the areoles and subtending leaves on the portion of the floral tube forming the outer layer of the ovary. *6 & 7.* Fruit in external view and in section, ×⅓. *8.* Seed, the outer part enclosing the curving embryo strongly differentiated, ×2.

var. *rufispina*, as shown, for example, by specimens from Kyle Canyon, Charleston Mountains, Clark County, Nevada (*L. Benson 15,054, Pom*). Plants appearing to include genes of var. *erinacea*, var. *utahensis*, and *O. polyacantha* var. *rufispina* are represented on four herbarium sheets collected near Cardinal Lodge west of Bishop, Inyo County, California (*E. F. Wiegand 78, 79, 109*, and *111* in 1951, *Pom*).

Opuntia erinacea Engelm. & Bigelow; *O. hystricina* Engelm. & Bigelow var. *Bensonii* Backeberg, *nom. nov.* for *O. erinacea,* but an illegitimate epithet because *O. hystricina* had been reduced to varietal status under *O. erinacea* by the writer in 1944. Mojave River.

O. xerocarpa Griffiths. Fifteen miles southeast of Kingman, Arizona.

Fig. 37, 38; Distribution Map, p. 124.

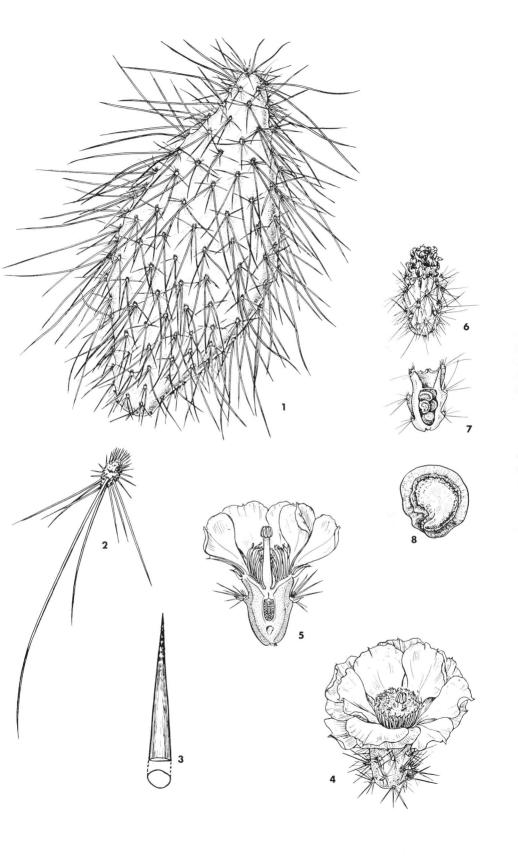

13*b*. **Opuntia erinacea** var. **ursina** (Weber) Parish
GRIZZLY BEAR CACTUS

Rocky soils in the desert, 4,000 to 5,500 feet elevation. Upper Mojavean Desert. California in the Mojave Desert region from the White Mountains, Inyo County, to northern Riverside County. Nevada in Mineral, Clark, and Lincoln counties; southwestern Utah; northern Arizona.

The variety is known best for its long, flexible, undulating, deflexed spines from the bases of the lower joints.

Opuntia ursina Weber; *O. erinacea* Engelm. & Bigelow var. *ursina* Parish. South of Barstow.

O. Ursus horribilis Walton. Mojave Desert.

FIG. 39; DISTRIBUTION MAP, this page.

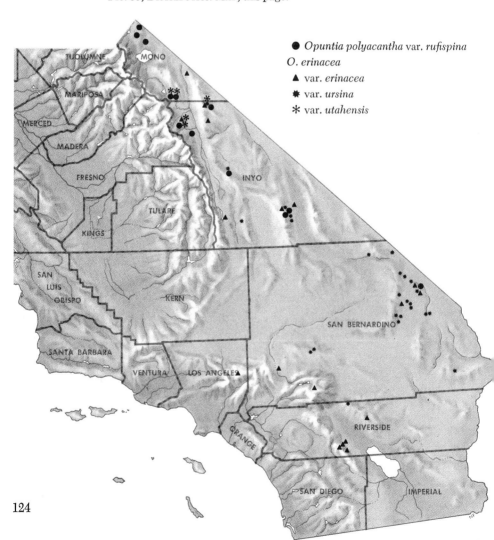

● *Opuntia polyacantha* var. *rufispina*
O. erinacea
▲ var. *erinacea*
✳ var. *ursina*
✳ var. *utahensis*

Fig. 39. The grizzly bear cactus, *Opuntia erinacea* var. *ursina. Above,* plants in the Rancho Santa Ana Botanic Garden, Claremont; the long, white or pale gray, flexible lower spines make this variety a favorite for cultivation. *Right,* the upper joints, which do not develop the long, flexible, white or pale gray spines appearing on the lower joints. Photograph *right* by David Griffiths.

	Var. *basilaris*
JOINT SHAPE	Obovate or sometimes orbiculate
JOINT SIZE	2 to 6(13) inches long, 1½ to 4(6) inches broad
SPINES	None
GEOGRAPHICAL DISTRIBUTION	California mountains in and near the deserts. Southern Nevada; Utah (rare); western Arizona. Mexico in northernmost Sonora

13c. **Opuntia erinacea** var. **utahensis** (Engelm.) L. Benson

Sandy, gravelly, or rocky soils in woodlands; (3,000)5,600 to 8,000 feet elevation. Juniper-Pinyon Woodland or the upper edge of the Sagebrush Desert. California along the eastern side of the Sierra Nevada in Mono and Inyo counties. Idaho to the middle levels of Nevada and Utah, western Colorado, northern Arizona, and New Mexico.

Var. *utahensis* is the plant long cultivated as *Opuntia rhodantha* and *O. xanthostemma.*

Opuntia sphaerocarpa Engelm. & Bigelow var. *utahensis* Engelm., not *O. utahensis* J. A. Purpus; *O. erinacea* var. *utahensis* L. Benson. West of Steptoe Valley, Nevada.

O. rhodantha K. Schum.; *O. erinacea* Engelm. & Bigelow var. *rhodantha* L. Benson. "Colorado bei 2000–2300 m. Höhe."

O. xanthostemma K. Schum.; *O. rhodantha* K. Schum. var. *xanthostemma* Rehder; *O. erinacea* Engelm. & Bigelow var. *xanthostemma* L. Benson. Grand Mesa, near Grand Junction, Colorado.

O. rhodantha K. Schum. var. *spinosior* Boissevain. "Southwestern Colorado desert variety."

PLATE 3; DISTRIBUTION MAP, p. 124.

Var. *brachyclada*	Var. *Treleasei*
Elongate, oblong, or spatulate	Narrowly elliptic or obovate
2 to 3(5) inches long, 1 to 1¼(1¾) inches broad	3 to 10 inches long, 2 to 4 inches broad
None	As described for the species
California, on the desert sides of the San Gabriel Mountains, on Vulcan Mountain in San Diego County, and on the Providence Mountains in the eastern Mojave Desert	California in Kern County northeast to southeast of Bakersfield and in the Turtle Mountains in the Mojave Desert and perhaps the San Gabriel Mountains. Arizona near the Colorado River

14. Opuntia basilaris Engelm. & Bigelow   BEAVERTAIL CACTUS

Plants forming clumps usually 6 to 12 inches high and 1 to 6 feet in diameter; joints blue-green, sometimes in cold weather also irregularly purplish with a betacyanin pigment, sometimes glabrous but usually minutely canescent (then ashy blue-green and velvety), obovate or sometimes circular or narrowly elongate or spatulate, 2 to 6(13) inches long, (1)1½ to 4(6) inches broad; spines *none, except* in var. *Treleasei*, in which they are yellow to brownish, 1 to 5 per areole, spreading, straight or rarely curving, ¼ to ¾(1¼) inches long, ⅛₈(¹⁄₂₄) inch in diameter, nearly circular in cross section, not barbed; glochids troublesome; flower about 2 to 3 inches in diameter; petaloid perianth parts cerise or (in one variety) yellow; fruit green but changing to tan or gray, dry at maturity, not spiny except for a few spines in var. *Treleasei*, 1 to 1¼ inches long; seed bone-white or grayish, nearly circular, smooth, the margin neither conspicuous nor corky, about ¼ inch long.

127

14a. Opuntia basilaris var. basilaris BEAVERTAIL CACTUS

Sandy, gravelly, or rocky soils in the desert; sea level to 4,000 feet elevation or sometimes up to 5,000(9,000) feet. Mojavean and Colorado deserts and the edge of the Sagebrush Desert; occasional in the California Oak Woodland, California Chaparral, Pacific Grassland, and Juniper-Pinyon Woodland; rare in the Sierran Montane Forest. California, at intervals on the coastal sides of the mountain axis from southern Tulare County to San Diego County, common in Inyo County and in the Mojave and Colorado deserts, and rare in the mountains, as on the east side of the Sierra Nevada in Inyo County and in the San Bernardino Mountains. Nevada from southern Mineral and southern Lincoln counties to Clark County; southern Utah; northern Arizona. Mexico in northern Sonora.

Opuntia basilaris Engelm. & Bigelow. "Cactus Pass, Bill Williams fork, etc." Arizona.

O. basilaris Engelm. & Bigelow var. *ramosa* Parish. Bear Valley, San Bernardino Mountains.

O. basilaris Engelm. & Bigelow var. *cordata* F. Fobe. No specimen or locality mentioned.

O. intricata Griffiths. San Bernardino.

O. humistrata Griffiths; *O. basilaris* var. *humistrata* W. T. Marshall. Canyons above San Bernardino.

O. whitneyana Baxter; *O. basilaris* Engelm. & Bigelow subsp. *whitneyana* Munz. Alabama Hills, Inyo County.

O. whitneyana Baxter var. *albiflora* Baxter, not *O. albiflora* K. Schum., not *O. basilaris* var. *albiflorus* Walton. Eastern Sierra Nevada near Mt. Whitney.

FIG. 40; PLATES 3, 5; DISTRIBUTION MAP, p. 130.

14b. Opuntia basilaris var. brachyclada (Griffiths) Munz

LITTLE BEAVERTAIL

Sandy soils just above the deserts, 3,000 to 6,000 feet elevation. Desert-edge phase of the California Chaparral. California on the desert sides of the San Gabriel and San Bernardino mountains in Los Angeles and San Bernardino counties and on Vulcan Mountain, San Diego County; and in the Providence Mountains, San Bernardino County.

Opuntia brachyclada Griffiths; *O. basilaris* Engelm. & Bigelow var. *brachyclada* Munz. Mountain valleys above San Bernardino.

FIG. 41; DISTRIBUTION MAP, p. 130.

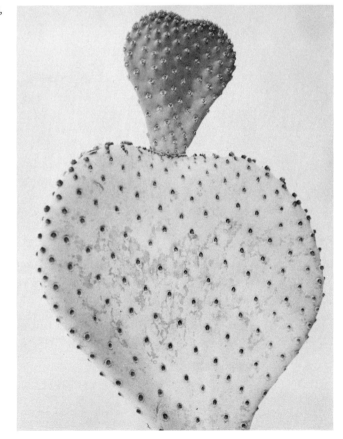

Fig. 40. Beavertail cactus, *Opuntia basilaris* var. *basilaris*. *Above*, at Kingman, Mohave County, Arizona. *Below*, a young joint with leaves and an old one without them, showing the small areoles with minute but strongly barbed and effective glochids. Photographs: *above*, by A. A. Nichol; *below*, by David Griffiths.

Opuntia basilaris
- ● var. *basilaris*
- ▲ var. *brachyclada*
- ✳ var. *Treleasei*

14c. Opuntia basilaris var. **Treleasei** (Coulter) Toumey

KERN CACTUS

Sandy soils of flats and low hills, mostly in grasslands; 400 to 1,000 feet elevation. Pacific Grassland and Mojavean Desert. California in the San Joaquin Valley in Kern County northeast, east, and southeast of Bakersfield; Turtle Mountains, eastern Mojave Desert, San Bernardino County. Northwestern Arizona near the Colorado River.

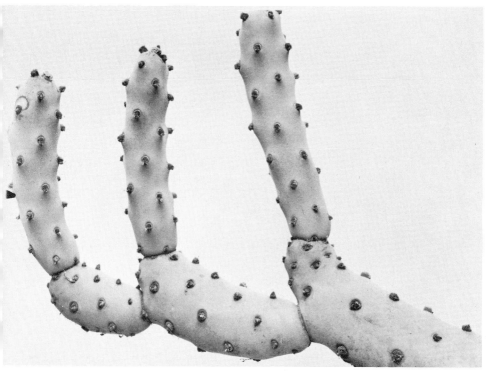

Fig. 41. Little beavertail cactus, *Opuntia basilaris* var. *brachyclada*. Joints showing the small areoles and minute glochids. Photograph by David Griffiths.

A specimen (*E. Wiegand 134* in 1950, *Pom*) collected near Big Pine Recreation Area, San Gabriel Mountains, has similar spines, and appears to be this variety.

Opuntia Treleasei Coulter; *O. basilaris* Engelm. & Bigelow var. *Treleasei* Toumey. Caliente, Kern County.

O. Treleasei Coulter var. *Kernii* Griffiths & Hare. Kern (East Bakersfield).

PLATE 5. DISTRIBUTION MAP, p. 130.

15. Opuntia macrorhiza Engelm.   PLAINS PRICKLY PEAR

Clump-forming, usually 3 to 5 inches high, the clumps 1 to 6 feet in diameter; main root(s) usually tuberous, other (adventitious) roots along the joints often fibrous; joints bluish-green, orbiculate to obovate, 2 to 4 inches long, 2 to 2½(3) inches broad; spines from the upper areoles white or gray or rarely brownish or reddish-brown, 1 to 6 per areole, mostly deflexed, straight or slightly curving, 1½ to 2¼ inches long, slender, ⅟₆₆ or ⅟₄₈ inch in diameter, not flattened, not barbed; flower 2 to 2½ inches in diameter; petaloid perianth parts yellow or tinged basally with red; fruit purple or reddish-purple, fleshy, 1 to 1½ inches long; seed pale tan or gray, irregular but more or less discoid, about ³⁄₁₆ inch in diameter, the margin (covering the embryo) about ⅟₂₄ inch broad, roughened.

Sand, gravel, or rocky soils; 2,000 to 7,000(8,000) feet elevation. Great Plains Grassland, Juniper-Pinyon Woodland, and lower Rocky Mountain Montane Forest; sometimes in the Prairie or along the edges of the Deciduous Forests. California on Clark Mountain, San Bernardino County. Utah (rare) and high plains of Arizona to the Great Plains and to Michigan (Muskegon County), Illinois (Oquawka), Texas, and Louisiana (Cameron); introduced east of Cincinnati, Ohio.

Opuntia macrorhiza Engelm.; *O. mesacantha* Raf. var. *macrorhiza* Coulter; *O. compressa* (Salisb.) Macbr. var. *macrorhiza* L. Benson. Between the Perdenales and Guadaloupe rivers, Texas.

O. tortispina Engelm. & Bigelow. Camanche plains, near the Canadian River, east of the Llano Estacado, New Mexico or Texas.

O. cymochila Engelm. & Bigelow; *O. mesacantha* Raf. var. *cymochila* Coulter; *O. tortispina* Engelm. & Bigelow var. *cymochila* Backeberg. Tucumcari hills, New Mexico.

O. cymochila Engelm. & Bigelow var. *montana* Engelm. & Bigelow. Sandia Mountains, New Mexico.

O. stenochila Engelm. & Bigelow. Zuñi, New Mexico.

O. fusiformis Engelm. & Bigelow. Kansas and Nebraska, in the regions of the Cross-Timbers.

O. mesacantha Raf. var. *Greenei* Coulter; *O. Greenei* Engelm., *pro syn.*; *O. Greenei* Britton & Rose. Golden, Colorado.

O. mesacantha Raf. var. *oplocarpa* Coulter; *O. oplocarpa* Engelm. ex Coulter, *pro syn.* Golden, Colorado.

O. plumbea Rose. San Carlos Indian Reservation, Arizona.

O. utahensis J. A. Purpus. Piñon Valley, La Sal Mountains, Utah.

O. Roseana Mackensen. Kerrville, Texas.

O. leptocarpa Mackensen. San Antonio, Texas.

O. Mackensenii Rose. Kerrville, Texas.

O. seguina C. Z. Nelson. Seguin, Texas.

O. MacAteei Britton & Rose. Rockport, Texas.

O. Loomisii Peebles. Prescott, Arizona.

Fig. 42; Distribution Map, p. 135.

16. Opuntia littoralis (Engelm.) Cockerell

Suberect or sprawling, usually 1 or 2 feet high and 2 to 4 feet in diameter; trunk none; joints green to blue-green, narrowly to broadly obovate or elliptic or sometimes nearly orbiculate, (3)5 to 7(12) inches long, (2)3 to 4(5) inches broad; spines over the entire joint or only the upper part (in var. *austrocalifornica* none), brown, tan, pink, gray, or various combinations of these and yellow, 1 to 11 or none per areole, spreading or some deflexed, 1 to $2\frac{1}{4}$ inches long, up to $\frac{1}{24}$ inch in diameter, not flattened, not barbed; flower 2 to 3 inches in diameter; petaloid perianth parts yellow with red or magenta bases or sometimes magenta or rose-purple, the largest obovate or obovate-cuneate, 1 to $1\frac{7}{8}$ inches long, $\frac{5}{8}$ to $\frac{7}{8}$ inch broad, rounded and mucronate, nearly entire; filaments yellow, $\frac{3}{8}$ to $\frac{1}{2}$ inch long; anthers yellow, $\frac{3}{32}$ inch long; style yellowish, $\frac{1}{2}$ to $\frac{3}{4}$ inch long, $\frac{1}{8}$ to $\frac{5}{16}$ inch in diameter, basally swollen; stigmas 8 to 12, $\frac{1}{8}$ to $\frac{3}{16}$ inch long, thick; fruit reddish to reddish-purple, fleshy, $1\frac{3}{8}$ to $1\frac{5}{8}$ inches long; seed light tan or gray, irregular but nearly discoid, with the margin enclosing the embryo conspicuous and irregular, $\frac{1}{8}$ to $\frac{1}{4}$ inch in diameter.

Today the species consists of remnants persisting where they are protected from the effects of land disturbance by man or fire. This may be in washes or on flood plains where growth of grass on the gravelly soil is irregular and fires do not travel for great distances, under trees where the plant is not enveloped in high grasses, or in mountain areas partly shielded from disturbance by man. The species enters into formation of hybrid swarms of the "*Opuntia occidentalis*" type. The other parent of the hybrids is *Opuntia Ficus-Indica*; see pp. 157–71.

The nearest relative of this species is *O. macrorhiza*. *O. phaeacantha* is less closely related.

16*a*. Opuntia littoralis var. **littoralis**

Sandy or rocky soils; 10 to 500 feet elevation. Disturbed areas in natural or induced grasslands. Southern California, islands and along the coast and in valleys up to 15 or sometimes 40 miles in-

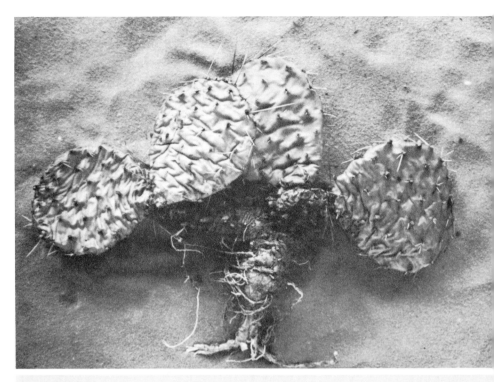

Fig. 42. Plains prickly pear, *Opuntia macrorhiza*. *Above*, near Amarillo, Texas; showing the large, tuberous taproot characteristic of the species. *Below*, joints showing the two or three needlelike spines in each upper areole of the joint and also the glochids; one joint with a young fruit, and with the fibrous roots commonly growing from the lower joints. Photograph *below* by David Griffiths.

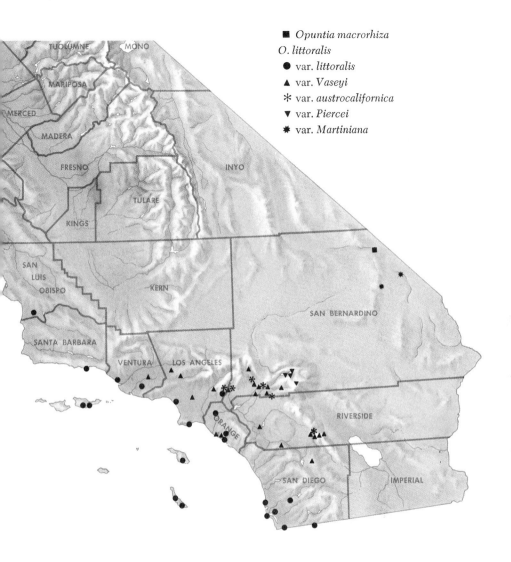

■ *Opuntia macrorhiza*
O. littoralis
● var. *littoralis*
▲ var. *Vaseyi*
＊ var. *austrocalifornica*
▼ var. *Piercei*
✳ var. *Martiniana*

land (Pomona and Fullerton); Santa Barbara County to San Diego County. Mexico in northwestern Baja California.

The *Opuntia littoralis* of authors is, for the most part, *Opuntia oricola* Philbrick.

Opuntia littoralis (Engelm.) Cockerell; *O. Engelmannii* Salm-Dyck var. *littoralis* Engelm.; *O. Lindheimeri* Engelm. var. *littoralis* Coulter; *O. littoralis* Cockerell; *O. occidentalis* Engelm. var. *littoralis* Parish. Santa Barbara, California.

Fɪɢ. 43; Pʟᴀᴛᴇ 8; Dɪsᴛʀɪʙᴜᴛɪᴏɴ Mᴀᴘ, this page.

16b. Opuntia littoralis var. **Vaseyi** (Coulter) Benson & Walkington

Sandy or gravelly soils of hillsides, alluvial fans, and washes in open parts of the chaparral region; 1,000 to 2,000(4,500) feet elevation. California Chaparral (disturbed areas). Southern California, mostly near the west and south bases of the San Gabriel, San Bernardino, and San Jacinto mountains; Los Angeles, San Bernardino, and Riverside counties and rare in Orange county.

Opuntia mesacantha Raf. var. *Vaseyi* Coulter; *O. Rafinesquei* Engelm. var. *Vaseyi* K. Schum.; *O. humifusa* Raf. var. *Vaseyi* Heller; *O. Vaseyi* Britton & Rose; *O. occidentalis* Engelm. & Bigelow var. *Vaseyi* Munz; *O. littoralis* (Engelm.) Cockerell var. *Vaseyi* Benson & Walkington. "Yuma, Arizona."

O. Covillei Britton & Rose; *O. occidentalis* Engelm. & Bigelow var. *Covillei* Parish; *O. phaeacantha* Engelm. var. *Covillei* Fosberg. San Bernardino, California.

Figs. 6, 44, 62; Plates 6, 8, 9; Distribution Map, p. 135.

16c. Opuntia littoralis var. **austrocalifornica** Benson & Walkington

Sandy soils of washes or mostly in the shade under trees; 800 to 2,000(4,000) feet elevation. California Chaparral. Southern California along the bases of the San Gabriel and San Bernardino mountains; Los Angeles and San Bernardino counties; rare in interior Riverside County.

Opuntia littoralis (Engelm.) Cockerell var. *austrocalifornica* Benson & Walkington. Indian Hill, Claremont, Los Angeles County.

The following names are based upon plants intermediate between var. *austromontana* and var. *Vaseyi* or nearer var. *Vaseyi* in their characters: *Opuntia magenta* Griffiths; *O. Vaseyi* (Coulter) Britton & Rose var. *magenta* Parish. Redlands.

O. intricata Griffiths. San Bernardino.

O. rubiflora Davidson, not *O. rubiflora* Griffiths. San Fernando Valley.

Fig. 45; Plate 6; Distribution Map, p. 135.

Fig. 43. *Opuntia littoralis* var. *littoralis*. *Above*, large plant near Puddingstone Reservoir, Pomona, Los Angeles County. *Below*, joint with a fruit.

Characters of the Varieties of Opuntia littoralis

	Var. *littoralis*	Var. *Vaseyi*
GLAUCOUSNESS	Green, not glaucous	Moderate
JOINT SHAPE	Narrowly obovate or narrowly elliptic	Obovate or narrowly so
JOINT SIZE	5 to 9 inches long; 3 to 4 (5) inches broad	4 to 6(7) inches long; 3 to 4(4½) inches broad
SPINE DISTRIBUTION	Over the entire joint	On nearly all of the joint
SPINE COLOR	Some gray, some yellow, some mixtures of these and red	Brown or dark gray
SPINE LENGTH	1¼ to 1⅞ inches	1 to 1¼ inches
SPINES PER AREOLE	5 to 11	1 to 4(6)
FLOWER COLOR	Yellow	Yellow
GEOGRAPHICAL DISTRIBUTION	Low elevations; 10 to 500 feet. Coast of California from Santa Barbara County south and inland 15 or rarely 40 miles	Low elevations in the interior on the coastal side of the mountains; 1,000 to 2,000 feet. California from Newhall to San Bernardino and the area east of Temecula; Los Angeles, San Bernardino, and Riverside counties

Var. *austrocalifornica*	Var. *Piercei*	Var. *Martiniana*
Strong; joints bluish	Moderate	Moderate
Narrowly obovate to nearly orbiculate	Narrowly obovate to elliptic or orbiculate	Obovate to orbiculate
3 to 5(8) inches long; 2 to 2½(3¼) inches broad	(4)4½ to 10(12) inches long; (2¾)4 to 6⅖ inches broad	(4)5 to 7 inches long; 3 to 5½ inches broad
No spines or a few along the top of the joint	On the upper half to three-fourths of the joint	Usually on most or all of the joint
White, gray, straw-colored, or golden	Reddish with yellow or white tips, but becoming gray	Red and yellow to gray
(¼)½ to ⅘ inch, when present	(1)1¼ to 2 inches	(1)1½ to 1¾ inches
0 or 1 to 2 and rudimentary	1 to 4(6)	1 to 4(6)
Red, flame, or magenta	Yellow or the center reddish	Yellow or the center red
Mostly in shade at low elevations in the interior on the coastal side of the mountains; 800 to 2,000 (4,000) feet. California from eastern Los Angeles County (near Glendora) to Riverside County	Higher elevations; 5,800 to 7,250 feet. California in the San Bernardino and San Jacinto mountains	Commonly at 4,500 to 6,500 feet. California in the eastern Mojave Desert; east to southern Nevada, the southern margin of Utah, and northern Arizona

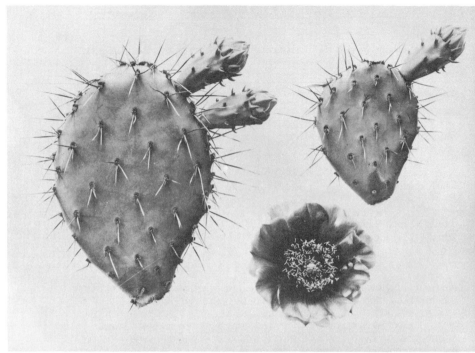

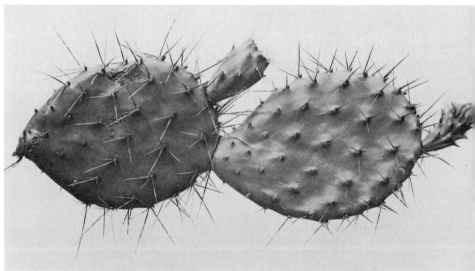

Fig. 44. *Opuntia littoralis* var. *Vaseyi. Above*, joints with spines and flower buds; top view of a flower, showing the petaloid perianth parts, the stamens, and the stigmas. *Below*, joints with a flower bud and a young fruit. Photographs by David Griffiths.

Fig. 45. *Opuntia littoralis* var. *austrocalifornica.* This small, glaucous, essentially spineless variety grows under trees, often but not necessarily in the shade, as here.

16d. Opuntia littoralis var. Piercei (Fosberg) Benson & Walkington

Sandy and gravelly soils of flats, washes, and mountainsides in forests and woodlands; 5,800 to 7,250 feet elevation. Lower Sierran Montane Forest and the area of junipers and pinyons in the desert-edge California Chaparral. California in the San Bernardino Mountains, San Bernardino County.

Much of the positive information concerning this variety has been obtained through the studies of John Adams as a student at Pomona College.

Opuntia phaeacantha Engelm. var. *Piercei* Fosberg; *O. Covillei* Britton & Rose var. *Piercei* Munz; *O. occidentalis* Engelm. & Bigelow var. *Piercei* Munz; *O. littoralis* Cockerell var. *Piercei* Benson & Walkington. Gold Mountain, San Bernardino Mountains.

DISTRIBUTION MAP, p. 135.

Fig. 46. *Opuntia littoralis* var. *Martiniana.* This variety occurs in the mountains of the eastern Mojave Desert and in northern Arizona and adjacent Utah. Photograph by A. A. Nichol.

16e. Opuntia littoralis var. Martiniana (L. Benson) L. Benson

Sandy or gravelly soils in forests or woodlands or along the edge of the desert; (2,000)4,500 to 6,500(8,500) feet elevation. Rocky Mountain Montane Forest, Juniper-Pinyon Woodland, and the Mojavean Desert. Southern California in the New York Mountains, eastern San Bernardino County. Nevada in Lincoln and Clark counties; Utah near the Arizona border; northern Arizona.

The variety hybridizes with *Opuntia erinacea* and shades into *O. phaeacantha*, *O. macrorhiza*, and especially *O. violacea*.

Opuntia charlestonensis Clokey; *O. phaeacantha* Engelm. var. *charlestonensis* Backeberg. Griffith's mine, Charleston Mountains, Nevada.

O. macrocentra Engelm. var. *Martiniana* L. Benson; *O. littoralis* (Engelm.) Cockerell var. *Martiniana* L. Benson. Hualpai Mountain, Mohave County, Arizona.

FIG. 46; DISTRIBUTION MAP, p. 135.

17. Opuntia phaeacantha Engelm.

Prostrate or sprawling, in clumps 2 to 8(20) feet in diameter and 1 to 2(3) feet high, in some varieties in other states sometimes with chains of several joints on edge along the ground; trunk lacking; joints somewhat bluish-green, in cold weather with some lavender to purple pigmentation, obovate or sometimes narrowly so or sometimes orbiculate, (4)6 to 10(16) inches long, 3 to 9 inches broad; spines over the entire joint or only the upper part, reddish-brown or dark brown, also with yellow or grayish or sometimes lighter red or red-and-gray coloring, all sometimes nearly white (pale gray), 1 to 6(10) per areole, spreading more or less at right angles or some deflexed, straight or bent downward or, uncommonly, curved or twisted, usually (1)2 to 3 inches long, up to $\frac{1}{32}$($\frac{1}{16}$) inch broad, some flattened, not barbed; flower 2½ to 3¼ inches in diameter; petaloid perianth parts yellow or the bases red; fruit wine color or purplish, fleshy, usually obovate, sometimes elongate, 1¼ to 2½ inches long; seed light tan or grayish, irregularly discoid, $\frac{3}{16}$ inch long.

Opuntia phaeacantha is highly variable, and many segregate species have been proposed. These have been based upon individual variants in hybrid swarms resulting from natural interbreeding with other species or from intergradation between the varieties (see Fig. 47). The two varieties described below are not discrete. They represent the extremes in a population system ranging across the deserts from California to Texas. Varietal status of the two is weakened by much intergradation in numerous areas. The segregation is erratic in California, and for many populations it is unconvincing. For others it seems clear. The problem of classification is complex.

17a. Opuntia phaeacantha var. major Engelm.

Joints broadly obovate or nearly orbiculate, usually 5 to 10 inches long, 4 to 8 inches broad; spines over usually the upper one-half, one-third, or less of the joint, dark brown, 1¼ to 2¼(2¾) inches long, usually from $\frac{1}{24}$ to $\frac{1}{16}$ inch broad, usually from 1 to 3 per areole.

Rock, gravel, or sand of hillsides or flats; 2,000 to 5,000 feet ele-

Fig. 47. Hybrid of *Opuntia phaeacantha* vars. *major* and *discata*. *Above*, occurring sporadically with hybrids having other gene combinations; the plant in cultivation at Chico. *Left*, close-up view of joint. This plant was the basis for *O. megacarpa* Griffiths, a name appearing commonly in books. The spines were very long, as in var. *major*, but white and distributed all over the joint, as in var. *discata*. Photographs by David Griffiths.

vation in California. Arizona and Chihuahuan deserts; Desert Grassland; Juniper-Pinyon Woodland; in California in the Mojavean Desert and in the desert-edge phase of the California Chaparral (including areas with junipers and pinyons) and rarely in the lower Sierran Montane Forest. California near San Luis Obispo and Santa Maria in San Luis Obispo County and eastward through Cuyama Valley, on the desert side of the mountain axis from Los Angeles County to San Diego County, and in the eastern Mojave Desert (rare); rare west of the mountain axis. Southern Nevada; southern edge of Utah; rare in southern Colorado; Arizona mostly below the Mogollon Rim; New Mexico, chiefly in the southern half of the state; rare in South Dakota, western Kansas, and Oklahoma; in Texas, common in the west and uncommon in the central and southern parts. Mexico in Sonora and Chihuahua.

Opuntia phaeacantha var. *major* is the most abundant prickly pear in the deserts of the Southwest. On the Colorado Plateau and in the southern Rocky Mountains it is replaced largely by var. *phaeacantha*, which is a localized variety of the highlands.

In California the plant has been overlooked or confused with other species. In books one form has been described under a synonym, *O. mojavensis*. Mountain populations have been confused with *O. littoralis* var. *Piercei*, with which it intergrades.

Opuntia phaeacantha Engelm. var. *major* Engelm. Santa Fé, New Mexico.
O. Engelmannii Salm-Dyck var. *cyclodes* Engelm. & Bigelow; *O. Lindheimeri* Engelm. var. *cyclodes* Coulter; *O. cyclodes* Rose. Hunah [Hanah?] Creek near the Pecos River, New Mexico.
O. mojavensis Engelm.; *O. phaeacantha* Engelm. var. *mojavensis* Fosberg. Mojave River.
O. phaeacantha Engelm. var. *brunnea* Engelm. El Paso, Texas.
O. arizonica Griffiths. Kirkland, Arizona.
O. gilvescens Griffiths. Santa Rita Mountains, Arizona.
O. Toumeyi Rose. Desert Laboratory, Tucson, Arizona.
O. Blakeana Rose. Desert Laboratory, Tucson, Arizona.
O. Gregoriana Griffiths. El Paso, Texas.
O. confusa Griffiths. Desert Laboratory, Tucson, Arizona.
O. expansa Griffiths. Anton Chico, New Mexico.
O. curvospina Griffiths. Searchlight, Nevada.
O. flavescens Peebles; *O. Engelmannii* Salm-Dyck var. *flavescens* L. Benson. Sells, Pima County, Arizona.

Figs. 48, 49; Plate 7; Distribution Map, p. 148.

Fig. 48. *Opuntia phaeacantha* var. *major*; the most abundant and widespread prickly pear of the Southwestern Deserts. The spines tend to spread, to be long and dark brown, and to be restricted to the upper areoles of the large joint. Photograph by David Griffiths.

Fig. 49. *Opuntia phaeacantha* var. *major. Above*, (*right*) young joint
with leaves; (*middle*) flower buds; (*left*) flowers in top view, showing
chiefly the petaloid perianth parts and the numerous stamens. *Below*, fruits.
Photographs by David Griffiths.

147

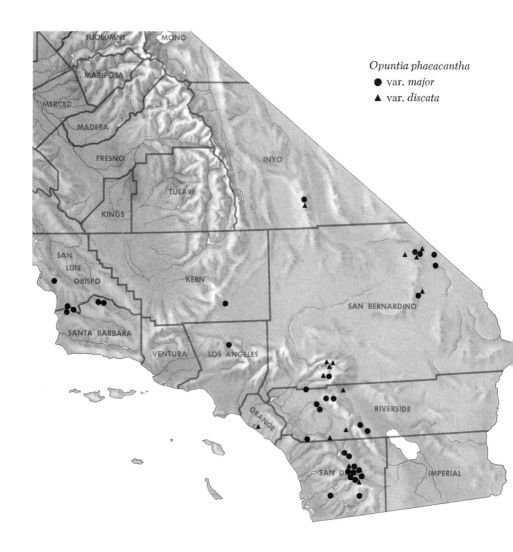

Opuntia phaeacantha
● var. *major*
▲ var. *discata*

17*b*. Opuntia phaeacantha var. discata (Griffiths) Benson & Walkington   Engelmann Prickly Pear

Joints broadly obovate or nearly orbiculate, usually 5 to 10 inches long, 4 to 8 inches broad; spines in all or all but a few basal areoles on the joint, white or ashy gray, 1 to 2 (rarely 2½, even 3) inches long, ¹⁄₂₄ to usually ¹⁄₁₆ inch broad, 1 to 4(10) per areole.

Sandy or gravelly soil of plains, washes, benches, arroyos, hillsides, valleys, and canyon bottoms in the desert and in grasslands;

148

(1,500)2,000 to 4,000(5,000) feet elevation. Arizona Desert, Chihuahuan Desert, and Desert Grassland; in California the Mojavean Desert and the upper edge of the Colorado Desert and especially the desert-edge phase of the California Chaparral. California in modified form near the southern coast and (mostly) on the desert side of the San Bernardino, San Jacinto, and Laguna mountains and in the Panamint, Clark, New York, and Providence mountains in the Mojave Desert. Nevada in Clark County (according to report); Utah near Springdale; mostly southern Arizona but occasional in northern Arizona; New Mexico mostly below 5,000 feet; Texas west of the Pecos River and sparingly eastward. Mexico in Sonora, Chihuahua, and Coahuila.

Var. *discata* is the largest and, especially in southern Arizona, the best-known native prickly pear of the Southwestern Deserts of the United States. It is variable in habit of growth, shape and size of joints, and size and distribution of spines because of much intergradation with var. *major,* with which it is almost always found. Var. *major* has longer brown spines restricted, or largely so, to the upper part of the obovate joint. Var. *discata* is nowhere stable, but apparently a fringe population extreme, tied in closely with the more abundant and wide-ranging var. *major.* Specific rank is untenable, and, also, the well-known name combination *Opuntia Engelmannii* was not applied to this taxon but to the spiny mission cactus, *O. Ficus-Indica,* from Mexico. Thus, unfortunately, the long-established pattern of reference cannot be retained on the basis of either classification or nomenclature.

Opuntia procumbens Engelm. & Bigelow. Aztec Pass, western Yavapai County between San Francisco Peaks and Cactus Pass in Mohave County, Arizona.

O. angustata Engelm. & Bigelow; *O. phaeacantha* Engelm. var. *angustata* Engelm. ex W. T. Marshall. Bill Williams River, Arizona. *O. discata* Griffiths; *O. Engelmannii* Salm-Dyck var. *discata* C. Z. Nelson; *O. phaeacantha* Engelm. var. *discata* Benson & Walkington. Santa Rita Mountains, Pima County, Arizona.

O. megacarpa Griffiths; *O. Engelmannii* Salm-Dyck var. *megacarpa* Fosberg; *O. occidentalis* Engelm. & Bigelow var. *megacarpa* Munz. Near Banning. In this form the maximum spine length is 2 to 3 inches. The epithet has been applied in California references to all material of var. *discata,* not to the specialized local material collected by Griffiths. Only fairly good matching material for the Griffiths collection has been collected (*Benson & Walkington*)

Fig. 50. Engelmann prickly pear, *Opuntia phaeacantha* var. *discata* (long known as *O. Engelmannii*, a name applied to another plant). *Above*, plants in fruit. *Below*, San Felipe Valley, San Diego County; plant in fruit. This is a relatively long-spined individual, the long spines being somewhat like those of var. *major*. Such intermediate plants are prevalent in California. Photograph *above* by David Griffiths.

Fig. 51. *Opuntia phaeacantha* var. *discata*; close-up view of joints of a plant similar to that in Fig. 48. For the type with stouter and somewhat shorter spines, prevalent from Arizona to Texas, see Fig. 1. Photograph by David Griffiths.

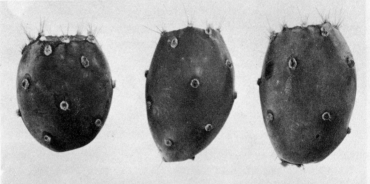

Fig. 52. *Opuntia phaeacantha* var. *discata. Above,* flower (*left*), showing the petaloid perianth parts, the stamens, and the stigmas; young joint with leaves (*right*). *Below,* fruits. Photographs by David Griffiths.

near Cabazon and near Redlands. The single plant was associated in each instance with others with numerous differing character combinations. Three older collections approach the type of *O. megacarpa* (San Bernardino, Riverside, and east of Jacumba). The long spines may have been acquired through interbreeding with *O. phaeacantha* var. *major,* which occurs nearby.

O. magnarenensis Griffiths. Southeast of Kingman, Arizona.

O. xerocarpa Griffiths. Fifteen miles southeast of Kingman, Arizona.

O. Woodsii Backeberg. "USA (Nevada)."

Figs. 1, 50, 51, 52; Distribution Map, p. 148.

18. Opuntia oricola Philbrick

Treelike, with a trunk up to 1 foot long or sometimes shrubby, about 3 to 10 feet high, spreading about 3 to 6 feet or more; joints green, broadly obovate or orbicular to broadly elliptic, some usually broader than long, 6 to 8(10) inches long, 5 to 8(9) inches broad; spines dense on the joint, yellow and at first translucent but in age brownish-gray to black as in other yellow-spined cacti, (4)8 to 16 per areole, spreading, the lower ones larger and with a downward trend, the longer ones gently and irregularly curving or twisting and ¾ to 1(1¼) inches long, ⅟₃₆ to ⅟₂₄ inch broad, flattened, not markedly barbed; flower about 2 to 2¼ inches in diameter; petaloid perianth parts yellow, cuneate to obovate-cuneate, 1¼ to 1½ inches long, ½ to ¾ inch broad, truncate and mucronate,

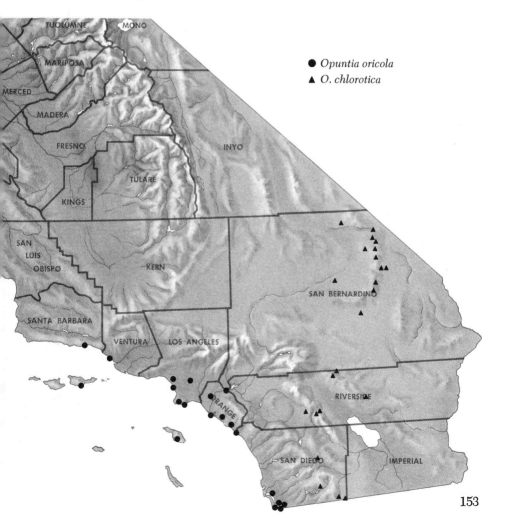

● *Opuntia oricola*
▲ *O. chlorotica*

153

Fig. 53. *Opuntia oricola*, long supposed to be *O. littoralis* and appearing in many publications under that name. The plants with flower buds and fruits. Photographs: *above* and *lower right* by David Griffiths; *lower left* by Edward F. Anderson.

Fig. 54. Flower of *Opuntia oricola* split lengthwise, showing the ovary, the style and stigmas, the floral cup bearing stamens, and the sepaloid and petaloid perianth parts. Photograph by David L. Walkington.

entire; filaments yellow, about ⅜ inch long; anthers yellow, linear-oblong, 1⁄16 inch long; style purplish-red, ⅝ to ⅞ inch long, ⅛ to 3⁄16 or the bulbous base up to ⅜ inch in diameter; stigmas green, about 10 to 12, 1⁄16 to 3⁄16 inch long, 1⁄24 inch broad; fruit red, fleshy, sub-globose, nearly as broad as long, 1 to 1¼ inches long; seed gray, discoid, with the rim enclosing the embryo narrow and smooth, ⅛ inch in diameter.

Sandy soils of flats and low hills; coastal grassy areas; 20 to 500 feet elevation. California Chaparral (coastal sagebrush phase). California near the coast and on the islands; Santa Barbara County to San Diego County; occurring inland as far as Santa Ana Canyon in Orange County. Mexico in northwestern Baja California.

The species appears in several books as *Opuntia littoralis* Engelm., a far different plant.

Opuntia oricola Philbrick. Montecito, Santa Barbara County.

Figs. 53, 54; Plate 11; Distribution Map, p. 153.

19. Opuntia chlorotica Engelm. & Bigelow   Pancake Pear

Arborescent or an erect shrub, (2)3 to 6 feet high, 3 to 4 feet in diameter; trunk about 1 foot long, 3 to 8 inches in diameter; joints blue-green, orbiculate to broadly obovate, 6 to 8 inches long, 5 to 7 inches broad; spines in all but a few basal areoles, light yel-

Fig. 55. Pancake pear, *Opuntia chlorotica*.
Above, miniature tree at the southeasternmost
extension of the Mojave Desert near Aguila,
Arizona. *Below, left*, smaller plant. *Below, right*,
joints with the characteristic yellow spines; near
Salome, Arizona. Photograph, *lower left*, by C.
Hope; Robert H. Peebles collection, courtesy
of the University of Arizona Herbarium.

Fig. 56. Pancake pear, *Opuntia chlorotica*. *1*. Joint with a flower bud and flowers, the areoles with the characteristic curving yellow spines and with glochids, ×¼. *2*. Areole with spines and glochids, ×2½. *3*. Flower in section, showing the inferior ovary and ovules, the style and stigmas, the floral tube above the ovary bearing stamens, and the sepaloid and petaloid perianth parts, ×¼. *4*. Fruit, external view, ×¼. *5*. Fruit in section, showing the seeds, ×¼. *6*. Seed, with the outer part enclosing the curving embryo clearly segregated, ×3⅓.

157

low to sometimes straw-colored, becoming black or dirty gray in age or in herbarium specimens, 1 to 6 per areole, all deflexed, straight or curving at the bases, 1 to 1⅝ inches long, ¼₄ or sometimes ¼₈ inch broad, flattened, tapering, not markedly barbed; flower about 1½ to 2½ inches in diameter; petaloid perianth parts light yellow, with an external reddish flush, broadly obovate to cuneate-obovate, ¾ to 1¼ inches long, ½ to ¾ inch broad, truncate or rounded and mucronate, nearly entire; filaments yellow, about ½ inch long; anthers yellow, ³⁄₃₂ inch long; style greenish-yellow, ¾ to 1 inch long, up to ³⁄₁₆ inch in diameter; stigmas about 10, ³⁄₁₆ inch long, thick; fruit grayish tinged with purple, fleshy, subglobose to ellipsoid, 1½(2½) inches long; seed light tan, nearly elliptic but asymmetrical, smooth, ³⁄₃₂ to ⅛ inch long.

Rocky or sandy soils of ledges, steep slopes, canyons, or sometimes flats in the desert or above it; (2,000)3,000 to 4,000(6,000) feet elevation. Colorado Desert (rare); Mojavean Desert; Arizona Desert; Southwestern Oak Woodland and Chaparral; Desert Grassland; desert-edge phase of the California Chaparral. California, southern and eastern Mojave Desert in San Bernardino County and the western edge of the Colorado Desert and the desert-edge chaparral from Riverside County to San Diego County. Southern Nevada, in the Charleston Mountains, Clark County; Arizona, except the lower deserts; southwestern New Mexico. Mexico in northern Baja California and Sonora.

Opuntia chlorotica Engelm. & Bigelow; *O. Tidballii* Bigelow, an inadvertence. Mojave River, 50 miles west of the Colorado.

Figs. 55, 56; Distribution Map, p. 153.

20. Opuntia Ficus-Indica (L.) Miller   Indian Fig

Tree 10 to 15 feet or more high; trunk 2 to 4 feet long, 8 to 12 inches in diameter; joints green, broadly to narrowly obovate or oblong, 12 to 24 inches long, 8 to 16 inches broad; spines none, few, or abundant, white or eventually some joints tan or pale brown, 1 to 6 per areole, some spreading, some deflexed, straight ½ to 1(1½) inches long, ¹⁄₃₂ inch broad, flattened, not barbed; flower 3 to 4 inches in diameter; petaloid perianth parts yellow or orange; fruit yellow to orange in the strain introduced in California but in some strains purple or purplish-red, fleshy and edible,

Fig. 57. The Indian fig of Mexico, *Opuntia Ficus-Indica*, the spineless
form. *Above*, plants currently in cultivation in a commercial cactus farm
at San Jose. *Below*, plants cultivated in 1916 during the "boom" of the spineless
cactus; United States Department of Agriculture Plant Introduction Garden,
Chico. Photographs, *above*, by Walter S. Phillips; *below*, by David Griffiths.

Fig. 58. Burbank's "Malta" spineless cactus, the Indian fig originally from Mexico, *Opuntia Ficus-Indica*. Photograph by David Griffiths, October 1908; plants received by the United States Department of Agriculture from Luther Burbank.

2 to 3(4) inches long, 1½ to 3½ inches in diameter, persistent for several months.

The species is probably native in Mexico, where there are numerous horticultural forms or cultivars and many hybrids with other species. Long cultivated or escaped in most of tropical America, the spineless cultivar probably having been prized for its fruit since prehistoric times and traded widely by the Indians; now cul-

Fig. 59. Indian fig of Mexico, *Opuntia Ficus-Indica*, the spineless form naturalized on a canyonside in southern California; chaparral in the background. Photograph by Burton Frasher, Sr., Frasher Fotos, courtesy of Burton Frasher, Jr., and the Pomona Public Library.

tivated throughout the warm parts of the world. Escaped here and there and naturalized and sometimes becoming a pest, as in Australia and eastern Cape Province, South Africa. In Southern California, occasional as an escape and commonly one of the parental types of the plants in the vast hybrid swarms of prickly pears; occasional as a local escape or as a relict around old dwellings. Occasional escape in southern Arizona, southern New Mexico, the southern portion of Texas, and Florida, and abundant on the dry sides of the islands of Hawaii. In southern California, the species becomes established only where there is deep soil and a little subirrigation, along valley washes or at the mouths of canyons. The pollen of this species is carried far and rapidly by bees and beetles, and has revolutionized the nature of the cactus populations in southern California. See discussion under the hybrid populations following the section on *Opuntia Ficus-Indica*.

Two major forms are common in cultivation in the warm, relatively dry regions of the world, particularly in Mediterranean climates. The spineless form, known as *O. Ficus-Indica*, is relatively less variable; the spiny form, known as "*O. megacantha*," is relatively variable in other characters. The "*megacantha*" type was postulated by Griffiths (see pp. 168–69) to be at least near the

161

Fig. 60. Indian fig, *Opuntia Ficus-Indica*, spiny form known as *"Opuntia megacantha,"* probably the wild type (but in this case with slight introgression of genes from varieties of *O. littoralis*); type locality of *"Opuntia occidentalis,"* near Cucamonga, San Bernardino County; growing in disturbed chaparral. The bird's-foot-like arrangement of white spines (*below*) is characteristic.

162

Fig. 61. Indian fig, *Opuntia Ficus-Indica*, spiny form; leafy young and leafless old joints and a flower bud; flowers in top view, showing the petaloid perianth parts, the stamens, and the stigmas. Photograph by David Griffiths.

wild type, the spineless form perhaps having arisen in cultivation. The introduced plants of both types vary from country to country, probably because of extensive propagation of a clone of a type introduced by chance, any form having been chosen in Mexico or tropical America to be taken abroad so long as the fruit was good. Thus, the spineless form covering the south face of the Acropolis of Athens differs from that in California, in Hawaii, or in eastern Cape Province in South Africa. The spiny forms differ too.

Cactus Ficus-Indica L.; *Opuntia Ficus-Indica* Miller. "*Habitat in* America *calidiore.*"

O. megacantha Salm-Dyck. "Habitat in Mexico."

O. Engelmannii Salm-Dyck. "Indigenous and cultivated, . . ." "north of Chihuahua, common as high up as El Paso." U.S. Senate Rept. Expl. & Surv.

R.R. Route Pacific Ocean. Botany 4: 38. *pl. 7. f. 1–2.* 1857. The type specimen is from cultivated material of *O. Ficus-Indica,* not from the native plant long called *O. Engelmannii,* which is *O. phaeacantha* var. *discata,* p. 148.

    O. occidentalis Engelm. & Bigelow; *O. Engelmannii* Salm-Dyck. var. *occidentalis* Engelm. Cucamonga. The plants long known by this name are transitory forms in the vast hybrid swarms of *O. littoralis* vars. *Vaseyi* and *austrocalifornica* and *O. Ficus-Indica.* The original plants were collected "On the western slope of the California mountains, from Quiqual Gungo, east of Los Angeles [J. M. Bigelow, Whipple Expedition], to San Pasquale and San Isabel [Santa Ysabel], northeast of San Diego (A. Schott), at an elevation of 1,000 to 2,000 feet, in immense patches often as large as half an acre." The following appears on p. 16: "At the Cajon Valley . . . At Cocomungo, in this valley, we [of the Whipple Expedition, which from 1852 to 1854 explored for a railroad route to the Pacific Ocean] found vast and dense patches of an *Opuntia,* nearly akin to *O. Engelmanni . . . .*" Quiqual Gungo and Cocomungo are transliterations of an Indian place-name, now Cucamonga. The main part of the description of *O. occidentalis* is drawn from the large joint, fruit, and seeds collected by Bigelow, and the illustrations were made from them. This collection has been designated as a lectotype. The identity of the Bigelow collection from Cucamonga determines which plant was named *O. occidentalis.* The vicinity of Cucamonga has been plowed up for planting of vineyards or citrus trees, but in a few waste places small native prickly pears flourish. These are unlike the lectotype specimen. However, on a water-spreading ground near the mouth of a canyon above Cucamonga, one very large plant was found, and it had joints nearly identical with the one collected by Bigelow, except that they were somewhat larger. However, selection of a medium or small joint to be carried on horseback is to be expected. The Cucamonga plant is the spiny mission cactus, known as *O. megacantha* Salm-Dyck, or possibly it may be a hybrid derived almost wholly from it. The plant now growing there may have been a more recent introduction, but it called attention to the nature of the type specimen. *O. occidentalis* cannot be used for any native California plant, but for only the spiny mission cactus. However, *O. occidentalis* is merely an unusable synonym for *O. megacantha,* applied much earlier. Furthermore, *O. megacantha* differs from the Indian fig only in presence of spines, and it is only one cultivar or horticultural variety in the vast complex of Mexican fruit trees for which the Linnaean name *O. Ficus-Indica* must be used. *O. occidentalis* and *O. megacantha* are mere synonyms for *O. Ficus-Indica.* The hybrids described in books as "*O. occidentalis*" are discussed below.

    FIGS. 57, 58, 59, 60, 61; PLATES 8, 9, 10.

Opuntia hybrid population "occidentalis" (*Opuntia occidentalis* of authors, not of Engelm. & Bigelow)

Following is a description summarizing the characters most commonly occurring in the vast irregular hybrid swarm resulting, according to morphological data as well as chemical evidence

1

2

PLATE 9. Hybrid of *Opuntia littoralis* var. *Vaseyi*, a prickly pear, with *O. Ficus-Indica* (Indian fig cactus). Detailed legends for all color plates follow Contents page.

PLATE 10. The hybrid of plate 9. The white spots on the upper fruit are the female cochineal insect, which yields various red dyes; this source of color has been replaced largely by aniline dyes.

PLATE 11. 1 & 2. *Cereus giganteus* (saguaro or giant cactus). 3 *Opuntia tomentosa*,
a cultivated prickly pear. 4. *O. oricola*, a coastal species.

1   2

3   4

PLATE 12. *Cereus Emoryi*. 1. A thicket, in fruit. 2. Branches. 3. Flower.
4. Fruits, and scars where two have been removed.

1

2   3

PLATE 13. *Echinocereus triglochidiatus* (hedgehog cactus). 1. Var. *melanacanthus*.
2. Var. *mojavensis*. 3. Flower position (in an Arizona variety).

1

2

PLATE 14. 1. *Echinocereus Engelmannii* var. *armatus*. 2. *E. Engelmannii* var. *chrysocentrus*.
Both plants are of the purple-to-magenta-flowered group.

PLATE 15. 1. *Mammillaria microcarpa.* 2. *M. tetrancistra.* 3 & 4. *Ferocactus acanthodes* var. *LeContei* (barrel cactus). 5. *Echinocactus polycephalus* (barrel cactus). 6. *Mammillaria dioica.*

PLATE 16. 1 & 2. *Neolloydia Johnsonii*. 3–5. *Coryphantha vivipara* (pincushion cactus).
3. Var. *rosea*. 4. Var. *Alversonii*. 5. Var. *desertii*. 6. *Sclerocactus polyancistrus*.

(Walkington, thesis, Claremont Graduate School, *ined.*), from interbreeding of *Opuntia littoralis* var. *Vaseyi* and, to a lesser extent, var. *austrocalifornica* mostly with the spiny form of *O. Ficus-Indica*.

Suberect or sprawling, 3 to 5(7) feet high, 3 to 15 feet or much greater in diameter; trunk none; joints markedly to slightly glaucous, narrowly elliptic, narrowly obovate, or sometimes broadly either one or rhombic, 7 to 15 inches long, 4 to 8 inches broad; spines in nearly all or all of the areoles, each brown or red on at least the lower part, sometimes all white or gray, 4 to 7 in the upper areoles, spreading or some deflexed, straight or rarely curving, ¾ to 1¼(1⅝) inches long, ¹⁄₂₄ to ¹⁄₂₀ inch broad, flattened, not

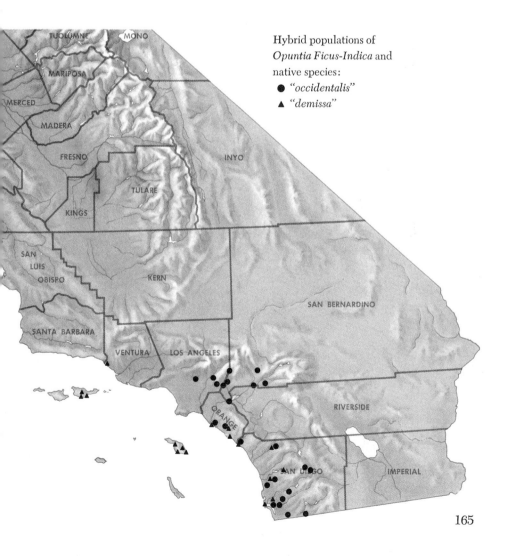

Hybrid populations of
Opuntia Ficus-Indica and
native species:
● *"occidentalis"*
▲ *"demissa"*

barbed; flower 3 to 4½ inches in diameter; petaloid perianth parts yellow to orange-yellow, becoming reddish in age; fruit red to purple, fleshy, obovoid, 1½ to 2¾ inches long; seeds variable, nearly orbiculate, the embryo-bearing margin from prominent and irregular to narrow and smooth, ⅛ to ¼ inch long.

Sandy, gravelly, or partly clay soils of hillsides and valleys or, less often, alluvial fans and washes; 500 to about 3,000 feet elevation. Naturally open places or disturbed areas in the California Chaparral. Coastal side of the mountain axis in southern California from eastern Los Angeles County to San Bernardino and Riverside counties and, less clearly, south through the interior foothill region to San Diego County.

In 1876, Engelmann (in Brewer & Watson, Bot. Calif. 1: 248) indicated the earlier collections from coastal southern California to represent varieties of "*O. Engelmannii*," i.e., *O. phaeacantha* Engelm. var. *discata* (Griffiths) Benson & Walkington, which occurs from California to Texas and adjacent Mexico, and the relationship of some plants to that taxon is close. Plants of var. *discata* grow along the desert edges of the southern California mountains from San Bernardino County to San Diego County and in the eastern Mojave Desert. They are rare near the coast in Orange County. The distinction is not always clear between some

Fig. 62. Effects of grass fires upon prickly pears. *Upper left*, the small native plant, *Opuntia littoralis* var. *Vaseyi*, almost completely enveloped (*center and upper left*) in weedy introduced Mediterranean grasses, principally wild oats (*Avena barbata*) and ripgut grass (*Bromus rigidus*). *Upper right*, grassy area after a fire, even the large prickly pears being almost destroyed; note regeneration of a small area of the plant in the foreground, a hybrid of *O. littoralis* var. *Vaseyi* and *O. Ficus-Indica* (spiny type) but a plant not large enough to exclude the fire from its center. *Lower left*, a hybrid swarm of prickly pears on a hillside; the larger plant at the left with genes derived about three-fourths from *O. littoralis* var. *Vaseyi*, one-fourth from the spiny type of *O. Ficus-Indica*; the small plants enveloped in the grass, var. *Vaseyi*; the others of mixed ancestry and intermediate. *Lower right*, portion of a hybrid clone covering about one-half acre from which fire is almost completely excluded; often, rodents, living under a hybrid cactus thicket, forage just outside its protection and reduce the number of grass plants. Plants near the Puddingstone Reservoir, between Pomona and San Dimas, Los Angeles County.

plants in the complex coastal southern California hybrid swarms and *O. phaeacantha* Engelm. var. *discata* as well as var. *major* Engelm., occurring at higher elevations in the same parts of southern California.

The distinction of the varieties of *O. littoralis* from the *O. phaeacantha* complex likewise is not wholly clear, because acicular spines shade into flattened spines. Consequently, segregation of species must be partly arbitrary. As in all classification, there is not necessarily a clear-cut answer to this problem. The complexity of the southern California prickly pears has been explained in a paper by Benson and Walkington,* reproduced here in its entirety insofar as the discussion is concerned, as follows.

When Father Junipero Serra founded the Mission San Diego in 1769, he began unknowingly the transformation of the landscape of California and its vegetation. After founding of the missions, settlers from Mexico and Spain brought agriculture and livestock to the region. As range animals were taken from the Mediterranean region to Mexico and other parts of the world, weed seeds were carried along in the wool or hair and in mud on the hoofs. Wherever sheep walked or died, weeds sprang up. Through many centuries of hybridizing and selection, these plants were adapted to areas about dwellings of man and to his cultivated fields and pasturelands. The plants had evolved in Mediterranean areas of summer drought disturbed by fire and overgrazing, and they were adjusted perfectly to the similar California climate and to the newly disturbed areas. Ultimately they reached an ecological dynamic equilibrium with the native species—an equilibrium that shifts from year to year in correspondence with the highly erratic incidence of winter rainfall.

When the Franciscan fathers established the series of missions through coastal southern California, they brought with them, also, fruit-bearing plants from Mexico and Spain. These included grapes, figs, and other fruits of mild climates, among them the large cultivated fruit-tree cacti of Mexico—primarily of two kinds. These prickly pears have become known in California as the mission cacti, *Opuntia Ficus-Indica*, a spineless type, and "*O. mega-*

---

* Lyman Benson and David L. Walkington, Annals of the Missouri Botanical Garden 52: 262–4. 1965. (Slightly adapted.) Used by permission.

cantha," a similar plant with flattened, white spines at each of the areoles (spine-bearing areas) on the joint (but with the spines of some joints tending to be brownish). These two plants were similar to each other, and the evolutionary origin of *O. Ficus-Indica* from *O. megacantha*, as the wild type, was postulated by David Griffiths (Journal of Heredity 5: 222. 1914). Both are members of a complex of cultivated prickly pears abundant in Mexico, many of them representing horticultural forms of hybrids of *O. Ficus-Indica*. The mission fathers and others found these cacti useful not only for their fruit but also as a source of mucilaginous binding material for the adobe bricks of the mission buildings. In the course of time, the two cacti were planted also on the great Spanish ranchos, about both the ranch headquarters and the dwellings of ranch employees and others, and they appeared wherever there were Spanish, Mexican, and, later, American settlers.

In many places the large cultivated prickly pears hybridize with the small native species, as pointed out by Baxter, California Cactus 40. 1935. Recent field studies, especially in Los Angeles, San Bernardino, Riverside, and Orange counties, indicate this hybridization to be vastly more extensive than has been supposed. The introduced cacti often survive in the lowlands or on the edges of hills about the sites of old dwellings. Here and there they have spread a short distance, but they are restricted to the better-watered, deeper soils along washes in the valleys or at the mouths of canyons. However, their genes are given rapid air transportation by several species of native bees and beetles. Sometimes the local hillside population of cacti includes plants with character combinations ranging from almost those of the mission cacti, usually of the spiny type known as "*O. megacantha*," to those of the native species, but more commonly the character combinations are restricted. In a few areas the prevailing plants are near the end of the series approaching "*O. megacantha*," though this is rare. Commonly the population is composed of plants varying in characters from about those of the postulated F_1 generation* to

---

* The F_1 generation is the one derived from crossing two unlike parents, each of which has within itself only similar genes in the pairs being taken into consideration in studying the cross. The generation resulting from crossing two species is an F_1. See footnote, p. 20.

those of the native species, because individuals in this range of phenotypes are better adapted to the dry, shallow soils of south-facing slopes where cacti are most abundant. The hillside populations away from the immediate coast are dominated mostly by plants of about the middle of this series, i.e., "quarter-breeds." On the other hand, gravelly or sandy places in the beds of dry washes, or shady areas beneath trees, or mountain areas are strongholds of varieties of the native species.

Fire has been a major factor in the evolution of prickly pears in southern California. Cacti do not grow in the chaparral or brushland, because this is a fire-associated type of vegetation that is burned over, on the average, once in 5 to 30 years. A hot chaparral fire cannot be survived by cactus plants. Even a summer grass fire sweeping through a patch of prickly pears is devastating, for small plants are killed outright and often the larger ones are killed, except for parts below ground or those sheltered, as by a piling up of cactus stem joints during the fire. From any living fragment, new joints may arise. Among the weeds introduced into California from the Mediterranean region are many grasses, especially of the genus *Bromus*, and these have formed a dense cover in the lowlands and on hillsides. The plants of the modified grassy areas become like tinder in the dry summer months, and grass fires are intense and frequent. Thus, in each locality every few years for two centuries there has been a determination of which plants are best adapted to withstanding intense heat; the prickly pears have been subject to a rigid trial by fire.

Selection by fire has favored not the native species but the larger hybrid plants and especially the somewhat sprawling ones capable of forming dense patches from which grasses are more or less excluded. These thickets of cactus joints are vulnerable to fire only around the fringes. They form vigorous resistant centers, which grow rapidly outward and occupy more and more space after each grass fire. Sometimes a single clone may cover half an acre, and rodents living among the cacti may keep the area clear of grasses. The smaller native species, on the other hand, is enveloped in grass, and on the open hillsides each fire tends to reduce its numbers. For this reason, the tendency in the large areas of dry grass is toward the ascendancy of a vast array of hybrid types about intermediate between the postulated F_1 generation and the small native species. Both morphological and chemical characters (Walkington, *ined.*) indicate this.

During the last half of the nineteenth century and almost two-thirds of the twentieth, all botanical authors have used the name *Opuntia occidentalis* for elements in the populations of hybrid cacti common everywhere except along the immediate coast. However, each author has had a different mental image of this species, for each has had in mind a different plant or range of plants in the vast hybrid swarm. Usually this has been one or a few of the many combinations about midway between the F_1 generation and the native species. No population can be reconciled with the description of *O. occidentalis* appearing in any book or paper, for no two plants are alike and the total variation is extreme.[*] Thus, from the standpoint of classification, the common conception of "*O. occidentalis*" is a will-o'-the-wisp, because it was based in each work upon one or more transitory combinations of genes, which would disappear with the individual plant(s) or the clone(s) upon which the description was based.

Opuntia rugosa Griffiths. Pomona to Claremont.

Fig. 62; Plates 9, 10; Distribution Map, p. 165.

Opuntia hybrid population "demissa"

Joints elliptic, obovate, or rhombic, 8 to 15 inches long, 5 to 8(10) inches broad; spines *yellow*, 3 to 6 in each upper areole of the joint, up to ¾ to 1⅜ inches long; petals yellow or with some reddish pigment basally.

Sandy or clay soils of foothills and valleys or of ocean bluffs and dunes; 10 to 500(1,000) feet elevation. California Chaparral or more commonly in coastal grasslands. California from Ventura County south to San Diego County; mostly in the lower valleys along the coast, but inland for 10 or up to 25 miles in places; Santa Catalina Island.

Opuntia demissa Griffiths. East of San Diego.

Distribution Map, p. 165.

[*] This, of course, has worried the authors, for most of them have recognized the extreme complexity of the "species," even though the source of complexity was not understood.

21. Opuntia tomentosa Salm-Dyck

Trees up to 10 to 25 feet high, spreading, 9 to 15 feet in diameter; trunk up to 3 to 5 feet long, up to 1 foot in diameter; larger terminal joints dark green, with a whitish sheen from a dense tomentum, velvety to the touch, 8 to 12 inches long, 3 to 5 inches broad; spines none or sometimes 1 or a few in some upper marginal areoles (plants from the Valley of Mexico reportedly often spiny), when present brown, spreading, straight, the longer ones observed about ⅛ inch long but probably sometimes longer, about ¹⁄₉₆ inch in diameter, not flattened, not markedly barbed; flower 1½ to 2 inches in diameter; petaloid perianth parts red in the middle and orange on the margins; fruit red, fleshy, densely tomentose, obovoid, 1¼ to 1½ inches long; seed light tan, orbiculate, with the rim enclosing the embryo about ¹⁄₂₄ inch thick and smooth, ¼ inch or a little less in diameter.

Deep soils where water is available. Central Mexico; escaped occasionally and especially so in Australia. California, near Thompson Creek north of Claremont, Los Angeles County, 1,500 feet elevation (*Louis C. Wheeler* in 1962, *Pom*).

Opuntia tomentosa Salm-Dyck; *Cactus tomentosus* Link. No specimen or locality mentioned; native of central Mexico.

Plate 11.

Cereus Miller

Stems branching, elongate, cylindroid to prismatic, at maturity 15 to 100 times as long as their diameter, 1 to 50 feet long, ¼ to 2½ feet in diameter; ribs 3 to 20 or more. Leaves not discernible. Spines smooth, gray, yellow, straw-colored, tan, brown, red, or white; central spines usually undifferentiated, the spines 1 to many per areole, straight, ¹⁄₁₆ to 3 inches long, ¹⁄₂₅₆ to ¹⁄₁₆ inch in diameter, acicular, broadly elliptic in cross section. Flowers and fruits on the old growth below the growing tip of the stem in a felted area within at least the edge of the spine-bearing part of the areole or merging into it. Flower 1 to 6(9) inches in diameter; superior floral tube almost obsolete to funnelform or tubular. Fruit fleshy, usually pulpy, often edible, with or without tubercles, scales, spines, hairs, or bristles, usually orbicular to ovoid or ellipsoid, ½ to 3 inches long, indehiscent. Seeds usually black, smooth to reticulate or papillate, longer than broad (hilum to opposite side); hilum obviously basal or sometimes oblique.

An undetermined, great number of species from California to Texas, Florida, and South America; two species native in California.

KEY TO THE SPECIES

1. Tree, the trunk with 1 to 15(50) branches, 25 to 50 feet high, 6 inches to 2½ feet in diameter, narrower at ground level than above; spines gray with a tinge of pink; superior floral tube slender, at least 1½ inches long; fruit fleshy, but splitting lengthwise along 3 or 4 lines, green outside but brilliant red inside; petaloid perianth parts white; desert . . . . 1. *C. giganteus*
1. Shrub, the sprawling stems forming dense colonies often several to many yards in diameter; stems branching below, 1½ to 2 inches in diameter; spines yellow but turning black in age; superior floral tube below the attachment of the stamens broad, up to only ⅝ inch long; ovary *not* scaly, densely spiny, in fruit forming a burlike sphere, dry at maturity; petaloid perianth parts yellow; coastal . . .
. . . . 2. *C. Emoryi*

1. Cereus giganteus Engelm.   SAGUARO, GIANT CACTUS

Tree 10 to 50 feet high; trunk 1 to 2½ feet in diameter, with 1 to 15(50) branches, these curving abruptly upward, located well above the base of the stem, with little rebranching; ribs 12 to 30, prominent, 1 to 1½ inches high; spines gray or with a pink tinge, 15 to 30 per areole, spreading in every direction, on younger stems deflexed and up to 3 inches long, on the upper parts of older stems spreading and 1 to 1½ inches long; flower opening at night but remaining open most of the next day, 2 to 3½ inches in diameter; petaloid perianth parts white; ovary at flowering time covered densely with green scales; fruit green tinged with red, fleshy, somewhat scaly (scale growth having ceased as the fruit enlarged), otherwise smooth, obovoid to ellipsoid, 2 to 3 inches long, about 1 to 1¾ inches in diameter; maturing in July, splitting open usually along three regular vertical lines and exposing the conspicuous red lining; seed irregularly obovoid, 1/12 inch long; hilum oblique.

Rocky or gravelly soils of hills and canyons and along washes in the desert at 600 to 3,600 feet elevation. Arizona Desert and the upper edge of the Colorado Desert. California sparingly near the Colorado River from the Whipple Mountains to the Laguna Dam. Arizona from near the Bill Williams River in Mohave County to western Graham County, Yuma County, and Pima County. Mexico in Sonora.

The Indian name (pronounced "sa-hwar-o") has been transliterated in more than one way; the best choice is saguaro. Giant cactus is common usage in the United States as a whole, but not in Arizona.

The "red flowers" appearing on picture postcards are the opened

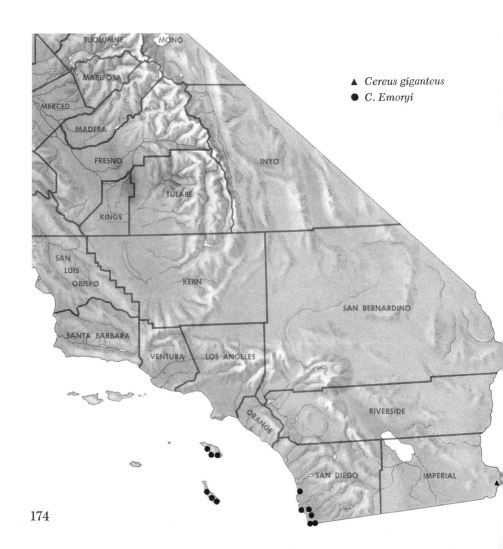

▲ *Cereus giganteus*
● *C. Emoryi*

Fig. 63. Flowers of the saguaro or giant cactus, *Cereus giganteus*, showing the elongate scaly floral tube above the scale-leaf-covered ovary, the white petaloid perianth parts, the innumerable stamens, and the elongate stigmas. Photograph by Robert H. Peebles; courtesy of the Herbarium of the University of Arizona.

fruits, the pulp of which is red. Arizona Indians gather the fruit for conserves and beverages and for the nutritious seeds.

Cereus gigantens [*giganteus*] Engelm.; *Pilocereus giganteus* Rümpler; *Carnegiea gigantea* Britton & Rose. Just northeast of the Coolidge Dam, Arizona.

Figs. 4, 63; Plate 11; Distribution Map, p. 174.

2. Cereus Emoryi Engelm.

Shrubs with sprawling or ascending to erect branches, the plants forming colonies 1 to 2 feet high and several yards in diameter; joints cylindroidal, 1 to 2 feet long, 1½ to 2 inches in diameter; ribs 12 to 16, inconspicuous, about ⅛ inch high; spines dense, obscuring the joint, clear yellow but blackening in age, about 20 to

Fig. 64. *Cereus Emoryi. Above*, thickets on a hillside southwest of San Diego. *Below*, two of the exceedingly spiny fruits with the seeds being extruded in a gelatinous mass of pulp. Photographs: *above*, by Edward F. Anderson; *below*, by Reid V. Moran.

30 per areole, central spines 1 to 3, the chief one deflexed, the others spreading in all directions, straight or the chief one curving slightly, up to 2 inches long; flower 1⅛ to 1½ inches in diameter; petaloid perianth parts yellow; fruit drying at maturity, densely spiny, globose, 1 to 1¼ inches in diameter; seed flattened-obovoid, ⅛ inch long; hilum oblique.

Sandy soils of hills near the coast at up to 200 feet elevation. Baja Californian phase of the California Chaparral. Southern California on Santa Catalina and San Clemente islands and in coastal San Diego County from Del Mar south. Mexico in northwestern Baja California.

Cereus Emoryi Engelm.; *Echinocereus Emoryi* Rümpler; *Bergerocactus Emoryi* Britton & Rose. San Diego.

Fig. 64; Plate 12; Distribution Map, p. 174.

Echinocereus Engelm. (Hedgehog Cactus)

Stems solitary or much branched near ground level, the branches sometimes as many as 500, usually cylindroidal, 2 to 24 inches long, 1 to 3(4) inches in diameter; ribs 5 to 13; tubercles coalescent through half to usually nearly all their height. Leaves not discernible. Spines smooth and white, gray, tan, brown, yellow, pink, red, or black; central spines straight or curving, 1/24 to 4 inches long, acicular. Flowers and fruits on the old growth, below (usually far below) the apex of the stem, bursting through the epidermis of the stem just above the spine-bearing areole, not quite connected with it, the irregular scar persisting for many years after the fall of the fruit. Flower ¾ to 5 inches in diameter; superior floral tube funnelform to obconic, green or tinged with the color of the perianth. Fruit fleshy, with the ultimately deciduous areoles bearing spines, globular to ellipsoid, not regularly dehiscent. Seeds black, obovoid or domelike, reticulate or papillate, longer than broad (hilum to opposite side), 1/24 to 1/16 inch long; hilum obviously basal, large.

About 20 to 30 species from California to South Dakota and Oklahoma and south to Mexico City; two species native in California.

1. Petaloid perianth parts red or red-and-yellow (without any trace of blue, the pigment not water-soluble); areoles of the mature parts of the stems bearing white felt or cobwebby hairs; flowers *not* closing at night, open two or three days; central spine(s) not flattened ... . 1. *E. triglochidiatus*
1. Petaloid perianth parts lavender to purple (a mixture of red and blue); the pigment water-soluble; areoles of the mature *vegetative* parts of the stems *not* bearing white felt or cobwebby hairs, the felt of the young areoles persisting one or rarely two years; flowers closing each night or in hot weather sometimes withering at the end of a single day; principal central spine flattened . . . . 2. *E. Engelmannii*

1. Echinocereus triglochidiatus Engelm.

Stems usually branching several to many times from the bases, commonly forming dense mounds up to 1 foot high and 1 to 4 feet in diameter; joints cyindroid to ovoid-cylindroid, 2 to 6(12) inches long, 1 to 3(4) inches in diameter; ribs 5 to 10(12), slightly tuberculate; spines sparse to dense, usually gray but sometimes pinkish or straw-colored or pale gray or black, (2–3)8 to 12(16) per areole, exceedingly variable in the varieties; flower 1¼ to 2 inches in diameter; petaloid perianth parts red (with no admixture of blue; fruit red, obovoid to cylindroid, ½ to 1 inch long; seed papillate, ¹⁄₁₆ to ¹⁄₁₂ inch long.

The forms composing *Echinocereus triglochidiatus* are deceptive, because the extreme types seem to differ radically. Variation is largely in such striking characters as size of stems and number, size, twisting, and angularity of spines. This produces diversity of appearance among the varieties, and has been responsible for the proposals of segregated "species."

Although within each of the several varieties some natural populations are composed largely of individuals whose character combinations fall within some definable range of variability, even these include a broad spectrum of genetic (hereditary) character combinations. Investigation in the field shows in every population some individuals that cannot be included clearly within the variety represented by the general population, because they have too many characters more abundant in other varieties. In any direction each population system undergoes a reduction in the frequency of oc-curence of some gene combinations, and there is an irregular trend toward the combinations prevalent in other geographical varieties.

The central type in the complex is var. *melanacanthus*, which ranges from California to Texas. This variety is in contact at one point or another with each of the others, all of which are local-ized, and it intergrades with all of them.

Var. *melanacanthus* has not appeared in accounts of the flora of California. However, one collection is clearly of this variety, and numerous plants not or barely distinguishable from it occur in the populations of var. *mojavensis* in the hills above the Mojavean Desert from California to southwestern Utah and northwestern Arizona. An example of plants matching var. *melanacanthus* but occurring in the highly variable local populations of var. *mojaven-sis* is to be seen in the following series: Cushenberry Canyon, *Par-ish 11,718, UC*; *Parish 11,717, UC*; *L. & R. Benson 15,633A–E, Pom*. The same phenomenon may be observed, for example, in Joshua Tree National Monument near Hidden Valley. In the Charleston Mountains, Nevada, the percentage of *melanacanthus*-like plants is higher (e.g., between Lee Canyon and Deer Creek, *L. & R. Benson 15,067–15,069, Pom*).

1a. Echinocereus triglochidiatus var. melanacanthus
(Engelm.) L. Benson

Spines gray, black, pink, or basally tan, or sometimes straw-colored, up to 1 to 2½ inches long, nearly straight, smooth or rarely angled; central spines 1 to 3, light or dark, spreading or the longest deflexed, up to ⅟₃₂ inch in basal diameter; flower slen-der, 1 to 1½ inches long.

Rocky or grassy hillsides, ledges, and canyons; on mostly igne-ous rocks; 3,500 to 8,000(9,600) feet elevation. Rocky Mountain Montane Forest, Juniper-Pinyon Woodland, and the edge of the Desert Grassland and the Great Plains Grassland. California on Clark Mountain, Mojave Desert, San Bernardino County (*C. & A. Bonner* in 1961, *Pom*). Nevada in Eureka County; Utah; Colorado; Arizona, except the lower desert regions of Yuma, Maricopa, and western Pima counties; New Mexico; Texas in the trans-Pecos re-gion and in granitic areas of the Edwards Plateau and its escarpment as far east as Granite Mountain, Burnet County. Mexico in the Sierra Madre Occidentál as far south as Durango.

In California and southern Nevada the variety is represented by individuals in the populations of var. *mojavensis* displaying some or all of the characters of var. *melanacanthus*. The segregation of var. *mojavensis* is rarely clear.

Variations in characters of the spines are common. Long- and short-spined individuals grow in the same natural populations, and intergrading forms occur with them.

> *Echinocereus coccineus* Engelm.; *Cereus phoeniceus* Engelm., *nom. nov.* for *C. coccineus* (Engelm.) Engelm. (this being necessary under *Cereus*); *E. phoeniceus* Engelm. ex Rümpler; *E. polyacanthus* Engelm. var. × *phoeniceus* Frič, *nom. nud.*; *E. triglochidiatus* Engelm. var. *coccineus* Engelm. Wolf Creek, east of Santa Fe, New Mexico.
>
> *C. Roemeri* Mühlenpfordt; *E. Roemeri* Rydb. North of Fredericksburg, Gillespie County, Texas.
>
> *Echinopsis octacantha* Mühlenpfordt; *C. octacanthus* Coulter; *Echinocereus coccineus* Engelm. var. *octacanthus* Boissevain; *Echinocereus triglochidiatus* Engelm. var. *octacanthus* Mühlenpfordt ex W. T. Marshall. No locality or specimen.
>
> *Mammillaria aggregata* Engelm.; *Cereus aggregatus* Rydb.; *Coryphantha aggregata* Britton & Rose; *M. vivipara* (Nutt.) Haw. var. *aggregata* L. Benson; *Escobaria aggregata* F. Buxbaum; *Coryphantha vivipara* (Nutt.) Britton & Rose var. *aggregata* W. T. Marshall. Between Santa Rita and the Mimbres River, New Mexico.
>
> *Cereus Roemeri* Engelm., not Mühlenpfordt; *Echinocereus Roemeri* Engelm. ex Rümpler. Llano River, Texas.
>
> *C. coccineus* (Engelm.) Engelm. var. *melanacanthus* Engelm.; *Echinocereus triglochidiatus* Engelm. var. *melanacanthus* L. Benson; *E. melanacanthus* Engelm. ex W. H. Earle. Santa Fe, New Mexico.
>
> *C. coccineus* (Engelm.) Engelm var. *cylindricus* Engelm. Santa Fe.
>
> *C. hexaedrus* Engelm.; *Echinocereus hexaedrus* Engelm. ex Rümpler; *E. paucispinus* (Engelm.) Engelm. ex Rümpler var. *hexaedra* K. Schum.; *E. triglochidiatus* Engelm. var. *hexaedrus* Boissevain. In Arizona near Zuñi, New Mexico.
>
> *C. conoideus* Engelm. & Bigelow; *C. phoeniceus* Engelm. subsp. *conoideus* Engelm.; *E. phoeniceus* Rümpler (illegitimate name) var. *conoideus* K. Schum. Upper Pecos River, New Mexico.
>
> *C. mojavensis* Engelm. & Bigelow var. *zuniensis* Engelm. & Bigelow; *C. Bigelovii* Engelm. var. *zuniensis* Engelm.; *E. zuniensis* (Engelm.) Engelm. ex Rümpler. Colorado Chiquito, Arizona.
>
> *E. Krausei* De Smet. "Vaterland unbekannt."
>
> *E. canyonensis* Clover & Jotter. Below Hermit Creek Rapids, Grand Canyon, Coconino County, Arizona.

PLATE 13; DISTRIBUTION MAP, p. 181.

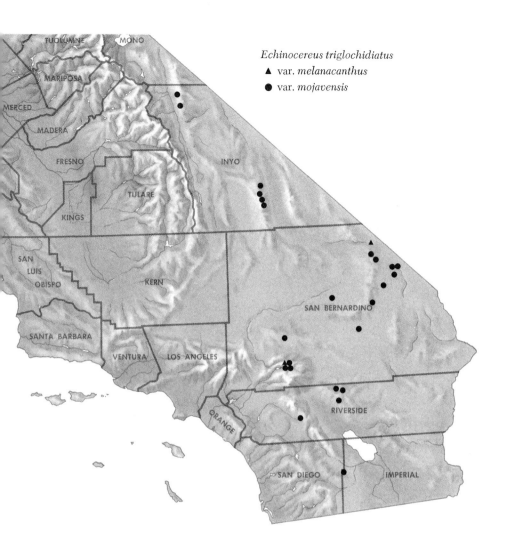

Echinocereus triglochidiatus
▲ var. *melanacanthus*
● var. *mojavensis*

1*b*. **Echinocereus triglochidiatus** var. **mojavensis** (Engelm. &
    Bigelow) L. Benson   Mojave Hedgehog Cactus

Spines gray, pink, or at first straw-colored, usually 1¾ to 3¾
inches long, striate, smooth or angled; central spines 1 or 2, light,
usually twisting, often striate, about ⅓₂ inch in basal diameter;
flower slender, 1½ to 2 inches in diameter, 1½ to 2 inches long.

Rocky hills and canyons in woodland above the deserts and in
the deserts; 3,500 to 8,000(10,000) feet elevation. Juniper-Pinyon

Woodland and the California Chaparral (desert-edge phase) and the upper Mojavean Desert or the Rocky Mountain Montane Forest. California from Inyo County to the desert sides of the San Bernardino Mountains and to the Little San Bernardino and San Jacinto mountains in Riverside County and eastward. South-central and southern Nevada in Nye and Clark counties; Utah in Washington County; Arizona in western Mohave County.

As pointed out above, even the extreme populations of this variety include some plants with characters of var. *melanacanthus*, and the reverse is true along the zone of contact with that variety in Washington County, Utah. In the Charleston Mountains, Nevada, the characters of var. *melanacanthus* are proportionately more common.

Cereus mojavensis Engelm. & Bigelow; *Echinocereus mojavensis* Engelm. ex Rümpler; *E. triglochidiatus* Engelm. var. *mojavensis* L. Benson. Mojave River. *E. Sandersii* Orcutt. Black Canyon, Providence Mountains.

PLATE 13; DISTRIBUTION MAP, p. 181.

2. Echinocereus Engelmannii (Parry) Lemaire

Stems 5 to 60, the mounds open or dense, up to 1 to 2 feet high and 2 to 3 feet in diameter; stems cylindroidal, usually elongate, 6 to 24 inches long, (1¼)2 to 3 inches in diameter; ribs commonly 10 to 13, tubercles *not* prominent; spines *not* obliterating the surface of the stem; central spines variable in the varieties (see table), 2 to 6 per areole, the lower principal one declined and flattened, the others variable, straight or curved or twisted, up to 1 to 2½ inches long, ¹⁄₂₄ to ¹⁄₁₆ inch broad, flattened; radial spines variable in the varieties (see table), 6 to 12 per areole, spreading parallel to the stem, straight, ½ to 1 inch long, about ¹⁄₄₈ inch broad, acicular; flower 2 to 3 inches in diameter; petaloid perianth parts purple to magenta or lavender; fruit green, but turning to red at maturity, ¾ to 1¼ inches long; seed deeply reticulate-pitted, ¹⁄₁₆ inch long.

The fruits are edible; the ovary is rich in sugar, and the seeds are rich in fats. The fruits are eaten by birds and rodents. The Indians used both fruits and seeds for food.

2a. Echinocereus Engelmannii var. Engelmannii

Gravel, sand, and rock; hills, washes, and canyons in the desert; 2,000 to 5,000 feet elevation. Mojavean Desert but chiefly the Colorado Desert. California in Inyo County (rare) and in the lower Mojave Desert; in mountains of northern and western Colorado Desert from San Bernardino County to San Diego County and western Imperial County. Rare in Arizona from Yuma County to northeastern Maricopa and Cochise counties. Mexico in northern Baja California and northwestern Sonora.

Cereus Engelmannii Parry ex Engelm.; *Echinocereus Engelmannii* Lemaire. San Felipe, San Diego County.

Distribution Map, this page.

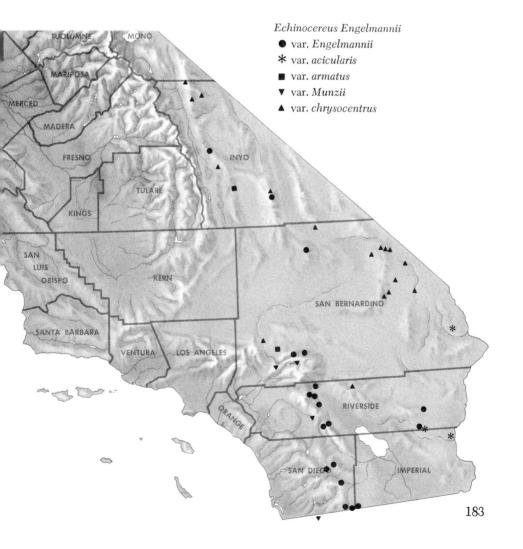

Echinocereus Engelmannii
- ● var. *Engelmannii*
- ✳ var. *acicularis*
- ■ var. *armatus*
- ▼ var. *Munzii*
- ▲ var. *chrysocentrus*

183

	Var. *Engelmannii*	Var. *acicularis*
STEMS	5 to 15, not crowded, erect, 6 to 8 inches long, 2 inches in diameter	Commonly 5 to 15 but up to 50 or more, usually erect, usually 6 to 8 inches long, $1\frac{1}{2}$ to 2 inches in diameter
SPINE COLOR	Yellowish, pink, or gray; lower central a little lighter	Pinkish or yellowish; lower central like the others
LOWER DEFLEXED AND FLATTENED CENTRAL SPINE	$1\frac{1}{4}$ to $1\frac{3}{4}$ inches long, about $\frac{1}{20}$ inch broad, stout, rigid, nearly straight	1 to $1\frac{1}{2}$ inches long, up to $\frac{1}{24}$ inch broad, rather weak and flexible
OTHER CENTRAL SPINES	Straight, the largest nearly equaling the lower central, basally $\frac{1}{24}$ inch in diameter	Straight, weak and flexible, up to 1 inch long, basally about $\frac{1}{48}$ inch in diameter
GEOGRAPHICAL DISTRIBUTION	Mostly Colorado Desert. California from southern San Bernardino County to San Diego County and western Imperial County. Rare in southern Arizona; Mexico in Baja California	Mostly Arizona Desert. Eastern edge of California in Riverside County. Arizona from near the Bill Williams River to Yuma, Yavapai, western Graham, and western Pima counties

Var. *armatus*	Var. *Munzii*	Var. *chrysocentrus*
5 to 25, suberect or erect, usually 6 to 8 (12) inches long, about 2 inches in diameter	5 to 60, crowded in mounds or clumps, suberect or erect, 4 to 8 inches long, about 2 inches in diameter	3 to 10, erect, 5 to 8 (13) inches long, 2 to 2½ inches in diameter
Pink to yellowish, the lower central like the others	All at first pink, pale gray to tannish in age; lower central often paler	Reddish to reddish-brown or yellow, dark or light; the lower central white
1½ to 1¾ inches long, basally ⅟₁₆ inch broad, stout and rigid, curving and somewhat twisted	1 to 2 inches long, basally ⅟₂₄ to ⅟₂₀ inch broad, rather flexible, markedly curving and twisted	1½ to 2¼ inches long, basally ⅟₂₀ to ⅟₁₆ inch broad, stiff and sword-like, straight or a little twisted
Curving and twisting, some equal to the lower central, basally ⅟₁₆ inch in diameter	Curving and twisting, similar to the lower central but half as long, basally ⅟₄₈ to ⅟₂₈ inch in diameter	Straight, shorter than the lower central, usually dark-colored, but sometimes yellow, basally about ⅟₂₄ inch in diameter
Mojavean Desert. California in the Argus Mountains, Inyo County, and east of Victorville, San Bernardino County	Pine forest and chaparral. California on the eastern sides of the San Bernardino, San Jacinto, and Laguna mountains. Mexico in Baja California	Mojavean Desert. California from the White Mountains, Inyo County, to Riverside County and east. Nevada to western Utah and to Mohave County and northern Yuma County, Arizona

Fig. 65. A hedgehog cactus, *Echinocereus Engelmannii* var. *acicularis*; near Papago Well, Camino del Diablo, westernmost Pima County, Arizona. Photograph by A. A. Nichol.

2*b*. Echinocereus Engelmannii var. acicularis L. Benson

Rock, sand, or gravel of hills, washes, and plains in the desert; 1,000 to 3,000 feet elevation. Arizona Desert and the edges of the Mojavean and Colorado deserts. California in eastern Riverside County. Arizona from southern Mohave County to Yavapai, Graham, and western Pima counties. Mexico in adjacent parts of Baja California.

Echinocereus Engelmannii Parry var. *acicularis* L. Benson. New River, near Black Canyon Game Refuge, Maricopa County, Arizona.

Fig. 65; Distribution Map, p. 183.

2*c*. Echinocereus Engelmannii var. armatus L. Benson

Granite hills in the desert; 3,000 feet elevation. Mojavean Desert. California in the Argus Mountains, Inyo County, and east of Victorville, San Bernardino County. Nevada in Nye County.

Echinocereus Engelmannii Parry var. *armatus* L. Benson. East of Victorville, California.

Plate 14; Distribution Map, p. 183.

Fig. 66. A mountain hedgehog cactus, *Echinocereus Engelmannii* var. *Munzii*, showing the twisting spines; northeastern side of the San Barnardino Mountains, San Bernardino County.

2*d*. **Echinocereus Engelmannii** var. **Munzii** (Parish) Pierce & Fosberg

Rock, gravel, or sand of mountains and canyons in pine woods and chaparral (which may resemble superficially the Juniper-Pinyon Woodland); 6,500 to 8,000 feet elevation. Southern California in the San Bernardino, San Jacinto, and probably the Laguna mountains. Mexico in adjacent Baja California.

Superficially this variety resembles *Echinocereus triglochidiatus* var. *mojavensis*. It is distinguished by the betacyanin pigmentation (magenta, i.e. red with blue, coloring) of the flowers (neither a pure red nor with yellow) and by the 4 central spines (except in an occasional areole) instead of 1.

Cereus Munzii Parish; *Echinocereus Engelmannii* (Parry) Lemaire var. *Munzii* Pierce and Fosberg; *E. Munzii* L. Benson. Below Kenworthy, Thomas Valley, San Jacinto Mountains, Riverside County.

Fig. 66; Distribution Map, p. 183.

2e. Echinocereus Engelmannii var. chrysocentrus (Engelm. & Bigelow) Engelm. ex Rümpler

Gravel or sand of hills, low mountains, and washes in the desert; 3,000 to 5,000(7,200) feet elevation. Mojavean Desert. California in the White Mountains, Inyo County, and southward to the eastern Mojave Desert; "Victorville" and the higher desert mountains in Riverside County. Southwestern Nevada from Esmeralda County to Clark County and occasionally northeast to Nye and Elko counties; Utah in the Great Salt Lake Desert (rare) and in Washington County and southern Kane County; Arizona in Mohave County and northern Yuma County.

The conspicuous long, white, lower central spine resembles a sword.

Cereus Engelmannii Parry var. *chrysocentrus* Engelm. & Bigelow; *Echinocereus Engelmannii* (Parry) Lemaire var. *chrysocentrus* Engelm. ex Rümpler; *E. chrysocentrus* Orcutt; *E. chrysocentrus* Thornber & Bonker. Bill Williams River, Arizona.

Plate 14; Distribution Map, p. 183.

Mammillaria Haw.

Stems simple or branching, ovoid to cylindroid, globose, or turbinate, 1 to 4(12) inches long, 1 to 3(8) inches in diameter; tubercles separate. Leaves not discernible. Spines smooth; central spines none to several or not differentiated, straight, curved, or hooked, ¼ to ¾(1) inch long, slender, usually $\frac{1}{256}$ to $\frac{1}{72}$ inch in diameter, acicular; radial spines usually smaller and lighter in color, 10 to 80 per areole, not hooked, acicular. Flowers and fruits on the old growth of preceding seasons, below the apex of the stem or branch, between the tubercles and not obviously connected with them or with the areoles upon them, sometimes in minor spine-bearing areoles between tubercles. Flower usually ¼ to 1(2) inches in diameter; superior floral tube funnelform or obconic, green as in the perianth. Fruit fleshy, without surface appendages, globular to elongate, not splitting open, the floral tube deciduous. Seeds black to brown, rugose-reticulate, reticulate-pitted, or smooth and shiny and with the surface more prominent than the pits, or tuberculate, longer than broad (hilum to opposite side); hilum usually obviously basal but sometimes oblique.

Perhaps 100 species, greater numbers having received names, native from California to southwestern Utah, New Mexico, western Oklahoma, and Texas, and south to Mexico, Central America, the Caribbean, and Venezuela; three species in California.

KEY TO THE SPECIES

1. Hooked central spine 1; base of the seed *not* corky (i.e., the aril about the hilum or attachment scar *not* markedly thickened or corky); radial spines 12 to 28 per areole; stems of older plants usually branching:
   2. Stem with minor areoles between the tubercles, these bearing tufts of hairs and a few weak, undifferentiated spines; radial spines 12 to 18 per areole; plants tending to be unisexual (dioecious), stamens being emphasized in the flowers of some plants, pistils in others; coastal near San Diego and along the western edge of the Colorado Desert and in Baja California . . . . 1. *M. dioica*
   2. Stem *not* with spine-bearing areoles between the tubercles; radial spines 18 to 28 per areole; plants not tending to be unisexual, the flowers all clearly bisexual; near the Colorado River in the Whipple Mountains, San Bernardino County, and common in the Arizona Desert, Arizona . . . . 2. *M. microcarpa*
1. Hooked central spines (1)2 to 4; base of the seed corky (with an enlarged aril or outgrowth next to the attachment scar or hilum), the corky portion half as large as the seed body in dried specimens or, in undried material, larger and with three inflated areas; radial spines 30 to 46(60) per areole; stems unbranched . . . .
   . . . . 3. *M. tetrancistra*

Fig. 67. *Mammillaria dioica*; southwest of San Diego.

1. Mammillaria dioica K. Brandegee

Stems of older plants usually branching and often forming small clumps, nearly cylindroid but enlarging gradually upward, 4 to 6(12) inches long, mostly 1½ to 2(2½) inches in diameter; tubercles protruding ⅜ inch; minor spine-bearing areoles produced between the tubercles; spines more or less obscuring the stem; central spines 1 to 4 per areole, the principal or most nearly central one hooked, dark red (accompanied by 1 to 3 shorter, basally white, straight accessory centrals), in the coastal form the longer ones ⅜ to ½(⅝) inch long, in the desert form 5/12 to ⅝(⅘) inch long, 1/96 to 1/48 inch in diameter; radial spines light tan to red, mostly 12 to 18 per areole, parallel to the stem, straight, in the coastal form the longer ones ⅕ to ⅓(⅜) inch long, in the desert form ⅕ to ⅜(⅖) inch long, about 1/128 inch in diameter, acicular; flower ¾ to 1(1½) inches in diameter; plant with a strong tendency to be dioecious (i.e., for the flowers of some plants to have small, sterile anthers and larger stigmas and those of other plants the opposite); petaloid perianth parts with the midribs sometimes purplish, the rest light yellow to pale cream or white; fruit red, fleshy, cylindroidal or enlarged gradually upward, ½ to 1 inch long, ⅛ to ¼ inch in diameter; seed black, the reticulate pattern evident, ¹⁄₂₄ to ¹⁄₂₀ inch long.

Rock or gravel or coarse sand of hills and washes in the chaparral or the desert; 50 to 500 feet elevation near the coast or 1,000 to 5,000 feet in the immediate rain shadow on the desert side of the mountains. California Chaparral (Baja Californian phase) and Colorado Desert. California near the ocean from Del Mar south in San Diego County and on the western side of the Colorado Desert from the San Jacinto Mountains south. Mexico in Baja California.

Mammillaria dioica K. Brandegee; *Neomammillaria dioica* Britton & Rose; *Ebnerella dioica* F. Buxbaum; *Chilita dioica* F. Buxbaum. Southwest corner of San Diego County.

Figs. 67, 68; Plate 15; Distribution Map, p. 194.

2. Mammillaria microcarpa Engelm.

Stems solitary or branching, cylindroid, the bases truncate, 3 to 6 inches long, 1½ to 2 inches in diameter; tubercles protruding about ½ to ⅝ inch; spine-bearing areoles only at the apices of the tubercles; central spine usually dark red or sometimes black-purple, strongly hooked, solitary (or accompanied by a straight, short, light-colored, accessory central spine), the apical hook ¹⁄₁₂ to ⅛ inch across, usually ½ to ⅝ inch long, acicular; radial spines light tan to red, 18 to 28 per areole, parallel to the stem, ¼ to ½ inch long; flower ¾ to 1 inch in diameter; petaloid perianth parts lavender; fruit red, fleshy, cylindroid to clavate, ½ to 1 inch long, ³⁄₁₆ to ¼ inch in diameter; seed black, shiny, the pits in the surface more prominent than the reticulum, about ¹⁄₂₄ inch long, without an aril.

Sand or gravel or rocky places in the desert; 1,000 to 3,000 feet elevation. California, reported from the Whipple Mountains near the Colorado River in San Bernardino County by Mrs. R. T. Craig, Cactus & Succulent Journal 10: 8. 1938. "The specimens could not be

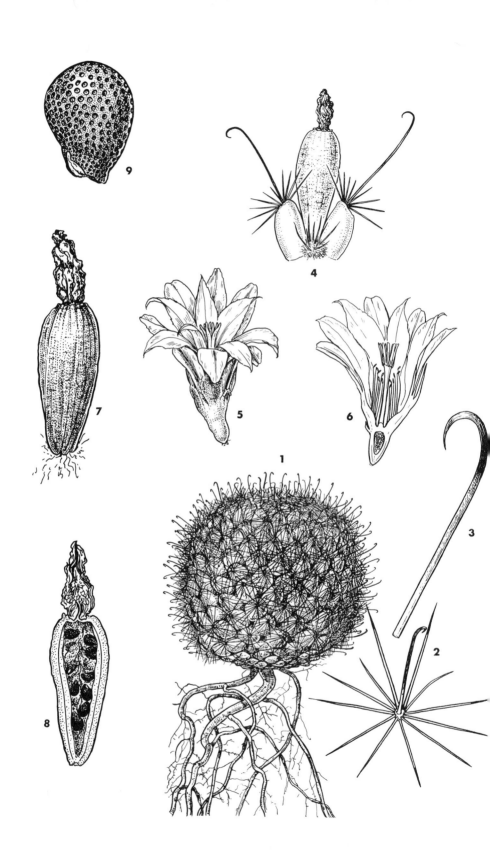

confused with *Phellosperma tetrancistra* [*Mammillaria tetrancistra*] as the dried seed pods present in the axils [of the tubercles] contained typical *Mammillaria* seed without the corky base which is the characterstic of *Phellosperma*." Dr. and Mrs. Craig are authorities on *Mammillaria*, and doubtless the report is correct, although the writer has seen no California specimens. The species is abundant in the Arizona Desert in Arizona.

Mammillaria microcarpa Engelm.; *Neomammillaria microcarpa* Britton & Rose; *Ebnerella microcarpa* F. Buxbaum; *Chilita microcarpa* F. Buxbaum. Near Winkelman, Gila County, Arizona.

N. Milleri Britton & Rose; *M. Milleri* Bödeker; *M. microcarpa* Engelm. var. *Milleri* W. T. Marshall. Phoenix, Arizona.

M. microcarpa Engelm. var. *auricarpa* W. T. Marshall. Pinnacle Peak, Maricopa County, Arizona.

PLATE 15; DISTRIBUTION MAP, p. 194.

3. Mammillaria tetrancistra Engelm.

Stems solitary, ovoid-cylindroid to cylindroid, 3 to 6 inches long, 1½ to 2½ inches in diameter; tubercles elongate, protruding ½ to ⅝ inch; spine-bearing areoles none between the tubercles; spines obscuring the stem; principal (hooked) central spines 1 to 4 per areole, grading from red to nearly black above, white below; straight central spines none to several, colored (like the principal centrals) to white, the longer central spines ½ to 1 inch long, ¼₄ to

Fig. 68. *Mammillaria dioica*; plant from near San Diego. *1.* A small individual, showing the fibrous root system, the separate tubercles on the stem, and the spine-bearing areoles, ×¼. *2.* Areole with radial spines, one (principal and lower) hooked central spine, and two straight, lighter-colored centrals, ×1½. *3.* Hooked central spine, ×6. *4.* Fruit, illustrating the position of the flower and later the fruit, developed clearly from a minor spine-bearing areole between the tubercles—not upon them as in other genera, ×1½. *5.* Flower, showing the naked ovary (actually the floral tube forming its outer coat) and the transition from sepaloid perianth parts to larger ones and then to petaloid perianth parts, also showing the slender stigmas. *6.* Flower in section, showing the ovary enclosing ovules, the upper portion of the floral tube bearing stamens, the transition from scale leaves on the floral tube to sepaloid to petaloid perianth parts, and the style and stigmas, ×1. *7.* Fruit, external view showing the bare ovary and the persistent perianth, ×1½. *8.* Fruit in section, showing the seeds, ×1½. *9.* Seed, showing the hilum or attachment scar at the base and the pits in the seed coat, ×15.

● *Mammillaria dioica*
✳ *M. microcarpa*
▲ *M. tetrancistra*

Fig. 69. *Mammillaria tetrancistra. 1.* Plant, showing the fibrous root system and the spine clusters formed in the areoles, ×¼. *2.* Areole with three large hooked central spines and with accessory straight, lighter-colored central spines grading into the numerous radial spines, ×1½. *3.* Flower, showing the bare ovary, the scales on the floral tube above it grading into sepaloid perianth parts and then into petaloid perianth parts, the numerous stamens, and the slender stigmas, ×1. *4.* Flower in section, showing the ovary containing ovules, the more or less elongate floral tube internally bearing stamens and externally on its upper part scale leaves and sepaloid and petaloid perianth parts, ×1. *5.* Fruit in external view, the surface bare, ×1. *6.* Fruit in section, showing the seeds, ×1. *7.* Seed, showing the strongly roughened surface (*above*) and the large aril (*below*), which even in the dried condition shown here rivals the size of the seed body, ×4½.

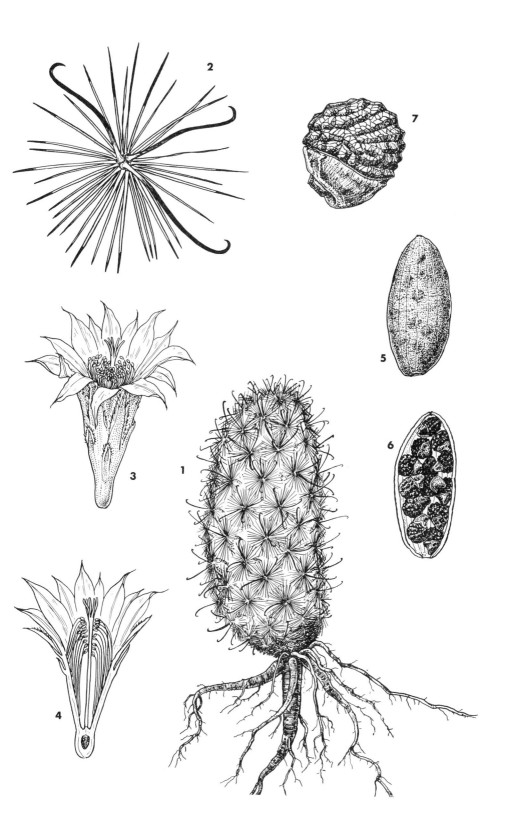

1/96 inch in diameter, acicular; radial spines white or sometimes the larger ones tipped with red or red-to-black, 30 to 46(reportedly 60) per areole, up to 3/8 to 1/2(1) inch long, 1/128 inch in diameter, acicular; flower 1 to 1 1/2 inches in diameter, all the flowers alike; petaloid perianth parts rose-pink to purple; fruit red, cylindroid to club-shaped, 3/4 to 1 1/4 inches long, 1/4 to 7/16 inch in diameter; seed black, dull, tuberculate, nearly spheroidal, the hilum invested in the nearly white corky tissue of an aril almost as large as the seed, the seed proper 1/12 inch long, the aril about 1/24 to 1/16 inch long in dried specimens, 1/12 to 1/8 inch long when fresh. In living material the aril has 3 symmetrical inflated areas.

Sandy soils of hills, valleys, and plains in the desert; 450 to 2,400 feet elevation. Colorado Desert and the lower edges of the Mojavean and Arizona deserts. California from the Panamint Mountains in Inyo County to San Diego and Imperial counties. Nevada in the Charleston Mountains in Clark County; Utah near St. George; western Arizona.

Mammillaria tetrancistra Engelm.; *M. phellosperma* Engelm., unnecessary *nom. nov.* for *M. tetrancistra*; *Cactus phellospermus* Kuntze; *C. tetrancistrus* Coulter; *Phellosperma tetrancistra* Britton & Rose; *Neomammillaria tetrancistra* Fosberg. Colorado Desert.

FIG. 69; PLATE 15; DISTRIBUTION MAP, p. 194.

Ferocactus Britton & Rose (BARREL CACTUS)

Stems unbranched or, after injury to the terminal bud, branched, cylindroid to ovoid or depressed-globose, 1/2 to 10 feet long, 1/6 to 1 1/2(2) feet in diameter, ribs 13 to 30, the tubercles coalescent for nearly their full height. Leaves not discernible. Spines annulate or smooth, red, pink, white, tan, brown, or yellow, often with a surface layer of ashy gray, gray in age; central spines 4(1 to 8), either straight, curved, or hooked, up to 6 1/2 inches long, 1/48 to 1/6 inch in diameter, acicular to subulate; radial spines either colored like the radial or more often lighter or white, 6 to 20 per areole, straight or curved, 3/8 to 3 inches long, 1/96 to 1/24(1/8) inch in diameter or width, acicular or subulate. Flowers and fruits on the new growth of the current season, near the apex of the stem or branch, at the apex of the tubercle in a felted area adjacent to the spine-bearing part of the areole. Flower 1½ to 3 inches in diameter; superior floral tube obconical to barely funnelform, green or tinged with the color of the perianth. Fruit fleshy, with numerous or sometimes only 10 to 15 broad scales (these marginally scarious, fimbriate, or denticulate), short-cylindroid, ovoid, or globular, ⅓ to 1¾ inches long, ⅛ to 1⅜ inches in diameter, with the floral tube persistent, opening by a short crosswise or lengthwise slit between the base and the middle. Seed black, finely reticulate, reticulate-pitted, or papillate, narrowly compressed-obovoid to semicircular or obovoid, with the base flaring around the micropyle, longer than broad (hilum to opposite side), ¹⁄₂₄ to ⅛ inch in greatest dimension; hilum obviously basal or "subbasal."

Twenty or 30 species native from California to Texas; two species in California.

KEY TO THE SPECIES

1. Outer radial spines bristle-like, flexible, white, bending irregularly back and forth, *not* straight or simply curved; principal central spine *not* pointing downward through its entire length; stems solitary except after injury to the terminal bud; mature plants at least 2 feet high and 8 to 24 inches in diameter; deserts . . . .
. . . . 1. *F. acanthodes*
1. Outer radial spines *not* bristle-like, rigid, straight or simply curved; principal central spine very stout, rigid, strongly deflexed, i.e., pointing downward through its entire length; plants depressed, i.e., short and broad and indented apically, usually about 1 foot high; coastal near San Diego and south to Baja California . . . .
. . . . 2. *F. viridescens*

1. Ferocactus acanthodes (Lemaire) Britton & Rose

Columnar to (uncommonly) barrel-shaped plants; nearly always solitary, unbranched except after injury to the terminal bud, cylindroidal and usually elongate, usually 3 to 10 feet long, averaging about 1 foot in diameter; ribs mostly 18 to 27; spines partly obscuring the stem; central spines yellowish or red-and-yellow when young, usually turning red except apically (yellow in one Arizona variety), later often becoming gray, usually 4 per areole, these in the form of a cross, the upper one and lower one broader, longer, and thicker, the lower usually apically curving a little or sometimes curving up to 90°, but never hooked, up to 2(5½) inches long, ½ to ⅛(¹⁄₁₆) inch broad; radial spines colored like the centrals, the 6 to 8 inner ones 1½ to 2½ inches long, basally ¹⁄₂₄ to ¹⁄₁₆ inch in diameter, the 6 to 12 outer ones as long as the inner but about ¹⁄₄₈ inch in diameter, flexible, curving irregularly in and out; flower 1½ to 2½ inches in diameter; petaloid perianth parts yellow with some red especially along the basal portions of the veins; fruit yellow, fleshy, with numerous rounded scarious-margined scales, the wall thick, 1¼ to 1½ inches long, about ⅝ to ¾ inch in diameter; seeds minutely reticulate-pitted, compressed-obovoid, ¹⁄₁₂ to ⅛ inch long; hilum clearly basal.

1a. Ferocactus acanthodes var. acanthodes

Principal (lower) central spine 3 to 6 inches long, ¹⁄₁₂(⅛) inch broad, the apex curving up to about 90° but not recurved; inner 6 to 8 radial spines 1½ to 2½ inches long; petaloid perianth parts ³⁄₁₆ to ¼ inch broad; seed about ⅛ inch broad.

Gravel or rock of hills, canyons, alluvial fans, and washes in the desert; 200 to 1,500(2,000) feet elevation. Colorado Desert. California in San Bernardino County (New York and Whipple mountains); perhaps rare in Riverside and San Diego counties. Arizona near the lower Gila River. Mexico in adjacent Baja California.

Echinocactus acanthodes Lemaire; *Ferocactus acanthodes* Britton & Rose; *E. viridescens* Nutt. var. *cylindraceus* Engelm.; *F. cylindraceus* Orcutt. San Felipe, San Diego County.

DISTRIBUTION MAP, p. 200.

1b. Ferocactus acanthodes var. LeContei (Engelm.) Lindsay

Principal (lower) central spine 2 to 3 inches long, basally (¹⁄₁₂)⅛(³⁄₁₆) inch broad, the apex curving a little; inner 6 to 8 radial spines 1½ to 2 inches long; petaloid perianth parts ¼ to ⅝ inch broad; seed about ¹⁄₁₂ inch broad.

Gravel or rock of hills, canyons, alluvial fans, and washes or sandy flats in the desert; 2,500 to 5,000 feet elevation. Mojavean and Arizona deserts and the upper edge of the Colorado Desert. California in the mountains of the eastern and southern Mojave Desert and perhaps rare on the upper edge of the Colorado Desert in Riverside and San Diego counties. Nevada in southern Clark County; Utah probably near St. George in Washington County; Arizona from Mohave County to Coconino, Gila, Yuma, and (mostly western) Pima counties. Mexico in adjacent Sonora and probably northern Baja California.

Echinocactus LeContei Engelm.; *E. Wislizenii* Engelm. var. *LeContei* Engelm.; *Ferocactus LeContei* Britton & Rose; *F. acanthodes* (Lemaire) Britton & Rose var. *LeContei* Lindsay. Bill Williams River, Arizona.

FIG. 3; PLATE 15; DISTRIBUTION MAP, p. 200.

2. Ferocactus viridescens (Nutt.) Britton & Rose

Stems depressed-globose or hemispheroidal to ovoid or cylindroidal, often broader than long, 6 to 12(18) inches long, 8 to 15 inches in diameter; ribs usually 15 to 20; central spines red, in age becoming gray or yellowish, 4 per areole, forming a cross, spreading at about 45° angles, the principal (lower) one slightly curving, strongly cross-ribbed, 1¼ to 1¾ inches long, ¹⁄₁₂ inch broad, flattened; radial spines similar to the central but smaller, 10 to 20 per areole, spreading irregularly, stiff, straight, the longer ones ½ to ¾ inches long, ¹⁄₂₄ inch broad, flattened, subulate; flower 1¼ to 1¾ inches in diameter; petaloid perianth parts pink, green, and yellow; fruit red, fleshy, with about 30 fimbriolate-denticulate semi-circular scales, barrel-like, ⅝ to ¾ inch long and of equal diameter; seeds strongly but minutely reticulate, elongate-obovoid, ¹⁄₁₄ inch (1.8 mm.) long; hilum obviously basal but oblique.

Sand or gravel of hillsides in the chaparral; 30 to 50 feet elevation. California Chaparral (San Diego County phase). California along the coast from Del Mar south, inland nearly as far as Otay. Mexico in northwestern Baja California.

Echinocactus viridescens Nutt.; *Melocactus viridescens* Nutt.; *Ferocactus viridescens* Britton & Rose. Near San Diego.

E. limitus Engelm. Boundary line south of San Diego.

FIGS. 70, 71; DISTRIBUTION MAP, p. 200.

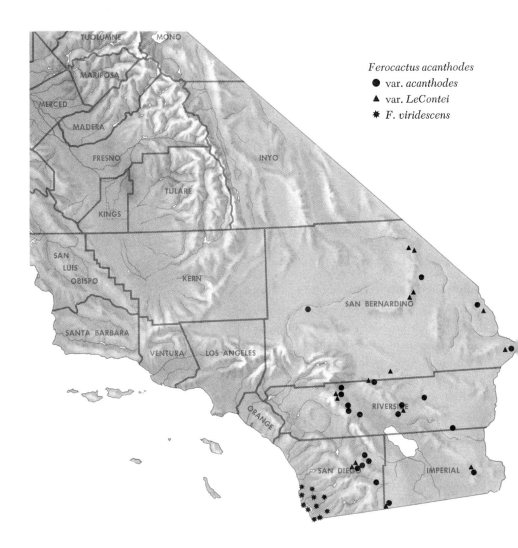

Ferocactus acanthodes
● var. *acanthodes*
▲ var. *LeContei*
✳ *F. viridescens*

Fig. 70. The barrel cactus of the coast, *Ferocactus viridescens*. *1.* Small
plant, showing the fibrous root system, the ribs of the stem, and the spine-
bearing areoles along the ribs, ×¼. As in this plant, commonly the stem is
depressed. *2.* Areole with felt and with four central and 13 radial spines,
×½. The lower radial spine is stout, flattened, and curved downward.
3. Flower in external view, showing the scale-leaves investing the ovary, the
transition from these to sepaloid and petaloid perianth parts, the stamens,
and the slender stigmas, ×⅓. *4.* Flower in section, showing the ovary
enclosing ovules, the style and the slender stigmas, the floral tube above
the ovary bearing numerous stamens, and the scale leaves transitional to the
sepaloid and petaloid perianth parts, ×⅓. *5.* The top of the style and
the 17 slender stigmas, ×1. *6.* Fruit, showing the scales (now proportionately
small) through which the seeds are freed, and the withered remains of
the persistent perianth, ×⅓. *7.* Fruit in section, showing the seeds, ×⅓.
8. Seed, showing the obviously basal hilum or attachment scar and the pits
in the wall of the seed coat, ×9.

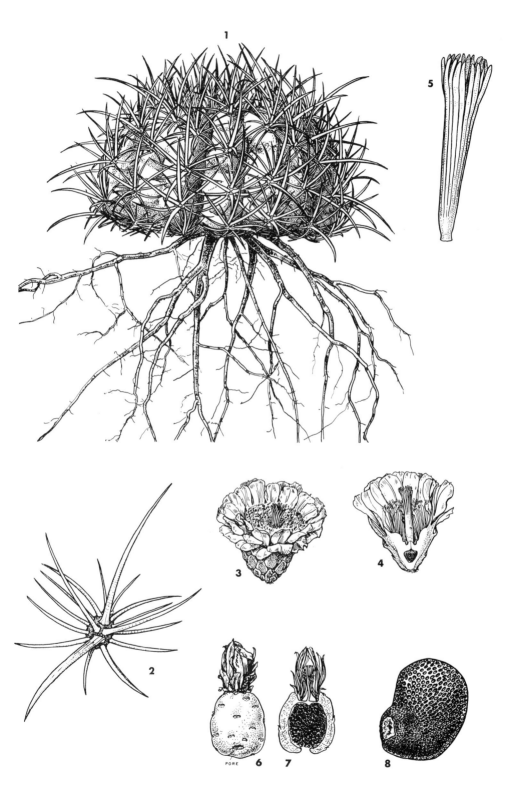

1

5

2

3

4

PORE 6 7 8

Fig. 71. The barrel cactus of the coast, *Ferocactus viridescens*, a species occurring in San Diego County and in Baja California. *Above,* plants on hills southwest of San Diego; note the attachment scars of the fruits (*right*). *Below left,* plants in the Rancho Santa Ana Botanic Garden. Photographs *above* by Edward F. Anderson.

Echinocactus Link & Otto (BARREL CACTUS)

Stems branching or unbranched, ⅙ to 2 feet long, ⅙ to 1 foot in diameter; ribs 8 to 27, the tubercles almost completely coalescent. Leaves not discernible. Spines, when present, annulate; central spines red, sometimes covered partly by ashy gray, (0)1 to 4 per areole, straight or curving, 1 to 3 inches long, ⅟₁₆ to ⅜ inch broad, nearly acicular to subulate; radial spines like the central but smaller, 5 to 11 per areole, ¾ to 2 inches long, ⅟₂₄ to ⅛ inch in width, nearly acicular to subulate. Flowers and fruits on the new growth of the current season near the apex of the stem or branch, each at the apex of a tubercle in a felted area adjacent to the spine-bearing part of the areole. Flower 1½ to 2¾ inches in diameter; superior floral tube obconical to slightly funnelform, green or tinted like the perianth. Sepaloid perianth parts aristate- or spinose-tipped. Fruit dry or fleshy, with scales and with hairs from beneath the scales, in some species the hairs obscuring the fruit, ⅝ to 2 inches long, ⅜ to 1½ inches in diameter. Seeds black or brown, reticulate, irregularly obovoid or ovoid or irregularly pyramidal, broader than long (hilum to opposite side), ⅟₁₂ to ⅙ inch in breadth.

Twelve or more species native from California to Texas and southward in Mexico to Querétero; one species in California.

1. **Echinocactus polycephalus** Engelm. & Bigelow

Stems branching, forming clumps of up to 30, these up to 2 feet high and 4 feet in diameter; stems gray-green, spheroidal to cylindroidal, 6 to 12(24) inches long, up to 8 to 10(12) inches in diameter; ribs 13 to 21; spines obscuring the stem; central spines red but with a conspicuous ashy surface layer, in the California (typical) variety with a dense felty canescence (this peeling off in sheets as the spine ages), 4 per areole, spreading irregularly, the principal lower one curving slightly downward, the others nearly straight, strongly cross-ribbed, 2½ to 3 inches long, ⅟₁₀ to ⅛ inch broad, flattened; radial spines similar to the centrals but smaller, 6 to 8 per areole, spreading irregularly or slightly curving in low arcs, 1¼ to 1¾ inches long, ⅟₂₄ to ⅟₁₆ broad, somewhat flattened;

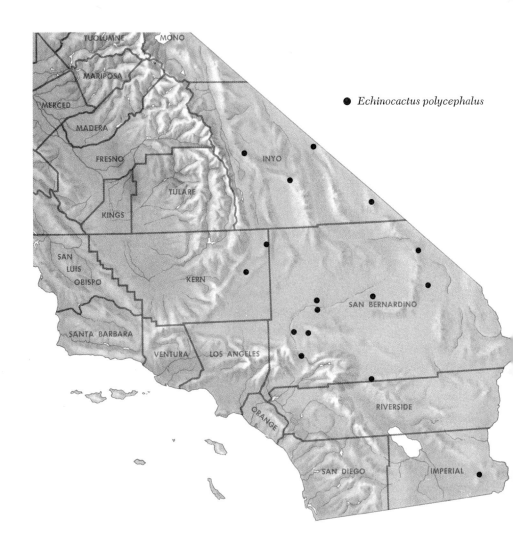

flower about 2 inches in diameter; petaloid perianth parts yellow or the midribs tinged with pink; fruit dry, densely encased in matted woolly white hairs ½ to ¾ inch long, the ovary ¾ to 1 inch long, ⅜ to ½ inch in diameter; seeds black, strongly reticulate, irregularly obovoid in outline though sharply irregularly angled from compression, ⅙ inch broad, ¹⁄₁₆ inch thick; hilum appearing "lateral."

Rock or gravel of dry, hot slopes of low mountains or clay soils of valleys in the deserts; 100 to 2,500 feet elevation. Mojavean Desert. California in the Mojave Desert from Kern and Inyo counties to the Little San Bernardino Mountains, Riverside County, and to northeastern Imperial County. Nevada in southern Nye County and in Clark County; Arizona in western Mohave and Yuma counties. Mexico in northwestern Sonora.

Echinocactus polycephalus Engelm. & Bigelow. Mojave River.
E. polycephalus Engelm. & Bigelow var. *flavispina*[us] Haage, fil. Without reference to a specimen or locality.

PLATE 15; DISTRIBUTION MAP, p. 204.

Sclerocactus Britton & Rose

Stems solitary or occasionally branching (perhaps because of injury to the terminal bud), cylindroid, ovoid, globose, or depressed-globose, 2 to 8(16) inches long, 1½ to 4(6) inches in diameter; ribs 12 to 17; tubercles coalescent into the ribs through one-half to four-fifths of their height, these protruding ⅛ to ¼ inch. Leaves not discernible. Spines smooth, not annulate (i.e., not with crosswise ridges); central spines gray, white, yellow, red, or brown, (0)1 to 6(11) per areole, usually of two or three distinctive types, usually 1 or more hooked, the longer ones ½ to 3½ inches long, acicular or subulate or some of each type; radial spines white or gray or sometimes some of them pink or brown, 6 to 11(15) per areole, straight, shorter than the centrals, acicular or subulate. Flowers and fruits on the growth of the current season near the apex of the stem or branch, each on the side of a tubercle toward the apex in a felted area adjacent to and merging with the new spiniferous areole. Flower ¾ to 2¼ inches in diameter; superior floral tube short, funnelform; petaloid perianth parts white, yellow, or pink to reddish-purple. Fruit green, thin-walled, becoming reddish and dry, naked or with a few broad, thin scales, ⅜ to 1 inch long, ⅜ to ⁷⁄₁₆ inch in diameter, opening *either* along a circular, nearly horizontal line above the base to a little above the middle *or* along 2 or 3 short vertical lines. Seed black, papillate-reticulate, angled on one side of the hilum, rounded on the other, broader than long, (¹⁄₁₀)⅛ to ⅙ inch broad.

1. Sclerocactus polyancistrus (Engelm. & Bigelow) Britton & Rose

Stem solitary, green, cylindroidal, usually 4 to 6 inches long, 2 to 2½(3) inches in diameter; ribs 13 to 17, the tubercles basally strongly coalescent, protruding ¼ inch; spines almost obscuring the stem; central spines 9 to 11, the usually 6 to 8 lower and lateral ones red, the longer ones up to the length of the median upper central (see below), ⅟₃₂ inch in diameter, acicular, all but 1 or 2 hooked; the (usually) 3 upper central spines white, flat, conspicuous, erect (parallel to the stem), the median one 3 to 3½ inches long, the lateral about ⅛ to ⅔ as long; radial spines white, 10 to 15 per areole, spreading in a circle, white, straight, about ¾ inch long,

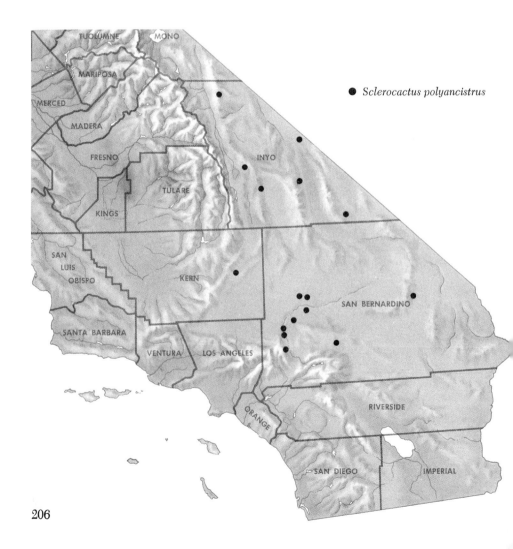

● *Sclerocactus polyancistrus*

206

⅟₄₈ inch broad, somewhat flattened; flower about 2 inches in diameter; petaloid perianth parts rose-purple to magenta; fruit green to tan, dry, with a few scales; fruit before maturity green, with a few fringed scales, ovoid-cylindroid, 1 inch long, ¾ inch in diameter; seeds (perhaps immature) brown, irregularly ovoid in outline, ⅟₁₂ inch long, ⅕ inch broad.

Usually on limestone; rocky soils of hills and canyons in the desert; 2,500 to 5,000(7,000) feet elevation. Mojavean Desert. California in the higher parts of the Mojave Desert. Nevada in Esmeralda County.

Echinocactus polyancistrus Engelm. & Bigelow; *Sclerocactus polyancistrus* Britton & Rose. Near the head of the Mojave River.

PLATE 16; DISTRIBUTION MAP, p. 206.

Neolloydia Britton & Rose

Stems branched or unbranched, ovoid or cylindroid, 2 to 6(15) inches long, 1 to 3(5) inches in diameter; ribs 8 to 21, the tubercles separate through half or less of their height. Leaves not discernible. Spines smooth, black to dark brown or tan, chalky blue, straw-colored, purplish, or pink, sometimes dark-tipped, becoming gray or black in age; central spines 1 to 8 per areole, straight or rarely (in Mexico) curved or almost hooked, ½ to ¾ inch long, ⅟₆₄ to ⅟₁₆ inch in diameter, acicular or subulate; radial spines white or similar to the central spines but usually smaller and lighter, 3 to 32 per areole, straight, ¼ to 1¼ inches long, ⅟₁₂₈ to ⅟₁₆ inch in diameter. Flowers and fruits on the new growth of the current season near the apex of the stem, each developed on the upper side of a tubercle in a felted area distant from the spine-bearing part of the areole and connected with it by an isthmus extending half the length to the full length of the tubercle. Flower 1 to 3 inches in diameter; superior floral tube funnelform to obconical, green and pink to purple. Fruit dry, with a few or up to 20 broad, membranous scales, ellipsoid to short-cylindroid, ¼ to ½ inch long, about ¼ to ⅜ inch in diameter, dehiscent basally or by 1 to 3 longitudinal slits. Seeds black, reticulate, reticulate-papillate, or papillate, either broader than long or longer than broad (hilum to opposite side), often crescentic-ellipsoid, ⅟₁₆ to ⅟₁₀ inch in greatest dimension; hilum either obviously basal or appearing "lateral."

Twelve to 15 species from California to Texas and south in Mexico to northern Sonora and San Luis Potosi; 1 species in California.

1. Neolloydia Johnsonii (Parry) L. Benson

Stem solitary or occasionally branching after injury to the terminal bud, ovoid- to ellipsoid-cylindroid, 4 to 6(10) inches long, 2 to 4 inches in diameter; ribs 17 to 21, strongly indented just above each tubercle and rising gradually to the next; tubercles protruding about ¼ inch; spines obscuring the stem; central spines pink to reddish, blackening in age, 4 to 8 per areole, spreading, straight or slightly curving, 1¼ to 1½ inches long, ¼₄ to ½₀(⅟₁₆) inch in diameter, acicular; radial spines smaller and sometimes lighter in color, mostly 9 to 10 per areole, ½ to ¾(1) inch long, ⅟₄₈ to ⅟₃₂ inch in diameter, acicular; flower 2 to 3 inches in diameter; petaloid perianth parts magenta to pink, or greenish-yellow; fruit green, drying to tan, with several scarious-margined fimbriate scales, ellipsoid-cylindroid, about ½ inch long, ⅛ inch in diameter, splitting along the dorsal side; seeds papillate, broader than long, ⅟₁₀ inch broad.

Granite hills and alluvial fans in the desert; 1,700 to 4,000 feet elevation. Mojavean Desert. California in the Death Valley Region in Inyo County. Nevada in Clark County; Utah in Washington County; Arizona in Mohave, western Yavapai, and northern Yuma counties.

Echinocactus Johnsonii Parry ex Engelm.; *Ferocactus Johnsonii* Britton & Rose; *Echinomastus Johnsonii* Baxter; *Thelocactus Johnsonii* W. T. Marshall ex Kelsey & Dayton; *Neolloydia Johnsonii* L. Benson. St. George, Utah.
Echinocactus Johnsonii var. *octocentrus* Coulter. Rusting [Resting] Springs Mountains, Inyo County.
Echinocactus Johnsonii var. *lutescens* Parish; *Echinomastus Johnsonii* var. *lutescens* Parrish [Parish] ex Glade *nom. nud.*; *Echinomastus Johnsonii* (Parry) Baxter var. *lutescens* Wiggins. Searchlight, Nevada.
Echinomastus arizonicus Hester. Butler Valley, Yuma County, Arizona.

PLATE 16; DISTRIBUTION MAP, p. 209.

Coryphantha Britton & Rose

Stems solitary or branching, in some species forming mounds of 100 or more, subglobose to cylindroid, 1 to 4(6) inches long, 1 to 3 inches in diameter; ribs none; tubercles separate. Leaves not discernible. Spines smooth, white to gray, pink, yellow, brown, or black; central spines usually 1 to 10 per areole, sometimes more and grading into the radial, straight, curved, hooked, or twisted, ⅛ to 1(2) inches long, ¹⁄₁₂₈ to ¹⁄₂₄ inch in diameter or width, acicular or sometimes subulate; radial spines usually the same color or lighter, 5 to 40 per areole, usually straight ⅛ to 1 inch long, ¹⁄₂₅₆ to ¹⁄₄₈ inch in diameter, acicular. Flowers and fruits on the new growth of the current season near the apex of the stem or branch, each at the base of the upper side of a tubercle, distant from the spine-bearing part of the areole, connected by a narrow isthmus; on immature stems the flower-bearing area about mid-level on the tubercle. Flower ½ to 2 inches in diameter; superior floral tube fun-

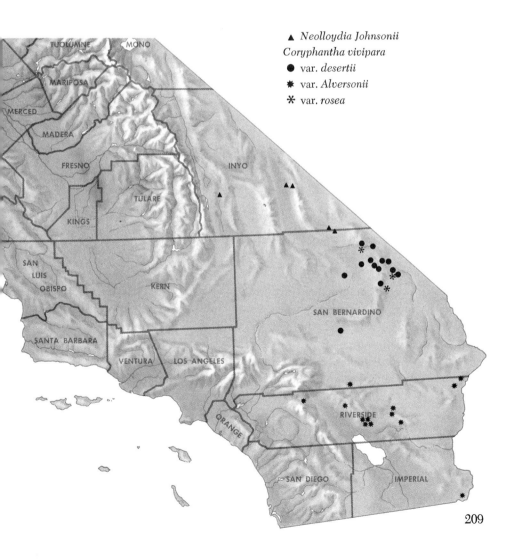

▲ *Neolloydia Johnsonii*
Coryphantha vivipara
● var. *desertii*
✳ var. *Alversonii*
✲ var. *rosea*

	Var. *desertii*
STEMS	Ovoid to cylindroid, usually solitary, 3 to 4½ inches long, 2½ to 3 inches in diameter
CENTRAL SPINES	4 to 6, white, tipped with pink, mostly about ½ inch long, with the radials forming a mass
RADIAL SPINES	About 20, white, about ½ inch long, ⅟₂₈ inch in diameter
FLOWER DIAMETER	1 to 1½ (1¾) inches
PETALOID PERIANTH PARTS	Straw-yellow to pink
GEOGRAPHICAL DISTRIBUTION	Southeastern California in the Clark and Ivanpah mountains, Mojave Desert. Nevada in the Charleston Mountains; western edge of Arizona

nelform, green or tinged with the color of the perianth (pink, magenta, reddish-purple, yellow-green, or yellow). Fruit fleshy, green or red, thin-walled, without surface appendages, usually ellipsoid, clavate, or cylindroid, ¼ to 2¼ inches long, ⅟₁₂ to ¾ inch in diameter, indehiscent. Seeds tan, brown, or black, smooth and shining or punctate or reticulate, *usually* broader than long (hilum to opposite side), ⅟₂₄ to ⅟₁₂ inch in greatest dimension.

Twenty or 30 species native from southern Alberta to central Mexico; 1 species in California.

Var. *Alversonii*	Var. *rosea*
Cylindroid, unbranched but from branching rhizomes beneath sand, 4 to 6 inches long, 2½ to 3 inches in diameter	Ovoid-globose, solitary or branching, 3 to 5(7) inches long, 3 to 4(6) inches in diameter
8 to 10, white, tipped with dark red or black, ½ to ⅝ inch long, stout, with the radials forming a remarkably dense mass	10 to 12, white with red tips, ¾ to 1 inch long, ¹⁄₂₄ inch in diameter, robust, with the radials forming a mass
About 12 to 18, white, ½ to ⅝(¾) inch long, about ¹⁄₆₄ inch in diameter	About 12 to 18, white, ⅝ to ¾(1) inch long, about ¹⁄₄₈ inch in diameter
About 1¼ inches	1¼ to 2 inches
Magenta to pink	Magenta to purplish, lanceolate
California in the Mojave and Colorado deserts in Riverside County. Pagumpa, Arizona	California in the New York Mountains, San Bernardino County. Nevada in the Charleston Mountains and east to Lincoln County

1. Coryphantha vivipara (Nutt.) Britton & Rose

PINCUSHION CACTUS

Stems depressed-globose, ovoid, or cylindroid, in some varieties forming clumps of 200 or more, green, 1½ to 6 inches long, 1½ to 3 inches in diameter; protruding ¼ to ¾ inch; spines more or less obscuring the stem, according to the variety; central spines usually white basally but tipped for various distances with pink, red, or black, 3 to 10 per areole, straight, ½ to ¾(1) inch long, ¹⁄₆₄ to ¹⁄₃₂ inch in diameter, acicular; radial spines white, 12 to 40 per areole,

Fig. 72. *Coryphantha vivipara* var. *Alversonii*; plant collected by Mr. and Mrs. Clarence Bonner in the region of the Eagle Mountains, Riverside County. The rhizomes or underground stems give rise to the aerial stems.

spreading, straight, up to ⅜(⅝) inch long, ¹⁄₁₂₈(¹⁄₆₄) inch in diameter, acicular; flowers open for only an hour or two, 1 to 2 inches in diameter; petaloid perianth parts pink, red, lavender, or yellow-green; fruit green, fleshy, rarely with a few scales (!), ellipsoid, ½ to 1 inch long, ⅜ to ⅝ inch in diameter; seeds brown, reticulate, about semicircular but a little broader on one side, ¹⁄₁₆ to ¹⁄₁₂ inch broad.

1a. Coryphantha vivipara var. **desertii** (Engelm.) W. T. Marshall

Limestone hills and flats in the desert; 1,000 to 5,400 feet elevation. Mojavean Desert. California in the Mojave Desert, eastern

San Bernardino County. Nevada from the Charleston Mountains south; Arizona in Mohave County north of Wolf Hole.

Mammillaria desertii Engelm.; *Cactus radiosus* (Engelm.) Coulter var. *desertii* Coulter; *M. radiosa* Engelm. var. *desertii* Engelm. ex K. Schum.; *Coryphantha desertii* Britton & Rose; *M. vivipara* (Nutt.) Haw. var. *desertii* L. Benson; *Coryphantha vivipara* (Nutt.) Britton & Rose var. *desertii* W. T. Marshall; *Escobaria desertii* F. Buxbaum. Ivanpah, San Bernardino County.

PLATE 16; DISTRIBUTION MAP, p. 209.

1b. Coryphantha vivipara var. **Alversonii** (Coulter) L. Benson

Sandy parts of the desert; 250 to 4,000 feet elevation. California in the border zone between the Mojave and Colorado deserts in Riverside County and near Bard, Imperial County. Arizona at Pagumpa.

Cactus radiosus (Engelm.) Coulter var. *Alversonii* Coulter; *Mammillaria Alversonii* Coulter ex Zeissold; *M. radiosa* Engelm. var. *Alversonii* K. Schum.; *M. vivipara* (Nutt.) Haw. var. *Alversonii* L. Benson; *Coryphantha vivipara* (Nutt.) Britton & Rose var. *Alversonii* L. Benson. McHaney's Mine, near Twentynine Palms.

FIG. 72; PLATE 16; DISTRIBUTION MAP, p. 209.

1c. Coryphantha vivipara var. **rosea** (Clokey) L. Benson

Limestone in woodlands in the mountains; 5,000 to 9,000 feet elevation. Juniper-Pinyon Woodland. California in northeastern San Bernardino County. Southern Nevada from western Clark County to eastern Lincoln County; northwestern Arizona.

Coryphantha rosea Clokey; *C. vivipara* (Nutt.) Britton & Rose var. *rosea* L. Benson. Between Kyle Canyon and Deer Creek, Charleston Mountains, Clark County, Nevada.

C. Alversonii (Coulter) Orcutt var. *exaltissima* Wiegand & Backeberg, *nom. nud.* No type specimen or locality designated.

PLATE 16; DISTRIBUTION MAP, p. 209.

Reference Materials and Index

Reference and Suggested Readings

The references appearing in the following list relate to the cacti in general, to those of California in particular, and to the subjects such as the Natural Vegetation of California discussed in the Introduction. Additional references, of historical interest, are listed on pp. 68–69.

A recommended reference on the cacti of California and other subjects concerned with both classification and growing of cacti is *The Cactus and Succulent Journal* (Charles Glass, editor, Box 167, Reseda, California 91335), a publication of the Cactus and Succulent Society of America, Inc. In addition to the general society, there are local affiliated cactus societies in all parts of the United States.

Axelrod, Daniel I. 1940. *Late Tertiary Floras of the Great Basin and Border Areas.* Bulletin of the Torrey Botanical Club 67: 477–488.

———. 1944. *The Sonoma Flora.* Carnegie Institution of Washington Publication (590): 1–22.

———. 1948. *Climate and Evolution in Western North America during Middle Pliocene Time.* Evolution 2: 127–144.

———. 1950a. *Classification of the Madro-Tertiary Flora.* Carnegie Institution of Washington Publication (590): 1–22.

———. 1950b. *Evolution of Desert Vegetation in Western North America.* Carnegie Institution of Washington Publication (590): 215–306.

———. 1956. *Mio-Pliocene Floras from West Central Nevada.* University of California Publications in Geological Sciences 33: 1–322.

———. 1957. *Late Tertiary Floras and the Sierra Nevadan Uplift.* Bulletin of the Geological Society of America 68: 19–45.

———. 1958. *Evolution of the Madro-Tertiary Geoflora.* Botanical Review 24: 433–509.

Backeberg, Curt. *Die Cactaceae; Handbuch der Kakteenkunde.* 6 vols. Gustav Fischer Verlag, Jena, 1958–62.

Baxter, Edgar M. *California Cactus.* Abbey San Encino Press, Los Angeles, 1935. This appeared first in parts, *Cactus & and Succ. Jour.* vols. 4–6.

Benson, Lyman. *The Cacti of Arizona.* University of Arizona Press, Tucson, 1940, 1950, 1969.

Borg, John. *Cacti, A Gardener's Handbook for Their Identification and Cultivation.* Blandford Press, London, 1937, 1951, 1959.

Britton, Nathaniel Lord, and Joseph Nelson Rose. *The Cactaceae.* 4 vols. Carnegie Institution of Washington, Washington, D.C., 1919–23.

Chaney, Ralph W. 1925. *A Comparative Study of the Bridge Creek Flora and the Modern Redwood Forest.* Carnegie Institution of Washington Publication (349): 1–22.

———. 1936. *The Succession and Distribution of Cenozoic Floras Around the North Pacific Basin.* Essays in Geobotany in Honor of W. A. Setchell, edited by T. H. Goodspeed. 55–85.

———. 1938. *Paleoecological Interpretation of Cenozoic Plants in Western North America.* Botanical Review 4: 371–396.

——— 1940. *Tertiary Floras and Continental History.* Bulletin of the Geological Society of America 51: 469–488.

———. 1951. *A Revision of Fossil Sequoia and Taxodium in Western North America based upon the Recent Discovery of Metasequoia.* Transactions of the American Philosophical Society. 40: 171–263.

———, Carlton Condit, and Daniel I. Axelrod. 1944. *Pliocene Floras of California and Oregon.* Carnegie Institution of Washington Publication (533).

———, and Daniel I. Axelrod. 1959. *Miocene Floras of the Columbia Plateau.* Carnegie Institution of Washington Publication (617): Part I. 1–134 by Ralph W. Chaney; Part II, Systematic Considerations, 135–237 by Ralph W. Chaney and Daniel I. Axelrod.

Dawson, E. Yale. *The Cacti of California.* University of California Press, Berkeley, 1966.

Kearney, Thomas H., and Robert H. Peebles. *Arizona Flora.* University of California Press, Berkeley, 1951, 1960. Cactaceae 567–586.

Marshall, W. Taylor, and Thor Methven Bock. *The Cactaceae.* Abbey Garden Press, Pasadena, Calif., 1941. (Intended as a supplement to Britton & Rose, *Cactaceae.*)

Munz, Philip A. *A Manual of Southern California Botany.* The Claremont Colleges, Claremont, Calif., 1935. Cactaceae 323–329.

Munz, Philip Alexander, in collaboration with David D. Keck. *A California Flora.* University of California Press, Berkeley, 1959. Cactaceae 309–320. Supplement by Philip Alexander Munz. 1968.

Parish, Samuel Bonsall, *in* Willis Lynn Jepson, *A Manual of the Flowering Plants of California.* University of California Press, Berkeley, 1923–25. Cactaceae 654–60.

————, *in* Willis Lynn Jepson, *A Flora of California.* 3 vols. University of California Press, Berkeley, 1909–. Cactaceae 2: 537–550.

Rümpler, Theodor. *Carl Friedrich Förster's Handbuch der Cacteenkunde.* 2d ed. Verlag von Im. Tr. Wöller, F.G.E. Kanzler, Leipzig, Germany, 1885.

Schumann, Karl. *Gesamtbeschreibung der Kakteen (Monographia Cactacearum).* Verlag von J. Neumann, Neudamm, Germany, 1898; with supplement, 1902, 1903.

Shreve, Forrest, and Ira L. Wiggins. *Vegetation and Flora of the Sonoran Desert.* 2 vols. Stanford University Press, Stanford, Calif., 1964. Cactaceae 2: 958–1037.

Trelease, William, and Asa Gray. *The Botanical Works of George Engelmann.* John Wilson & Son, University Press, Cambridge, Mass., 1887.

Wiggins, Ira L., *in* Leroy Abrams, *Illustrated Flora of the Pacific States: Washington, Oregon, and California.* 4 vols. Stanford University Press, Stanford, Calif., 1923–60. Cactaceae 3: 143–160. (Text on *Opuntia* jointly with Carl Brandt Wolf.)

Biographical Data

The following biographical list indicates some of the persons who have made important contributions to the study of the native cacti of California. Some of those in the list contributed indirectly through major works on the Cactaceae of larger areas or through botanical works in which accounts of the cacti were included. In keeping with long-established botanical custom, reference to some persons appears after the names of taxa in the text in the form of abbreviations; these names appear in the alphabetical list according to their abbreviations.

Much information has been contributed by persons who were not botanists but cultivators of cacti, and special appreciation is due to the Cactus and Succulent Society of America, founded in the Los Angeles area in 1929 and now worldwide in its membership. The Society publishes *The Cactus and Succulent Journal*, a high-quality horticultural and botanical periodical, which has carried innumerable papers on the native as well as the cultivated cacti. Field observations by members of the Society have added much to knowledge of the native species. The editors and publishers of the Journal, Scott E. Haselton (from 1929 to 1965) and Charles E. Glass (since 1966), have been at the center of the work of the Society.

For an account of early discovery of cacti in the state, see pp. 63–69.

Baxter, Edgar Martin, 1903–67. Los Angeles area during his period of cactus study. *California Cactus.*

Benson, Lyman, 1909–. Professor of Botany, Pomona College, Claremont, Calif. *Plant Classification; Plant Taxonomy, Methods and Principles; The Cacti of Arizona* (3 eds.); *The Trees and Shrubs of the Southwestern Deserts* (with Robert A. Darrow, 2 eds.); *A Treatise on the North American Ranunculi.* Specialist in *Ranunculus, Pleuropogon* (a genus of grasses), the Cactaceae of the United States and

Canada, and the flora of western North America, especially of the deserts.

Bigelow, John Milton, 1804–78. Surgeon and botanist of the Mexican Boundary Survey and the Whipple Expedition of the Pacific Railroad Surveys.

Brandegee (Lane, Curran), Katherine, 1844–1920. Botanist and physician, California. With her husband, T. S. Brandegee, among the most important early botanists of California.

Brewer, William Henry, 1828–1910. Leader of the field expeditions of the California State Geological Survey. *Botany of California* (with Sereno Watson).

Britton, Nathaniel Lord, 1859–1934. Director, New York Botanical Garden, New York City. *The Cactaceae* (with J. N. Rose); many other botanical works.

Clokey, Ira Waddell, 1878–1940. Colorado; California. *Flora of the Charleston Mountains, Nevada.* The Clokey Herbarium is a large unit in the Herbarium of the University of California, Berkeley.

Coulter, John Merle, 1851–1928. Professor and Head, Dept. of Botany, University of Chicago. *Manual of Botany of the Rocky Mountain Region*; founder and editor of the *Botanical Gazette.*

Cov. Coville, Frederick Vernon, 1867–1937. Curator of the U.S. National Herbarium, Smithsonian Institution, Washington, D.C. Botanist of the Death Valley Expedition, 1891, and consequently a collector of cacti.

Davidson, Anstruther, 1860–1932. Physician, Los Angeles, Calif. *Flora of Southern California* (with G. L. Moxley).

DC. Candolle, Augustin Pyramus de, 1778–1841. Geneva, Switzerland. Professor of botany; first of several in a famous botanical family. *Prodromus Systematis Naturalis Regni Vegetabilis.* Papers on the Cactaceae, including *Revue de la Famille des Cactées.*

Emory, William Hemsley, 1811–87. U.S. Army Corps of Topographical Engineers; ultimately, during the Civil War, a major general; chief engineer of the Army of the West and in charge of a military reconnaissance from Fort Leavenworth, Kansas, to San Diego in 1846; in 1854 appointed commissioner and astronomer of the Mexican Boundary Survey. Keen observer of plants and a contributor of much knowledge of the cacti.

Engelm. Engelmann, George, 1809–84. Physician and the leading student of cacti of the United States; St. Louis, Mo. An outstanding botanist of the nineteenth century and a specialist in several plant groups.

Förster, Carl Friedrich, middle nineteenth century. Germany. *Handbuch der Cacteenkunde,* 1st ed. (1846). (See Rümpler.)

Fosberg, Francis Raymond, 1908–. Botanist, U.S. Geological Survey, Washington, D.C. Outstanding student of the flora of the islands of the Pacific Ocean; earlier an author of papers on the Cactaceae of the United States.

Gray, Asa, 1810–88. Fisher Professor of Natural History, Harvard University, Cambridge, Mass. *Manual of Botany of the Northern United States*, now in 8th edition; *Synoptical Flora of North America*; sympetalous plants of Brewer and Watson's *Botany of California*; innumerable papers. The leading botanist in North America in his time and the biologist who in Darwin's time introduced the concept of evolution to this hemisphere.

Griffiths, David, 1867–1935. University of Arizona, Tucson, Ariz. (briefly); then botanist, U.S. Department of Agriculture, Washington, D.C. A serious student of *Opuntia* in the period of land sales promotion and speculation connected with Burbank's spineless cactus. The first set of the Griffiths collection of cactus specimens is at the U.S. National Herbarium, Smithsonian Institution; a second set, in exchange for curating and identification, is at Pomona College.

Haw. Haworth, Adrian Hardy, 1767–1833. Entomologist and student of succulent plants, Great Britain. *Miscellanea Naturalia*; *Synopsis Plantarum Succulentarum*; *Supplementarum Plantarum Succulentarum*.

Hester, J. Pinckney. Fredonia, Ariz. Collector and author of papers on succulent plants.

Knuth, F. M. 1904–. Germany. *Kaktus—ABC* (with Curt Backeberg).

Kuntze, Carl Ernst Otto, 1843–1907. Berlin and Leipzig, Germany. *Revisio Generum Plantarum*; author of more than 30,000 unacceptable changes of names of plants, based upon individual policy.

L. Linnaeus, Carolus (later Carl von Linné), 1707–78. Professor of Botany, University of Uppsala, Uppsala, Sweden. *Species Plantarum* (1753) and *Genera Plantarum* (5th ed., 1754), the starting points for botanical nomenclature; many other botanical, zoological, and medical books. The first person to employ the binomial system of nomenclature (naming by genus and species) consistently.

Lemaire, Charles Antoine, 1801–71. Professor in the University, Ghent, Belgium. *Les Cactées*; *Cactacearum Genera et Speciesque Novae et omnium in Horto Monvilliana . . .* ; *Cactacearum Aliquot Novarum . . . in Horto Monvilliano*; and numerous other works.

Lindsay, George Edmund, 1916–. Director, San Diego Natural History Museum, and now California Academy of Sciences, San Francisco. Specialist primarily in succulent plants and especially in *Ferocactus*.

Marshall, William Taylor, 1886–1957. Director (1946–57), Desert Botanical Garden in Papago Park, Phoenix, Ariz. *The Cactaceae* (with

Thor Methven Bock); *Arizona's Cactuses*; editor, *Saguaroland Bulletin*.

Munz, Philip Alexander, 1892–. Professor of botany, Pomona College, Claremont, Calif., 1917–44; Bailey Hortorium, Cornell University, 1944–46; Director, Rancho Santa Ana Botanic Garden, 1946–60. *A Manual of Southern California Botany*; *A California Flora* (in collaboration with David D. Keck); and numerous botanical papers.

Nutt. Nuttall, Thomas, 1786–1859. Philadelphia, Pa. Curator of the Botanical Garden, Harvard University, Cambridge, Mass. Explorer, especially of western North America; botanist and ornithologist. *The Genera of North American Plants*; *The North American Sylva*.

Orcutt, Charles Russell, 1864–1929. Horticulturist and collector of desert plants, especially cacti, San Diego, Calif. Author of several botanical papers.

Parish, Samuel Bonsall, 1836–1928. San Bernardino, Calif. Correspondent of Asa Gray; pioneer in the study of the flora of southern California; author of the texts on the Cactaceae for W. L. Jepson's *A Manual of the Flowering Plants of California* and *A Flora of California*.

Parry, Charles Christopher, 1823–90. Colorado and Iowa. One of the botanists of the Mexican Boundary Survey; collector in the Southwest.

Peebles, Robert Hibbs, 1900–1956. Director, U.S. Field Station, and agronomist studying the breeding of cotton, Sacaton, Ariz. Co-author (with Thomas H. Kearney) of *Flowering Plants and Ferns of Arizona* and its revision, *Arizona Flora*; specialist in cacti and author of the treatment of the family in the books mentioned above.

Philbrick, Ralph Nowell, 1934–. Biosystematist and Curator of the Herbarium, Santa Barbara Botanic Garden, Calif. *Opuntia*.

Rose, Joseph Nelson, 1862–1928. U.S. National Herbarium, Smithsonian Institution, Washington, D.C. *The Cactaceae* (with N. L. Britton); many papers on Cactaceae, Crassulaceae, and Umbelliferae.

Rümpler, Theodor, 1817–91. Generalsekretär des Gartenbauvereins, Erfurt, Germany. *Carl Friedrich Förster's Handbuch der Cacteenkunde*, 2d ed.

Salm-Dyck. Salm-Reifferscheid-Dyck, Prince Joseph Franz Maria Anton Hubert Ignaz, 1773–1861. Neuss, Germany. The estate of Prince Salm included a cactus garden upon which several books were based.

K. Schum. Schumann, Karl Moritz, 1851–1904. Curator of the Herbarium, Berlin Museum, Berlin-Dahlem. *Gesamtbeschreibung der Kakteen* (*Monographia Cactacearum*). Numerous botanical papers.

Torrey, John, 1796–1873. Professor of Chemistry and Botany, College of Physicians and Surgeons, New York. The leading botanist in North America in his time; classifier of plants collected on most of the expeditions and surveys in the West during his time.

Walkington, David L., 1930–. Associate Professor of Botany, California State College at Fullerton. Cactaceae of California and of the Galápagos; chemical characters of cacti.

Watson, Sereno, 1826–92. Curator of the Gray Herbarium, Harvard University, Cambridge, Mass. *Botany of California* (with W. H. Brewer); many other botanical works.

Wiggins, Ira Loran, 1899–. Professor of Botany and Director of the Natural History Museum, Stanford University, Stanford, Calif.; Director of the Arctic Research Laboratory at Point Barrow, Alaska. *Vegetation and Flora of the Sonoran Desert* (with Forrest Shreve, ecologist); botanical papers on various taxonomic subjects; special interest in the Cactaceae.

Wolf, Carl Brandt, 1905–. Botanist, Rancho Santa Ana Botanic Garden, in Orange County, Calif., 1930–45. *The New World Cypresses*; botanical papers, including some on the southern California cacti.

Glossary

ACCUMBENT. Said of a pair of *cotyledons* curved back down the hypocotyl in such a way that their edges are turned toward the hypocotyl. See INCUMBENT.

ACICULAR. Needlelike; said of an elongate, cylindroid, but tapering structure, circular to broadly elliptic in cross section.

ACUMINATE. Abruptly narrowed at the apex into a long, pointed structure.

ACUTE. In the form of an acute angle.

ADNATE. Joined with another structure of a different kind; said, for example, of the joining of the bases of sepals with petals, or of petals with stamens. See COALESCENT.

ADVENTITIOUS ROOT. A root developed from a stem or a leaf and therefore not part of the primary root system.

AMPHITROPOUS. Said of an ovule bent back along and adnate with its funiculus (stalk), but with the micropyle not close to the funiculus. See ORTHOTROPOUS, CAMPYLOTROPOUS, ANATROPOUS.

ANATROPOUS. Said of an ovule bent back along and adnate with its funiculus (stalk), with the micropyle very close to the funiculus. This is the common type of ovule in flowering plants. See ORTHOTROPOUS, CAMPYLOTROPOUS, AMPHITROPOUS.

ANNULATE. With horizontal projecting ringlike bands.

ANTHER. The upper, expanded portion of a stamen, composed largely of pollen sacs.

ANTHOCYANIN PIGMENTS. A group of water-soluble pigments dissolved in the fluid of living cells, ranging in color from pink to purple. Such pigments are indicators of acidity or alkalinity, turning toward red in an acid solution and toward blue in a basic solution, as does litmus paper. See BETACYANIN.

APICAL. Formed at the apex, or extremity.

APPRESSED. Turned upward and flat against the stem.

ARBORESCENT. Said of a plant intermediate between a tree and a shrub, having two to a few trunks from the base. Commonly arborescent plants are larger than most shrubs and smaller than most trees.

AREOLE (diminitive of area). In the cacti a usually sharply defined small area bearing spines and sometimes glochids. The contents of the areole are developed from the bud in the axil (angle) above a leaf (or of the rudiment of a leaf present during early development of the stem but not discernible in the mature plant).

ARISTATE. With the terminal point slender or forming a bristle.

ARISTULATE. Aristate, but with the point or bristle very small.

AXIL. The angle above a leaf, between the leaf and the stem or branch that bears it.

AXILLARY. Borne in an axil.

BETACYANIN. A pigment of a group similar in behavior to the anthocyanin pigments. So far as investigated, pigments of this type occurring in the cacti are betacyanins.

CAESPITOSE. With the stems in a dense, low tuft.

CAMPYLOTROPOUS. Said of an ovule curved so that the micropyle approaches the funiculus (stalk), though the body of the ovule is not coalescent with the funiculus. See ORTHOTROPOUS, ANATROPOUS, AMPHITROPOUS.

CANESCENCE. A dense covering of very fine, white or gray, usually short hair.

CANESCENT. Bearing canescence.

CARPEL. A specialized leaf forming all or part of a pistil of a flower. In the cacti there are usually 3 to 20 carpels coalescent lengthwise and forming the pistil; they are distinguishable by their divergence into separate stigmas.

CENTRAL SPINE. One of the spines in the central part of the areole; the distinction is sometimes obvious, sometimes arbitrary. See RADIAL SPINE.

CLAVATE, CLUBLIKE, or CLUB-SHAPED. Elongated and with the diameter increasing gradually upward (or increasing abruptly near the top).

CLONE. A group of individual plants propagated without sexual reproduction from a single individual. When joints of the stem of a single cholla or prickly pear fall to the ground, many joints may form new plants; the group of new plants thus established is a clone.

COALESCENT. Joined with another structure of the same kind; said, for example, of the growing together of the bases of petals or of stamens. See ADNATE.

CONICAL. Cone-shaped and attached at the broad end of the cone.

CORTEX. The mostly soft outer tissues of a stem, i.e., the tissues outside the woody cylinder.

COTYLEDONS. Leaves of the embryo in the seed (in the cacti becoming the first pair of leaves conspicuous in the seedling).

CULTIVAR. A horticultural strain of a plant species. Cultivars are not given names similar to those of species or varieties; a cultivar represents only a horticultural element of a species. The names of cultivars are derived from modern languages, and often the designation is the name of a person, which follows that of genus and species, e.g., *Camellia japonica* Julia Drayton. Cultivar replaces the obsolete term "horticultural variety."

CUNEATE. Wedge-shaped; of the form of an isosceles triangle attached at the apex of the odd angle.

CUTICLE. A layer of waxy material secreted by the surface cells of a stem or a leaf.

CYCLIC. Arranged in a circle at one level; said, for example, of leaves arranged in a single CYCLE about a stem.

DECIDUOUS. Falling away.

DECLINED. Turning downward.

DEFLEXED. Turning downward.

DEHISCENT. Splitting open, usually lengthwise, releasing seeds or pollen in the process.

DENTATE. With angular teeth projecting outward at right angles to the margin of a structure, e.g., a leaf.

DENTICULATE. Finely dentate.

DEPRESSED. Flattened from above, as if pushed downward.

DIOECIOUS. Said of a plant having unisexual flowers, all those on a single plant being of the same sex, i.e., all having stamens (male) or all having pistils (female).

DORSAL. In botany, the outer side of a structure, i.e., the side away from the axis of the organism. The dorsal side of a leaf is the back or lower side, i.e., the side that is away from the stem axis, because the leaf ordinarily slants upward facing the stem. See VENTRAL.

DORSOVENTRALLY. Along the (DORSOVENTRAL) measurement from front to back, or vice versa. A structure flattened dorsoventrally, e.g., a leaf, has the broadest faces on the front and back, rather than on the sides. See LATERALLY.

DRIP-TIP. A sharp, drawn-out point on which water accumulates until drops are large enough to fall off. Drip-tips are common on the leaves of tropical trees occurring in areas of much rainfall; the spines of some cacti behave as drip-tips.

ELLIPTIC, ELLIPTICAL. Forming an ellipse, i.e., having both ends rounded and the length on the order of twice the diameter; said of structures essentially two-dimensional in form, such as leaves.

ELLIPSOID. Three-dimensionally elliptic, i.e., with the ellipse rotated about its long axis.

EMBRYO. A new plant formed from the fertilized egg cell. In the flowering plants the embryo reaches its ultimate development in the seed, where it usually consists primarily of the rudiments of a root, a stem, and one or two primary leaves. In the cacti there are two primary leaves (cotyledons) in the embryo. See EPICOTYL, HYPOCOTYL.

ENTIRE. With the margin smooth and unindented.

EPIDERMIS. The surface layer of cells of a structure, usually secreting a layer of CUTIN (waxy material), which retards evaporation of water.

EPICOTYL. The part of the main axis of the embryo just above the cotyledons, in the seedling continuing into the developing stem. See HYPOCOTYL.

EPIGYNOUS. Said of a flower with a floral cup or tube enclosing the ovary and wholly or partly adnate with it, the two forming in fruit an inseparable unit. All cactus flowers but those of *Pereskia* are epigynous, the fruit consisting of the developed ovary (with its enclosed seeds) and an outer layer formed from the floral cup (or tube). The core of an apple is the ovary; the edible portion is mostly floral cup. Flowers of other plants may be *perigynous* or *hypogynous*. See HYPOGYNOUS, PERIGYNOUS, FLORAL CUP, FRUIT.

EPIPHYTE (adj. EPIPHYTIC). A plant that grows (without parasitism) upon another plant, as, for example, on the limb of a tree.

EPITHET. An adjective used as a noun; for example, *"alba"* (meaning "white") may be used as part of the botanical name of a plant species.

ESCAPE. An individual of a species introduced from another region and having spread from cultivation to areas where it grows without the intentional aid of man.

FILAMENT. The stalk of a stamen, bearing the anther or upper, expanded portion, which includes the POLLEN SACS.

FILIFORM. Very slender and threadlike.

FIMBRIATE. Fringed on the margin (like the fringe of the frontiersman's buckskin shirtsleeve).

FIMBRIOLATE. Finely fimbriate.

FLORAL CUP (or TUBE, according to shape). A structure investing the ovary, formed either by extension of the margin of the receptacle (a HYPANTHIUM) or by coalescence and adnation of the bases of the sepals, petals, and stamens. This structure, as in the cacti, may be adnate to the outer surface of the (inferior) ovary (see EPIGYNOUS), and it then appears to form the outer layer of the ovary, as seen most readily in the developed fruit. See EPIGYNOUS, INFERIOR OVARY, FRUIT.

FRUIT. The matured and usually enlarged ovary and its enclosed seeds. In the cacti and other plants with epigynous flowers the fruit is covered by and wholly adherent except across the top to the floral cup (or tube), which is considered part of the fruit—an outer coat. See EPIGYNOUS, FLORAL CUP.

FUNICULUS. The stalk of an ovule or, later, of a seed.

FUNNELFORM. Of the shape of a funnel.

GLAUCOUS. Covered with a bluish powdered wax.

GLOBOSE. Spheroidal.

GLOCHID. A fine, barbed bristle produced in the areole of a cholla or prickly pear (genus *Opuntia*). The glochids are markedly different from the larger spines and in the prickly pears are often more troublesome to man.

HETEROZYGOUS. With unlike genes (determiners of hereditary characteristics) in a given pair or pairs of genes. For example, in an individual plant both genes of the pair determining flower color may tend to produce white, or both may tend to produce red, or one may promote red and the other white. In the first two cases, the plant is homozygous with respect to flower color (i.e., with respect to this pair of genes); in the third case, the plant is heterozygous, and the color of its flowers (not of its progeny's flowers) depends upon which, if either, color is dominant to the other; if neither is dominant, the color will be pink. Reproduction between individuals that are homozygous for the red-flower character invariably produces red-flowered progeny; reproduction between individuals one or both of which is (are) heterozygous for this character has predictable but various outcomes.

HILUM. The scar on the seed coat marking the position where the seed stalk (funiculus) was attached; *the basal point* of the seed. In seeds that are broader than long, the hilum appears to be on the side of the seed, i.e., to be "lateral," but this is an illusion.

HOMOZYGOUS. Having like genes in a given pair or pairs of genes. See explanation under HETEROZYGOUS.

HYBRID. An individual derived from parents some of whose hereditary characters differ. Commonly used to describe individuals arising from crosses of different genera, species, or varieties. Since these taxa cannot be limited precisely, neither can intergeneric, interspecific, and intervarietal hybrids. See discussion on p. 20.

HYPANTHIUM. A floral cup or tube derived from stem tissue, as opposed to one derived through fusion of the parts of the flower.

HYPOCOTYL. The part of the main axis of the embryo in the seed just below the cotyledons, in the seedling continuing into the developing primary root. See EPICOTYL.

HYPOGYNOUS. Said of a flower with no floral cup or tube (see PERIGYNOUS, EPIGYNOUS).

INCUMBENT. Said of a pair of cotyledons curved back down the hypocotyl in such a way that the back of one is toward the hypocotyl and the back of the other is away from it (i.e., the direction of curving is perpendicular to the accumbent orientation). See ACCUMBENT.

INDEHISCENT. Not splitting open. See DEHISCENT.

INFERIOR OVARY. An ovary that is enclosed partly or completely by the floral cup or tube with which its surface is adnate. In all the cacti except *Pereskia* the ovary is inferior. See SUPERIOR OVARY.

INVESTED. Enclosed by another structure.

ISTHMUS. A narrow structure joining two broader ones (as in geography).

JOINT. A section or segment of a stem composed of a series of such units.

LANCEOLATE. Lance-shaped, 4 to 6 times as long as broad, acute at both ends, and attached at the broader end.

LATERAL. On, or extending to, the side or sides.

LATERALLY. From side to side or on the side. A structure compressed laterally is broad on each side and narrow on the back and the front. See DORSOVENTRALLY.

LECTOTYPE. A substitute for the type specimen, designated to take its place if it has been lost or was not designated in the first place. A lectotype is chosen from the original specimens mentioned in the work in which the name of the species (or other taxon) was first published by the original author of the taxon or from those clearly studied by the author.

LINEAR. Narrow and with the sides essentially parallel, the length about 8 or more times the width.

MAMMILLATE. Of the form of a human breast.

MARGIN. The edge or perimeter of, e.g., a leaf blade.

MICROPYLE. A microscopic or pinhole-like opening in the seed coat near the hilum. This is the passageway through which the pollen tube earlier entered the ovule.

MUCRONATE. With a short, sharp, terminal point, this of the same texture as the rest of the leaf or other structure.

MUCRONULATE. Mucronate, though with a minute point.

OB-. A prefix indicating attachment of a part in the way opposite from that expected. For example, ovate is egg-shaped (but flattened), with the attachment at the large end; obovate is the same, but with the attachment at the small end.

OBCONIC, OBCONICAL. Conical, but with the attachment at the apex of the cone.

OBLANCEOLATE. Lanceolate, but attached at the narrow end.

OBLIQUE. In a diagonal position.

OBOVATE. Ovate, but attached at the narrow end.

OBOVOID. Ovoid, but attached at the narrow end.

OBSOLETE. Not developed.

OBTUSE. In the form of an obtuse angle.

ORBICULATE. Forming nearly a circle.

ORTHOTROPOUS. Said of a straight ovule, i.e., one that is not curved or bent toward its funiculus (stalk). See CAMPYLOTROPOUS, AMPHITROPOUS, ANATROPOUS.

OVARY. The lower, swollen part of a pistil of a flower, containing the ovules that, after fertilization of the contained egg cells, enlarge and become seeds. In hypogynous and perigynous flowers the ovary is superior, in epigynous flowers, as in the cacti, inferior.

OVATE. Of the shape of a hen's egg (though essentially two-dimensional), with both ends rounded, about one and one-half times as long as broad, and the apex somewhat narrower than the base; said, for example, of many leaves. See OVOID.

OVOID. Ovate, but three-dimensional (not flat), nearly circular in cross section; said, for example, of a hen's egg.

OVULE. A structure in the ovary containing an egg (female reproductive cell). After fertilization the ovule develops into a seed, the fertilized egg forming a group of cells that becomes an embryo composed of a main axis (root and stem, or hypocotyl and epicotyl) and in the cacti two cotyledons (seed leaves).

PAPILLATE. With usually low and rounded projections (PAPILLAE).

PARIETAL. On the margin or outer side. A parietal placenta (seedbearing area) in an ovary is on the outer wall of the ovary rather than in the center.

PECTINATE. With rows of structures (e.g., spines) resembling the teeth of a comb.

PERIANTH. A collective term for the sepals and petals, or for structures corresponding to them in position but either not clearly differentiated into the two or of a fundamentally different origin from sepals and petals.

PERIGYNOUS. Said of a flower with a floral cup or tube, but in which the cup or tube is not coalescent with the ovary. See HYPOGYNOUS, EPIGYNOUS.

PERSISTENT. Remaining attached for longer than the usual or expected time.

PETAL. One of the usually highly colored series of flower parts attractive to insects (in the cacti, a petaloid perianth part and not a true petal). This series is interior to the sepals (in cacti, to the sepaloid perianth parts), which may be green to usually less highly colored than the petals. The leaves (usually scalelike) of the cacti grade into sepaloid and these into petaloid perianth parts, and all are of similar origin. Phylogenetically, the petals of most flowering plants were derived from sterilization of stamens or the forerunners of stamens.

PETALOID. Similar in position and appearance to a petal.

PETALOID PERIANTH PARTS. Structures resembling petals and in the position of petals but of different origin.

231

PHENOTYPE. The visible or at least detectable inherited characters of the individual; for example, a plant may be red-flowered or ovate-leaved.

PISTIL. The seed-producing (female) organ of a flower. At its extremity is the stigma (the pollen receptor); below the stigma is the tubular style, which supports the stigma and connects it with the ovary (which produces ovules, which become seeds). See CARPEL.

PITH. The central soft tissue of a stem, enclosed by the woody cylinder.

PLACENTA. The attachment point of the funiculi (stalks) of one or more ovules or seeds. Usually it is on the ovary wall or at the meeting lines of partitions of the ovary.

PLASTID. A structure within a cell, as, for example, a chloroplast. Usually plastids are colored, bearing pigments such as the chlorophylls and their associated pigments or other pigments producing such colors as yellow or red. These pigments are not water-soluble, and usually they persist with little change when a quickly dried plant specimen is made. Other plastids include no pigment.

POLLEN SAC. A segment of the anther of a stamen. In flowering plants there are usually four sacs (in two pairs) joined by a connective; each produces pollen.

PROLIFEROUS. Continuing to form new units; said, for example, of a cactus fruit that stays on the plant and gives rise to new flowers and therefore to new fruits from its areoles, a new fruit developing from the last often for season after season.

PULVILLUS (pl. PULVILLI). A cushionlike or padlike structure.

PUNCTATE. With dotlike glands on the surface.

RADIAL SPINE. One of the spines on the margin of the areole; the distinction is sometimes obvious, sometimes arbitrary. See CENTRAL SPINE.

RECEPTACLE. The end of the stem (often enlarged, occasionally narrowed, often neither) supporting the parts of a flower. The receptacle is composed of the upper, very short internodes (segments) of the stem and the nodes bearing the flower parts. In the cacti (except *Pereskia*) the receptacle is obscured by the combined (adnate) floral cup and ovary, which arise from it. The stalk of the flower beneath the receptacle is the PEDICEL, which in the cacti is usually small and obscure or essentially wanting.

REPAND. With the margin, as, for example, of a leaf, winding irregularly in and out.

RETICULATE. Forming a meshwork, resembling chicken wire.

RETICULUM. A network or meshwork.

RHIZOME. A horizontal, underground stem usually bearing roots at its joints (nodes).

RHOMBIC. Of the form of an equilateral parallelogram that is more or less diamond-shaped, and with the petiole attached to one of the sharper angles.

RIB. A vertical or spiral ridge along the side of the stem. In the cacti the rib is formed by the complete or incomplete coalescence of the tubercles of the stem, and the tops of these (bearing spine clusters) may protrude from the rib.

SCABROUS. With minute, rough projections, therefore rough to the touch.

SCALE or SCALE LEAF. A small leaf on the stem or floral tube of a flower or fruit, usually thin and somewhat flattened, but succulent.

SCARIOUS. Thin, translucent, and membranous; resembling parchment.

SEED. The developed ovule (in flowering plants) in an ovary, developing a usually hard coat and internally an embryo composed of an axis (root and stem, or hypocotyl and epicotyl) and in the cacti two cotyledons or seed leaves.

SEED CHAMBER. A walled-off segment of the ovary containing seeds. In other flowering plants there may be more than one chamber, but in the cacti there is only one.

SEPAL. One of the usually green outer parts (often with other colors) of the perianth (sepals and petals) (in the cacti a sepaloid perianth part). See PETAL.

SEPALOID. Similar in position and appearance to a sepal.

SEPALOID PERIANTH PARTS. Structures resembling sepals and in the position of sepals but of different origin. In the cacti, leaves (usually scalelike) on the floral tube grade into sepaloid perianth parts, which grade into petaloid perianth parts, all having a similar origin different from that of sepals and petals.

SERRATE. With sawlike teeth, i.e., with marginal, acutely angled, forward-projecting teeth.

SERRULATE. Finely serrate.

SHRUB. A woody plant with several to many stems from ground level, usually smaller than a tree. See ARBORESCENT.

SPATHULATE, SPATULATE. Narrowly oblong with rounded corners and with the basal end long and tapering and the apical end (often abruptly) broadened; of the shape of a spatula.

SPINE. A sharp-pointed structure derived from a leaf or part of a leaf. In the cacti the spines are formed from leaves produced by the bud in the areole or from its derivative buds. See CENTRAL SPINE, RADIAL SPINE.

SPINIFEROUS. Bearing spines.

SPINOSE. Ending in a spine or bearing spines.

STAMEN. The pollen-producing (male) organ of the flower. At its extremity are pollen sacs, in an anther, which is supported by a slender filament or stalk.

STIGMA. The pollen receptor of a pistil, formed at the apex of the style.

There may be more than one stigma from one style; in the cacti there are usually 3 to 20.

STRIATE. With longitudinal (lengthwise) markings.

STYLE. The tubular connection between the stigma or stigmas and the ovary of a pistil.

SUB-. A prefix meaning "almost."

SUBULATE. With the shape of a shoemaker's awl, i.e., flattened (forming a narrow ellipse in cross section) and gradually tapering to an apical point.

SUCCULENT. Fleshy, i.e., with much soft, watery tissue.

SUPERIOR OVARY. An ovary that is not adnate to a floral cup or tube. See INFERIOR OVARY.

TAXON (pl. TAXA). A unit of classification, such as a SPECIES (pl. SPECIES), or one of the varieties composing it, or a larger unit such as a GENUS (composed of species) or a FAMILY (composed of genera).

TOMENTOSE. Woolly.

TOMENTUM. Wool.

TREE. A large, woody plant having a single main trunk, which usually branches above. See ARBORESCENT, SHRUB.

TRUNCATE. Ending abruptly, appearing chopped off.

TUBER. A short, thickened, underground stem developed into a storage organ. A white potato is an example.

TUBERCLE. A projection.

TUBERCULATE. Bearing tubercles.

TUBEROUS. Of the form of a tuber.

TURBINATE. Of the shape of a top.

TYPE LOCALITY. The locality of collection of a type specimen.

TYPE SPECIMEN. A permanently preserved specimen designated by the author of a species or other taxon as representing the taxon being described. The name applied to the taxon is associated permanently with the type specimen, and it determines the application of the name.

VEGETATIVE. Said of a nonreproductive part of a plant. Vegetative organs are roots, stems, and leaves.

VENTRAL. In botany, the inner side of a structure, i.e., the side toward the axis of the organism or of its branch. The ventral side of a leaf is the front or upper side, because the leaf ordinarily slants upward facing the stem. See DORSAL.

Index

Page numbers in roman type (118) indicate a significant discussion of a subject on the page given; because some subjects appear throughout the book, not all the pages upon which they appear are listed. **Boldface type** (**118**) is used to indicate the first page of a major discussion or a critical explanation of a subject. *Italics* (*118*) indicate an illustration of the subject or a map of its distribution; "pl." indicates an illustration in the color plates (following p. 100 and p. 164). The names of accepted genera and species appear in roman type; the names of those not accepted are in *italics*.

Personal names are indicated only as they appear in the text or in a text reference to a publication. Those appearing in the list of contributors to study of the cacti of California (pp. 220–224) or as authors of publications suggested for reading (pp. 217–219) are not included in the Index.

Terms specially defined in the text are indexed; they may appear also in the Glossary (pp. 225–234), but the Index does not cover the Glossary. Neither is the endpaper indexed.

240

Temperate region, north, 31
Temperate regions, 33
Tertiary Period, 35, 36
Texas, 31
Thelocactus Johnsonii, 208
Topography of California, maps of, 48, 50
Torrey, John, 69
Trade winds, 32, 33, 34
Tree of heaven, Chinese, 37
Triassic, 36
Tropical calms, 34; belt of, 32
Tropical Flora, American, 46
Tropical regions, 34
Tropics, 32
Tubercles, 6, 7, 8
Tuberous structures, 6
Tunas fragilis, 119
Tundra, Alpine, West American, 46, 47; Arctic, 46
Type locality, 28
Type specimen, 27, 28

Umbellularia californica, 35
United States, cacti of, 30
United States and Canada, cacti of, 24
Uplift of mountain axis, 38, 39
Utah, 31

Vancouver, George, 63
Variety, 16, 24; determination of, 23
Vegetation of California, natural, maps of, 49, 51
Vernacular names, 30
Viscaino Desert, 63

Walkington, David L., 63, 165
Washingtonia filifera, *64*
Water, concentration of, 7
West American Alpine Tundra, 46, 47
Westerlies, prevailing, 31
Western Yellow Pine, *54*
Wheeler, Louis C., 172
Whipple Expedition, 68
Wiegand, E. F., 122
Winds: global, 31; polar, 31; prevailing westerly, 33, 34; trade, 32, 33, 34
Wing nuts, Chinese, 37
Wislizenus, A., 27
Wood, 7
Woodland, Juniper-Pinyon, 46, 57, 59

Xylem, 7

Yucca brevifolia, *62*

Occurrence of Cactus Species and Varieties in Natural Vegetation Types in California*

P = primary occurrence; S = secondary occurrence; s = slight occurrence

Species and Varieties	Page	Rocky Mt. Montane Forest	Sierra Montane Forest	Calif. Oak Wood-land	Calif. Chaparral (disturbed areas)	Pacific Grass-land	Juniper-Pinyon Wood-land	Sage-brush Desert	Moja-vean Desert	Colo. Desert
1. *Opuntia Parryi*	84									
1a. var. *Parryi*	85				P					
1b. var. *serpentina*	88				P					
2. *O. Wigginsii*	88									P
3. *O. echinocarpa*	89									
3a. var. *echinocarpa*	90								P	S
3b. var. *Wolfii*	93									P
4. *O. acanthocarpa*	94									
4a. var. *coloradensis*	96								P	s
4b. var. *major*	96									s
4c. var. *Ganderi*	96				s					P
5. *O. prolifera*	98				P					
6. *O. Munzii*	99									P
7. *O. Bigelovii*	102									
7a. var. *Hoffmannii*	104									P
7b. var. *Bigelovii*	106									P
8. *O. ramosissima*	106									P
9. *O. Stanlyi*	110									
9a. var. *Parishii*	114								P	
9b. var. *Kunzei*	114									P
10. *O. pulchella*	115						P			
11. *O. polyacantha*	117									
11a. var. *rufispina*	118	s					S	P		
12. *O. fragilis*	118	s					P	P		
13. *O. erinacea*	120									
13a. var. *erinacea*	121						s	S	P	s
13b. var. *ursina*	124								P	
13c. var. *utahensis*	126	s					P	s		
14. *O. basilaris*	127									
14a. var. *basilaris*	128	s	s	s	s	s	s	s	P	P
14b. var. *brachyclada*	128				P					
14c. var. *Treleasei*	130					P			s	
15. *O. macrorhiza*	131						P			
16. *O. littoralis*	133									
16a. var. *littoralis*	133	s			P					
16b. var. *Vaseyi*	136				P					
16c. var. *austrocalifornica*	136				P					
16d. var. *Piercei*	141		P		s					
16e. var. *Martiniana*	142	s					P		S	
17. *O. phaeacantha*	142									
17a. var. *major*	143		s		S		S		s	s
17b. var. *discata*	148				S				S	s

* An analytic key to all genera is given on pp. 74–76; the vegetation types are discussed on pp. 45–63.